D1248619

Décors de Bars
Bar Decors
Bar Dekor

Editorial Director • Directeur éditorial • Verlagsleiter
Nacho Asensio

Coordination and text • Rédaction • Redaktion
Victoria Gómez García
Nuria González
Agnès Gallifa Hurtado

Design and layout • Dessin et maquette • Gestaltung und Layoutrealisation
Núria Sordé Orpinell

Translation • Traduction • Übersetzung
English: Mike Eaude
Français: BEST TRADUCCIONS
Deutsch: BEST TRADUCCIONS

Production • Production • Produktion
Juanjo Rodríguez Novel

Copyright © 2002 Atrium Group
Proyecto editorial: Books Factory, S.L.
e-mail: books@booksfactory.org

Published by: Atrium Internacional de
México, S.A. de C.V.
Fresas n° 60 (Colonia del Valle)
03200 México D.F. MÉXICO

Tel: +525 575 90 94
Fax: +525 559 21 52
e-mail: atriumex@laneta.apc.org
www.atrium.com.mx

ISBN: 84-95692-09-0
National Book Catalogue Number:
B-36458-2002

Printed in Spain
Grabasa.

Copyright © 2002 Atrium Group
Progetto editoriale: Books Factory, S.L.
e-mail: books@booksfactory.org

Publié par : Atrium Internacional de
México, S.A. de C.V.
Fresas n° 60 (Colonia del Valle)
03200 Messico D.F. MESSICO

Tél.: +525 575 90 94
Fax: +525 559 21 52
e-mail: atriumex@laneta.apc.org
www.atrium.com.mx

ISBN: 84-95692-09-0
Dépôt légal: B-36458-2002

Imprimé en Espagne
Grabasa

Copyright © 2002 Atrium Group
Verlagsprojekt: Books Factory, S.L.
E-mail: books@booksfactory.org

Herausgegeben von: Atrium Internacional de México, S.A. de C.V.
Fresas n° 60 (Colonia del Valle)
03200 México D.F. MÉXICO

Tel.: +525 575 90 94
Fax: +525 559 21 52
E-mail: atriumex@laneta.apc.org
www.atrium.com.mx

ISBN: 84-95692-09-0
Depot der gesetzlichen
Pflichtexemplare: B-36458-2002

Druck in Spanien
Grabasa

Contents
TITLES

Index

Inhaltsverzeichnis

Introduction

Bars, cafeterias or discothèques are not just designed according to concepts of architecture or interior decoration. To use a comparison with painting, their image can depend more on chance inspiration or the influence of current trends, whether aesthetic, musical or just unclassifiable -- factors that are some distance from conventional reasoning.

Whereas a few years ago the search for an austere whole, reflected in the absence of fittings and in the use of cold materials, governed bar architecture, the wheel -- fortunately irrational -- of influences has thrown up today a rhythmic selection of "trend-setting furniture + bold colors + materials" as a magic recipe to spice up the dynamics of a locale. In consequence, we find aesthetically similar bars, regardless of the city where they are located. Words such as lounge, chill-out, night club and cool are now part of a global vocabulary of indoor leisure spots. In certain cases, this involves assimilating the everyday world of the home into the places where you go for a drink. In others, the muses have visited the creator and let loose imaginary stage-sets, living metaphors of free fantasy, nods to art for art's sake. As such, maximalist decor has been relegated to the back seat. As a counter to this trend, there has also been a certain refurbishing of ancient buildings under a more playful mask.

Setting aside for the moment evaluations of particular places, any card in the pack dealt in these pages responds to the current demand for "modern" premises, some *avant-garde*, others heirs of a legacy of the past recovered for our time. They are all up-to-date, even the spaces that occupy old warehouses. The art of creating social spaces is warmly applauded, except by those whose minds are still stuck in a rather antiquated idea of the creative process. The maxim of "design for design's sake", once so often cited, has now been replaced by the purest *chic*, which is transmitted by the distinction of a balanced selection of furniture, almost always brandname, and the delicate return to contemporary luxury.

The suggestive contrasting of fittings says a lot about the direction of the future of design: the fusion, disguised on occasions, of radical decors. Fine examples are those that have recourse to the cradle of New York, or to cinema or outer-space references. Anything goes as long as it manages to provoke surprise or at least challenge hidebound tradition in order to prophesy -why not?- decisive changes in creative capacity.

If one tried to find a word to express the entire range of decor suggestions, this word would be color, the use of which is the main way to highlight volumes in structures or different levels. Live colors, including acid ones, that give rise to a flow of synergy with the whole, arising too from the flowing through of people and the music chosen. The formula will make the visitor take part in this enigmatic way of communicating. Once this occurs, you will hear it said that the atmosphere is pleasant, as Warhol would say, because in short the factor that marks the difference is often the context, the proscenium arch around the social stage.

The best atmosphere I can think of is a movie, because it is physically three-dimensional and emotionally two-dimensional.

ANDY WARHOL

introduction

Pour réaliser le projet d'un bar, une cafétéria ou une discothèque il faut quelque chose de plus que des concepts d'architecture ou de décoration d'intérieurs. En faisant un rapprochement avec la peinture, la représentation, répond plus à l'inspiration hasardeuse, à l'influence de tendances actuelles de différent signe: esthétiques, musicales, et autres paramètres inclassables qui sont loin du raisonnement conventionnel. S'il y a quelques années, la recherche d'une austérité d'ensemble se traduisait par le dénuement de l'équipement, l'utilisation de matériaux froids, qui dominaient les créations architectoniques, actuellement l'évolution des influences (heureusement irrationnelle) a donné lieu à une sélection rythmée du "mobilier unique + couleurs audacieuses + matériaux", une recette magique qui dynamisme un local. Le résultat : des locaux gardant certaines similitudes esthétiques, indépendamment de la ville où ils se trouvent. Lounge, chill-out, night club ou cool font partie du vocabulaire universel pour les intérieurs des établissements. Dans certains cas, il s'agit d'assimiler le monde quotidien de l'habitat aux lieux où l'on va prendre un verre. Dans d'autres cas, les muses ont aidé le créateur à déployer des scénarios imaginaires, des métaphores vivantes de fantaisie libre, des clins d'oeil d'artiste per se. On constate également que les créations maximalistes ont été reléguées à un second plan. En contrepartie, on ne dédaigne pas de réadapter un certain patrimoine monumental pour le destiner à un usage plus ludique.

Mais laissons les appréciations particulières de côté, n'importe quel échantillon présenté dans ces pages répond à la demande actuelle de créations "modernes", d'avant-garde pour certaines, la plupart héritant d'un patrimoine rétro alimenté et récupéré pour notre temps. Toutes sont actuelles, mêmes celles logées dans ce qui autrefois devait être un vieil entrepôt. L'art de socialiser le processus de création est applaudi chaleureusement, sauf par ceux dont la perception est encore imprégnée d'une conception de la création tout à fait rance. L'application de la maxime "le design pour le design", si habituelle à un moment donné, a été remplacée par le plus pur style chic, transmettant le privilège d'un choix équilibré du mobilier, presque toujours signé, et la réversion délicate d'un luxe tout à fait contemporain.

La suggestive alternance des équipements en dit long sur l'avenir du design: la fusion déguisée, parfois, d'un décor radical. Il n'y a qu'à voir les exemples sortis du berceau new-yorkais, ou les références cinématographiques et galactiques. Tout est permis, pourvu que la surprise soit assurée, ou que la tradition ankylosée bouge un peu prédisant -pourquoi pas- d'éventuels sauts mortels de la créativité.

S'il fallait trouver une nuance d'unité dans l'éventail que nous proposons, ce serait la couleur; le recours à la couleur règne lorsqu'il s'agit de proposer des structures et des niveaux séparant les volumes. Des couleurs vives, acides même, qui provoquent la circulation de synergies avec l'ensemble, et également par la présence des différents personnages et le choix de la musique. La formule permettra au visiteur de prendre part à cette communication énigmatique. Dès que cela se produit on entend dire que "l'ambiance est agréable", comme dirait Warhol, parce que finalement ce qui fait la différence c'est souvent le cadre de la mise en scène.

La meilleure ambiance que je puisse imaginer c'est celle d'un film, parce qu'elle est physiquement tridimensionnelle et émotionnellement bi-dimensionnelle.

ANDY WARHOL

Bei der Auswahl der Bars, Cafeterias oder Diskotheken werden nicht nur die Architektonik oder die Innendekoration berücksichtigt. Beim Vergleich mit der Malerei entspricht die Darstellung eher einer zufälligen Inspiration oder dem Einfluß von verschiedenen aktuellen ästhetischen, musikalischen oder nicht zu klassifizierenden Tendenzen, also Parameter, die sich von herkömmlichen Urteilen entfernen.

Während noch vor einigen Jahren in der Innenarchitektur die Suche nach einem nüchternen Raum mit spärlicher Ausstattung und kaltem Material vorherrschte, hat das –glücklicherweise vernünftige – Aufkommen von Einflüssen einer rhythmischen Auswahl von "Muster-Möbeln + gewagten Farben + Materialien" Platz gemacht, was dem Lokal Dynamik verleiht. Das Ergebnis sind Lokale, die sich ästhetisch ähneln, ganz unabhängig von der Stadt, in der sie sich befinden. Deshalb gehören Wörter wie Lounge, Chill-Out, Nightclub oder cool zum universellen Wortschatz der Branche. In manchen Fällen geht es darum, die alltägliche Atmosphäre der Wohnung an die Lokale anzupassen, die man aufzusuchen pflegt. In anderen Fällen haben die Musen den Schöpfer beim Entfalten von imaginären Schauplätzen, lebenden Methaphern freier Phantasie und künstlerischen Tupfern per se inspiriert. Ebenso kann festgestellt werden, daß die maximalistischen Werke allmählich in den Hintergrund treten. Als Kontrapunkt sollte auch die Sanierung mancher historischer Gebäude, die als Lokale umfunktioniert wurden, hervorgehoben werden.

Abgesehen von persönlichen Meinungen, entsprechen alle Lokale dieser Auswahl der derzeitigen Nachfrage an "modernen" Produktionen, einige davon advantgardistisch, die meisten jedoch stellen ein für unsere Zeit zurückgewonnenes Retro-Vermächtnis dar. Alle Lokale sind aktuell, sogar diejenigen, die in ehemaligen Lagerräumen untergebracht sind. Die Kunst, diese Räume der Gesellschaft zugänglich zu machen, erhält heftigen Beifall, ausgenommen davon sind diejenigen, die immer noch einen recht veralteten Standpunkt bezüglich des Kreierungsprozesses vertreten. Der früher so geläufige Grundsatz "Design für Design" ist heute durch den reinsten Chic-Stil ersetzt worden, der sich in einer ausgeglichenen Auswahl der Möbel -wobei es sich fast immer um Markenartikel handelt- und in der feinen Umkehrung des zeitgenössischen Luxus widerspiegelt.

Der suggestive Ausstattungswechsel sagt viel darüber aus, wohin die Zukunft des Designs führt: zur gelegentlich als radikaler Dekor geschminkten Verschmelzung. Davon zeugen Beispiele, die sich entweder auf ihren New Yorker Ursprung oder auf filmischen und galaktischen Referenzen stützen. Es ist alles erlaubt, wenn damit Überraschung hervorgerufen, oder zumindest die veraltete Tradition umgewandelt wird, damit -und warum nicht- mögliche radikale Wendungen bei der kreativen Fähigkeit prophezeit werden können.

Wenn es darum ginge, eine Nuance zu finden, welche die Vorschlagspalette vereinheitlichen würde, wäre die Farbe das beste Mittel zur Planung von Strukturen und Ebenen, die die Räume abheben. Lebhafte, auch zitrusfarbene Töne, welche einen auch durch den Personentransit und die ausgewählte Musik verursachten Synergiefluß mit dem Raum hervorrufen. Diese Formel wird dazu führen, daß der Besucher an dieser rätselhaften Kommunikation teilhat. Wenn dies geschieht, wird man von den Leuten hören, daß die Stimmung angenehm ist, wie Warhol sagen würde, denn in den meisten Fällen liegt der Unterschied in der Aufmachung.

Die allerbeste Atmosphäre,
die ich mir vorstellen kann
ist die Stimmung eines Filmes,
denn sie ist physisch dreidimensional
und gefühlsmäßig zweidimensional.

ANDY WARHOL

Lux

Margarida Grácio Nunes, Fernando Sanchez Salvador

Lisboa, Portugal
1997
Photography | Photo | Fotografie: Ana Paula Carvalho,
Fernando Sanchez Salvador.

A bet on Portuguese longing melancholy. Favorite destination of night owls, sure of finding alternatives and enjoying gigs and wild dancing, without forgetting the joy of new concepts of interior design. Provocative and nostalgic, Lux honors its name by being an essential piece of the Lisbon night. Grandiose in its conception, Lux is on three levels with three independent areas —bar, disco and chill-out— defined by the choice of furnishings. Separating screens in blue, lilac and fuchsia coloring define the boundaries of the room. A fantastic collection of chairs, sofas and stools of every possible shape —don't miss that hand that moulds the seat— is the best feature of this club whose recipe takes us to a reinvented 1970s. Still more disconcerting are the images projected on the bar, that serve up a cocktail of often kitsch abstraction. If you choose the chill-out with its view over the Tagus to spend the small hours, touches of a contemporary oasis combine with ultramodern taste.

Un pari pour la saudade portugaise. Destination favorite des noctambules, sûrs de trouver des options alternatives et de profiter des concerts et de l'agitation de la danse, sans oublier le plaisir de se trouver dans un décor au concept tout nouveau. Provocateur et nostalgique, le Lux fait honneur à son nom car il est considéré comme un must dans la nuit de Lisbonne. Immense par sa conception, il est distribué sur trois plans, équivalant à trois ambiances distinctes -bar, discothèque et chill-out- marquées par le choix de l'équipement. Des panneaux de séparation indiquent par leur couleur aux nuances bleutées, lilas et fuchsias, la finalité de la salle. Une collection unique de chaises, de fauteuils et de tabourets ayant toutes les formes possibles et imaginables -entre autres, l'incontournable main- est ce qu'il y a de meilleur dans ce club qui vous transporte dans le monde des années 70, réinventé par sa recette particulière. Avec l'intention de déconcerter encore plus, les projecteurs du bar servent un cocktail d'images abstraites, souvent kitsch. Choisir le chill-out avec vue plongeante sur le Tage, pour laisser poindre le petit matin, c'est laisser l'atmosphère prendre des airs d'oasis contemporain, d'un goût ultramoderne.

Hier trifft man auf die portugiesische Saudade. Lieblingsziel der Nachtschwärmer, die hier ganz sicher alternative Angebote vorfinden und sich sowohl an Konzerten wie auch am Tanz erfreuen können, nicht zu vergessen sind dabei die hier zu bewundernden neuen Konzepte der Innenarchitektur. Das herausfordernde und nostalgische Lux macht seinem Namen alle Ehre, da es einfach zum Lissaboner Nachtleben gehört. Das überaus große Lokal besteht aus drei Flächen, welche dank der Auswahl der Ausstattung in drei unabhängige Ambienten aufgeteilt sind -Bar, Diskothek und Chill-Out-. Die Bestimmung des Saales wird durch die blauen, lila und rosa Farbtöne der Trennwände definiert. Eine geniale Sammlung von Stühlen, Sofas und Hokkern, die alle möglichen Formen aufweisen -wie die unübersehbare Hand im Raum- ist die Attraktion dieses Clubs, welcher die Gäste in eine Stimmung der 70er Jahre versetzt. Um die allgemeine Verblüffung noch mehr zu steigern, werden in der Bar abstrakte, oft sogar Kitsch-Bilder vorgeführt. Im Chill-Out, mit Aussicht auf den Tejo, wird der Gast eine Atmosphäre erleben, die an eine zeitgenössische Oase mit ultramodernen Flair erinnert.

The use of the separating screens recalls a television set opening and closing off spaces in order to highlight areas. On their own, the blue, lilac and fuchsia colors define the boundaries of the different spaces.

L'agencement des panneaux de séparation rappelle un plateau de télévision qui ouvre et ferme les espaces pour définir les sections. Les couleurs bleutées, lilas et fuchsias suffisent pour définir la finalité de chacune des salles.

Die Gliederung der Trennwände erinnert an ein Fernsehstudio, das zur Definierung von Abteilungen Räume öffnet bzw. schließt. Die blauen, lila und rosa Farbtöne definieren die Bestimmung eines jeden Saales.

Lux

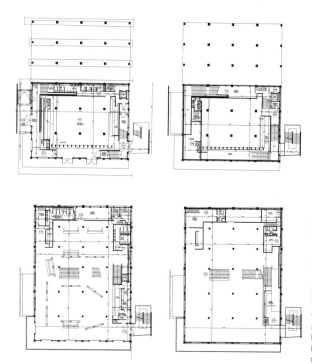

The fantastic collection of chairs, sofas and stools of every possible shape are more than just functional furniture. As on a journey to the world of the '70s, the ambiguous play of the furniture says it all at Lux, a club out of bounds to those ignorant of alternative concepts in fusion of interior decor.

La collection exceptionnelle de chaises, de canapés et de tabourets dépasse largement leur fonction d'équipement. Comme dans un voyage dans le mode des années 70, le jeu équivoque du mobilier, indique tout dans le Lux, club défendu à ceux qui ignorent les concepts alternatifs dans la fusion des intérieurs.

Die außergewöhnliche Sammlung von Stühlen, Sofas und Hockern ist etwas mehr als eine funktionale Ausstattung. Das mehrdeutige Spiel mit der Möbeleinrichtung, das wie eine Reise in die 70er Jahre anmutet, sagt viel aus über die Philosophie des Lux, ein Club, der für Personen gedacht ist, denen die alternativen Konzepte bei der Fusion des Mobiliars ein Begriff sind.

Neon beams focus on the bar. Acclaimed for its DJ's Lux is an essential piece of the Lisbon night. Its location in the Alcântara area and its closeness to the Tagus add to this feeling. The views from the chill-out confirm its distinctive concept.

Faisceaux de néon se fusionnent sur le comptoir. Très apprécié en raison de sa programmation de Dj's, le Lux devient indispensable dans les nuits de Lisbonne. Sa situation dans la zone de l'Alcântara et la proximité du Tage y contribuent sûrement. Les vues depuis le chill-out confirment sa conception particulière.

Neonstrahlen fallen auf die Theke. Das ausgezeichnete DJ-Programm des Lux ist ein Muß im Lissaboner Nachtleben. Vielleicht trägt dazu seine Lage im Alcântara-Viertel und die Nähe zum Tejo bei. Der Ausblick vom Chill-Out her bestätigt seine besondere Konzeption

Astro

Michael Young

Reykiavik, Iceland
2000
Photography | Photo | Fotografie: Ari Magg.

Conceptual design through colors and shapes. Symbiosis of cold effects from outer space in an imaginary world that has forgotten the outside. The walls of this bar are covered with fiberglass and painted in bright stucco. Green dominates, though some rooms, like the red room upstairs, have thermal walls with an advanced lighting system that transforms the pale pink into intense red, depending on the physical activity of the people in the room. Furniture is also used as a boundary between spaces. All the pieces, that recreate life in the open air or establish curving psychedelic lines, are designs by Young, produced by Capellini and Azuaya & Moroni. Another separator is the circular stone bath in the middle, inspired by the traditional geo-thermal pools of the island. Beside the bath stands the bar made of Corian, material repeated on the built-in shelving.

Langage conceptuel au moyen des couleurs et des formes. Symbiose aux effets froids et galactiques comme dans un monde imaginaire étranger à l'extérieur. Les murs de ce local sont recouvertes de fibre de verre et de stucs aux couleurs brillantes.

C'est le vert qui domine mais dans certaines salles comme la salle rouge à l'étage supérieur, les murs thermiques comportent un système d'illumination avancé qui fait que le rose pale se transforme en rouge intense selon l'activité qui s'y déroule. Le mobilier limite les zones. Toutes les pièces qui rappellent la vie à l'air libre ou produisent des lignes sinueuses et psychédéliques, sont design de Young produits par Capellini et Azuaza & Moroni. Le bassin rond en pierre situé dans la partie centrale est un autre séparateur de zones; il rappelle les piscines géothermiques traditionnelles de l'île. Toute près se trouve le comptoir en Corian, matière qui se retrouve dans les étagères qui sont intégrées dans les murs.

Konzeptsprache durch Farben und Formen. Eine Symbiose kalter und galaktischer Effekte, wie in einer imaginären, abgekapselten Welt. Die Wände des Lokals sind mit Glasfaser verkleidet und in buntem Stuck gearbeitet. Der grüne Farbton herrscht vor, wenn auch einige Räume, wie zum Beispiel der Red Room auf der oberen Etage, thermische Wände mit einem hochmodernen Beleuchtungssystem besitzen. Dieses bewirkt, daß sich das blaße Rosa durch die physische Tätigkeit im Raum in ein Tiefrot verwandelt. Alle Räume, von Young entworfen und von Capellini und Azuaya & Moroni gefertigt, geben das Leben im Freien wieder oder legen gewundene und psychedelische Linien fest. Ein weiteres trennendes Element ist der von den traditionellen geothermischen Schwimmbädern der Insel inspirierte kreisförmige Pool aus Stein, der sich in der Mitte befindet. Daneben steht die Theke aus Corian, dieses Material wurde auch bei den Wandregalen verwendet.

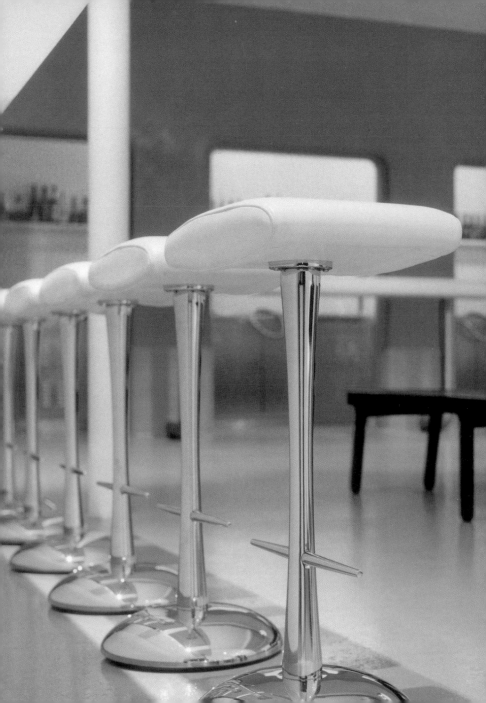

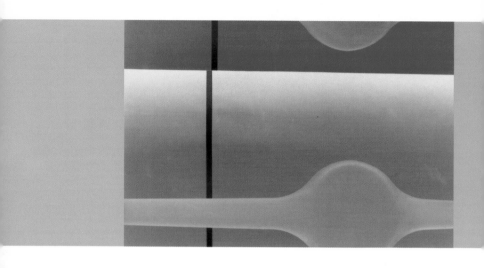

The luminous batons,
like the bar's overall
lighting system,
are by Eurolounge.

*Les bâtons lumineux, ainsi que le
système d'éclairage général du local
ont été produits par Eurolounge.*

Die Leuchtstäbe, ebenso auch das
allgemeine Beleuchtungssystem,
stammen von Eurolounge.

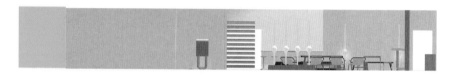

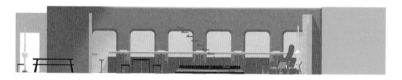

The seating is laid out round the stone pool in the middle: white arm-chairs by Capellini and the set of MY 71 wooden benches and table by Sawaya & Moroni.

Autour du bassin en pierre, au centre, on a disposé le mobilier: des fauteuils blancs de Capellini et l'ensemble de bancs et la table en bois MY 71 de Sawaya & Morini.

Um den in der Mitte liegenden Pool aus Stein herum ist das Mobiliar aufgestellt: weiße Sessel von Capellini, sowie Bänke und Tisch aus MY 71-Holz von Sawaya & Moroni.

Astro

Pharmacy

Damien Hirst, Mike Rundell

London, United Kingdom
1998
Photography | Photo | Fotografie: Alberto Ferrero.

The Pharmacy, located in bohemian Notting Hill, has become a well-known watering-hole for the most famous and beautiful figures of the London night, thanks to its owner, the controversial artist Damien Hirst. His artistic trajectory confers glamour on the Pharmacy, which evokes the chemical spirit of the nineties. The flat white front of this renowned bar is the setting for the works of art exhibited inside. It has two floors that are joined by a stainless-steel stairway. The leitmotiv of the decor is the world of a pharmacy: medicines in the cupboards and walls lined with medical scale paper. The famous *enfant terrible* of BritArt provokes his customers, who are surprised to find that, though the drinks served bear names of medicines, these are far from being classic prescriptions.

Le Pharmacy, situé dans le quartier bohème de Notting Hill, est devenu un établissement important grâce à sa clientèle, la plus célèbre et exquise des nuits londoniennes, attirée par la personnalité controversée du propriétaire, Damien Hirst. Sa propre trajectoire artistique est sa réclame, et ainsi le Pharmacy évoque un imaginaire bien propre à l'esprit chimique des années quatre-vingt-dix. La façade de cet emblématique établissement, lisse et blanche, sert de cadre des oeuvres d'art exposées à l'intérieur. L'espace est organisé en deux étages qui communiquent par un escalier en acier inoxydable. Le leitmotiv de la décoration intérieure est le monde de la pharmacie: médicaments dans les vitrines et murs tapissés de papier médical millimétré. Le mythique enfant terrible du BritArt provoque son client surpris en constatant que les boissons servies dans cet établissement portent des noms de médicaments mais ils sont bien loin des formules magistrales conventionnelles.

Das im Künstlerviertel Notting Hill gelegene Pharmacy ist dank des kontroversen Künstlers Damien Hirst, Besitzer des Lokals, zu einem Begriff für die Prominenz des Londoner Nachtlebens geworden. Der hervorragende Ruf des Künstlers hat eine anziehende Wirkung auf die Gäste, demzufolge evoziert das Pharmacy typische Bilder des chemischen Geistes der neunziger Jahre. Im Inneren des namhaften Lokals mit der weißen und glatten Fassade werden Kunstwerke ausgestellt. Der Raum ist in zwei durch eine Treppe aus rostfreiem Stahl miteinander verbundene Etagen gegliedert. Leitmotiv der Innendekoration ist die Apothekenwelt: Medikamente in den Schränken und mit medizinischem Millimeterpapier tapezierte Wände. Das mythische Enfant terrible des BritArt überrascht die Gäste mit Drinks, die wie Medikamente heißen, aber längst nicht nach Magistralformeln hergestellt sind.

The Pharmacy is an excellent space for exhibiting the works of Damien Hirst. There is nothing gratuitous in the artist's proposal of a flat, white facade as the front-drop to the works exhibited inside.

Le Pharmacy offre un espace idéal pour exposer les oeuvres de Damien Hirst. Le choix de l'artiste n'était pas gratuit: la façade blanche et lisse allait devenir le cadre pour les oeuvres exposées à l'intérieur de l'établissement.

Pharmacy ist der ideale Ausstellungsraum für die Kunstwerke von Damien Hirst. Nicht umsonst entwarf der Künstler eine weiße und glatte Fassade als passender Rahmen für die im Inneren ausgestellten Arbeiten.

Pharmacy

Damien Hirst has suggested an art space that breaks with the traditional idea of exhibition gallery. The provocative artist explained that the Pharmacy "is like a little creation where, at any rate, you can spend your time more agreeably than in most art galleries".

Damien Hirst propose un espace pour l'art qui rompt avec le concept traditionnel de salle d'exposition. L'artiste provocateur expliquait que le Pharmacy "est comme une petite création où, en tout cas, on peut passer un moment plus agréable que dans la plupart des galeries d'art".

Damien Hirst hat einen Raum für die Kunst gestaltet, der mit dem herkömmlichen Konzept des Ausstellungsraumes bricht. Der polemische Künstler sagte, daß das Pharmacy "wie eine kleine Schöpfung ist, wo der Gast sich auf jeden Fall mehr als in den meisten Kunstgalerien amüsiert".

Grand Central

Zoe Smith, Gareme Williamson (Block Architecture)
London, United Kingdom
1998
Photography | Photo | Fotografie: Chas Wilshere.

A fast-food American-style outlet right in the heart of Shoreditch. At Grand Central, you can have breakfast, lunch, dinner or just a drink. The food on offer is almost as spectacular as its decor, conceived by Block Architecture. The non-stop traffic outside is the restaurant's main source of inspiration. Even the name, referring to New York's main railway station, accentuates this feeling of motion. The element that best transmits this constant coming and going is the long winding bar, whose front is decorated with lines of different thickness and color. Also striking are all the cubes out of which the bottle racks are formed. The various groups of tables, chairs and benches, light in structure and softly colored, are laid out around these items.

Un restaurant au style américain où prendre un repas rapide, situé en plein centre de Shoreditch. Au Grand Central on peut prendre le petit-déjeuner, déjeuner, dîner ou simplement prendre un verre. Son offre gastronomique est aussi spectaculaire que sa décoration conçue par Block Architecture. Le mouvement continuel du trafic extérieur est la principale source d'inspiration de la décoration. Même son nom, qui fait référence à la gare centrale de New York, accentue encore plus la sensation de dynamisme. L'élément qui transmet le mieux ce va et vient constant est constitué par des lignes aux épaisseurs et aux couleurs différentes décorant le devant du comptoir, long et sinueux. La succession de cubes formant l'étagères à bouteilles attire l'oeil. Autour de ces éléments les différents ensembles de tables, chaises et bancs aux structures légères et aux couleurs aux nuances douces ont été disposés.

Ein mitten in Shoreditch gelegenes Fast-Food-Lokal im amerikanischen Stil. Im Grand Central kann man frühstücken, zu Mittag und zu Abend essen oder nur einen Drink nehmen. Das gastronomische Angebot ist fast so aufsehenerregend wie die von Block Architecture entworfene Dekoration. Das ständige Kommen und Gehen auf der Straße ist die hauptsächliche Inspirationsquelle des Lokals. Sogar sein Name, der an den New Yorker Hauptbahnhof erinnert, verstärkt das Gefühl der Dynamik. Das Element, welches dieses ständige Hin und Her zum Ausdruck bringt, ist die lange, geschwungene Theke, deren Vorderfront durch die unterschiedlich breiten und farbigen Streifen besticht. Auffallend ist das aus aufgestapelten Würfeln zusammengestellte Flaschenregal. Um diese Elemente herum wurden schlichte, in sanften Farben gehaltene Tische, Stühle und Sitzbänke gruppiert. .

Despite being conceived with function in mind, the restaurant is full of style details: for example, the lamps in the dining area or the spot-lights on the bottle-racks.

Malgré le fait d'avoir été conçu avec un critère de fonctionnalité, le local est plein d'éléments stylés: les lampes de la zone de la salle à manger ou les projecteurs qui éclairent le présentoir de bouteilles sont un bon exemple.

Trotz der Funktionalität des Lokals sind überall stilvolle Details vorhanden: die Lampen im Eßbereich und die das Flaschenregal beleuchtende Strahler sind gute Beispiele dafür.

Grand Central

The bar-front adorned with infinite colored lines transmits the dynamic motion of the city traffic that whizzes past the windows.

Le devant du comptoir décoré avec une infinité de lignes de couleurs transmet le dynamisme du trafic urbain qui passe à toute vitesse devant les baies vitrées.

Die mit unzähligen Farbstreifen dekorierte Vorderfront der Theke drückt die Dynamik des Straßenverkehrs aus.

The geometrical pieces out of which the spectacular bottle rack has been fashioned contribute still further to the feeling of movement that the restaurant exudes.

Les pièces géométriques composant le spectaculaire présentoir de bouteilles contribuent à augmenter encore la sensation de mouvement que transmet le local.

Die geometrischen Formen, aus denen das aufsehenerregende Flaschenregal besteht, unterstreichen das im Lokal zu spürende Gefühl der Betriebsamkeit.

Bbar

Studio X Design Group (Oscar Brito, Lara Rettondini)
Hannover, Deutschland
1999
Photography | Photo | Fotografie: Oscar Brito, Lara Rettondini.

Sky-blue flashes that transmit a feeling of insubstantiality. The Bbar is a white capsule that hides within it an encircling space. The different parts -ceiling, walls and floor- fuse, the boundaries between them obscured by curves and turns where they meet. The effect is one of continuous extension round which a long metallic surface bends sinuously. The deep recesses for lights in the ceilings, bar and pillars help display the fittings. Like magnets of light, each piece takes on a luminous character, but the bar alone stands out. This solid block is the focus of everyone moving through the locale. Effects of reddish and pink lightbeams are achieved on the "Cameo White" Corian coating of the bar. The flooring is treated with white epoxy resin. The walls and false ceiling bear a coating of plaster-board. Final vision: the assimilation of an intangible dimension in which floating entities take on the shapes of chairs and tables.

Des éclats célestes produisent une sensation d'immatériel. Le Bbar est une capsule blanche qui cache en son intérieur un espace enveloppant. Les différents plans -plafond, murs et sol- se fondent, effaçant leurs limites, se courbent et se retournent à leurs intersections. L'effet obtenu est une extension continuelle autour de laquelle une longue surface métallique est disposée de façon sinueuse. À partir de celle-ci, les profondes cavités éclairées pratiquées dans le plafond, le comptoir ou les colonnes permettent d'exposer l'équipement. Comme des aimants, chaque pièce prend un caractère lumineux, mais seul le comptoir garde le protagonisme. Conçu comme un bloc massif, projeté en faisceaux rougeâtres et rosés (effet obtenu sur le revêtement de Corian "Cameo White" qui le recouvre) il focalise le mouvement des personnes. Le sol est traité avec une résine époxy blanche. Sur tous les murs et le faux plafond on a appliqué une formule de carton-plâtre. Vision finale: l'assimilation d'une dimension intangible où des entités flottantes prennent la forme de chaises et de tables.

Eine himmlische Atmosphäre, die ein Gefühl der Unkörperlichkeit vermittelt. Die Bbar ist eine weiße Kapsel, die einen umhüllenden Raum in sich birgt. Die verschiedenen Flächen –Dkcke, Wände und Boden– verschmelzen miteinander, wobei die Grenzen zwischen ihnen sich krümmen und drehen, und schließlich ganz verschwinden. Das Ergebnis ist eine durchgehende Fläche, um die eine lange, geschwungene Metalloberfläche entlangläuft. Die tiefen, beleuchteten Nischen bzw. Vertiefungen in der Decke, in der Theke und in den Säulen dienen zum Ausstellen von Ausstattungselementen. Jedes Element strahlt Licht aus, als wäre es ein Lichtmagnet, aber lediglich die Theke steht im Mittelpunkt. An dieser als ein von rötlichen und rosa Strahlen beleuchteter massiver Block konzipierten Theke, mit einer Verkleidung aus Corian "Cameo White", herrscht stets ein geschäftiges Treiben. Der Fußboden wurde mit weißem Epoxydharz behandelt. Die Wände und die abgehängte Decke wurden mir Gipskarton verkleidet. Endergebnis: die Assimilierung einer unberührbaren Dimension, in der schwebende Wesen zu Stühlen und Tischen werden.

The Bbar is one of the additional services that Benetton has promoted in Hanover and Hamburg so far. Like a pirouette on stage, the tables seem to drop down from the rounded hollows dug out of the ceiling, dropping on the same axis, sliding down on their legs. Tables are in stainless steel, with a Scotch-Brite finish. The chairs and benches are the unmistakable Bombo model, by Magis.

Le Bbar est un des services annexes que Benetton a mis en place à Hannover et Hambourg. Comme dans une pirouette théâtrale, les tables semblent descendre des trous ronds creusés dans le plafond juste dans le même axe, en glissant sur leurs supports verticaux.
Ils sont en acier inoxydable, finition Scotch-Brite. Chaises et bancs sont des exemplaires du caractéristique modèle Bombo de Magis.

Die Bbar ist einer der Dienstleistungsbereiche, die bis jetzt von Benetton in Hannover und in Hamburg eröffnet wurden. Wie bei einer inszenierten Pirouette scheinen die Tische von den runden Deckenvertiefungen an den vertikalen Stangen herunterzugleiten. Diese Tische sind aus moosfarbenem rostfreiem Stahl gefertigt. Stühle und Sitzbänke entsprechen dem unverwechselbaren Modell Bombo von Magis.

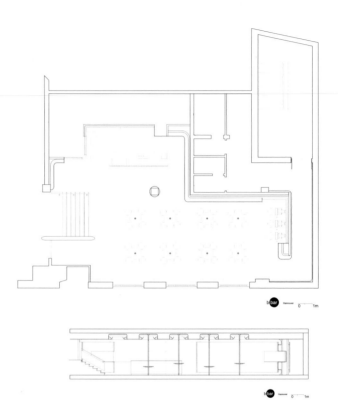

b bar Hannover 0 — 1m

b bar Hannover 0 — 1m

Lighting is the resource used to highlight the suspension of the metallic surface. These are lights within the fittings and controlled electronically. They create luminous masses inside, which in turn slowly change the color of the surrounding white light. The space achieved is mutant, whereby the atmosphere takes on different tones depending on the color changes.

L'éclairage est une ressource employée pour rehausser la suspension de la surface métallique. Il s'agit de lampes faisant un tout avec l'installation, contrôlées par un système électronique qui définit les masses lumineuses de l'intérieur et qui à leur tour, changent lentement la couleur de la lumière blanche enveloppante. Un espace mutant est ainsi obtenu où l'atmosphère prend différentes nuances selon les variations chromatiques.

Mit der Beleuchtung wird das Schweben der Metalloberfläche betont. Es handelt sich dabei um in die Einrichtungen eingebaute, elektronisch gesteuerte Lampen, mit welchen Lichtmassen definiert werden können, die den Farbton des umhüllenden weißen Lichtes allmählich verändern. Auf diese Art und Weise wird ein ständig mutierender Raum geschaffen, in dem die Atmosphäre sich je nach der Farbe ändert.

Bbar

Atelier Renault

Franck Hammoutène Architecte

Paris, France
2000
Photography | Photo | Fotografie: Olivier Martin Gambier (ARCHIPRESS).

Movement. Transparency. A live communications channel. Though it might look like a car showroom, Atelier Renault aims to be a space for surprising montages on art, sports, technology or any other theme of burning contemporary interest. The identity of the Renault company is transmitted through the juxtaposition of elements such as the five walk-ways placed at the same level as the spectators, to bring the fashion parades closer to the public. The glass wall allows a view of the Champs Elysés and offers the possibility of looking in from outside. Faithful to his reputation as avant-garde artist, Hammoutène devised modern volumes, letting them breathe, so that the spectator can enjoy each animation. The upper floor is for the restaurant, and the lower houses the visual effects. A visionary view of the new paths down which architecture is walking: fusion of creative concepts.

Mouvement. Transparence. Un moyen vivant de communication. Quoiqu'on pourrait penser qu'il s'agit d'un showroom automobile, Atelier Renault prétend être un espace témoin de mises en scène surprenantes sur l'art, le sport, la technologie ou n'importe quel sujet brûlant d'actualité. L'identité de la maison Renault est transmise à partir de la juxtaposition d'éléments comme les cinq passerelles disposées au niveau du public, pour en rapprocher les défilés de mode. De même, la façade en verre, avec vue sur les Champs Elysées, permet de voir l'intérieur, de l'extérieur. Fidèle à sa réputation de créateur d'avantgarde, Hammoutène a conçu des volumes modernes en les laissant respirer, pour que le visiteur profite de chacune des animations. Ainsi, le plan supérieur est destiné au restaurant et sur le plan inférieur sont présentés les spectacles. Une proposition visionnaire des nouveaux itinéraires que prend l'architecture : fusion des concepts créatifs.

Bewegung. Durchsichtigkeit. Ein lebendiges Kommunikationsmedium. Obwohl es eher wie ein Automobilausstellungsraum aussieht, soll Atelier Renault ein Ort für eindrucksvolle Events aller Richtungen sein: Kunst, Sport, Technik, oder brandaktuelle Themen. Die Identität der Firma Renault wird durch die aneinandergereihten Elemente wie die fünf Laufstege, die sich auf der gleichen Höhe der Zuschauer befinden, um die Models dem Publikum näherzubringen, zum Ausdruck gebracht. Außerdem ermöglicht die Glasfassade einen Blick auf die Champs-Elysées; von der Straße aus kann man sich ein Bild davon machen, was drinnen geschieht. Hammoutène, als avantgardistischer Designer bekannt, hat moderne, nicht streng voneinander abgegrenzte Räume konzipiert, damit die Gäste sich an jedem einzelnen Event erfreuen können. So befindet sich das Restaurant auf der oberen Ebene, während auf der unteren die visuellen Vorführungen stattfinden. Ein visionärer Vorschlag der neuen Richtungen der Architektur: Verschmelzung von kreativen Konzepten.

350 PIXELS U

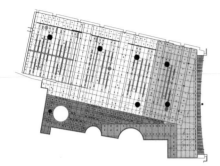

Atelier Renault is a live communications channel that brings animations within reach of the visitor. Unlike the cat-walks of the fashion firms, these walk-ways run at the same height as the spectator. They are an allegory of the Champs Elysés, place *par excellence* where people file past every day.

L'Atelier Renault a été conçu comme un moyen vivant de communication qui rapproche les animations du visiteur. Contrairement aux passerelles des firmes de mode, celles-ci se trouvent au même niveau que le spectateur. C'est comme une allégorie des Champs Elysées, paradigme des défilés quotidiens des gens.

Atelier Renault wurde als ein lebendiges Kommunikationsmedium konzipiert, das die Events dem Gast näher bringt.
Hier liegen die Laufstege, im Gegensatz zu denjenigen der Modefirmen, auf der gleichen Ebene der Zuschauer. Sie sind eine Allegorie der Champs-Elysées, eines Musterbeispiels des alltäglichen Vorbeiziehens der Leute.

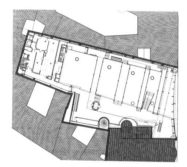

Atelier Renault

The objective is to be as non-elitist as possible. Making themes in form of animation or exhibition more accessible is the idea of putting the restaurant upstairs and placing the five walk-ways and the exhibition of "hanging cars" on the lower floor.

Le but : être le moins élitiste possible. Rapprocher les thèmes intéressants sous forme d'animation ou d'exposition est le fait de destiner le plan supérieur au restaurant et de situer les cinq passerelles et l'exposition de "voitures suspendues" à l'étage inférieur.

Ziel war, das Lokal so wenig elitär wie möglich zu gestalten.
Um die Events und Ausstellungen dem Publikum näher zu bringen, wurde die obere Ebene als Restaurant eingerichtet; die fünf Laufstege und die Ausstellung von "hängenden Autos" wurden hingegen im unteren Geschoß untergebracht.

The red room upstairs is reserved for private functions. Its thermal walls take on a more intensive red hue as physical activity rises.

La red room *située à l'étage supérieur est une salle réservée aux fêtes privées. Ses murs thermiques deviennent d'un rouge plus intense à mesure que l'activité augmente.*

Der im oberen Geschoß befindliche Red Room ist ein für private Parties reservierter Raum. Bei Zunahme der physischen Aktivität bekommen die thermischen Wände, ursprünglich rosa, einen tiefroten Farbton.

The curving shapes of the furniture
and sculptures at strategic points
reflect the style of the '70s.

*Les formes sinueuses de certaines
pièces de mobilier et de certaines
sculptures stratégiquement situées
renvoient à l'esthétique particulière
des années soixante.*

Die geschwungenen Formen einiger
Möbelstücke und strategisch
aufgestellten Skulpturen erinnern an
die Ästhetik der siebziger Jahre.

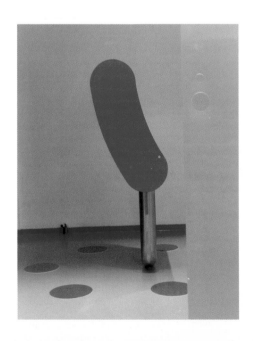

Atlantique

Fabio Novembre
Milano, Italia
1995
Photography | Photo | Fotografie: Alberto Ferrero.

All the offspring of November's imagination draw metaphors of more or less content. Mystic, sociologist and architect of passion, in Atlantique the apocalyptic creator evokes the difficulty Cupid's arrows have to reach people's hearts in the Milan of 1995 AD. The chaos of communication is shown by the blue of the Bisazza flooring as an ocean on which the circular bar floats and above which hangs a sumptuous chandelier of optic fiber. This is the masculine zone, a lounge with a clear Baroque style. Then, on the banister of a walkway constructed from glass fragments, disturbing caryatids and mutant *omenoni*, made of scrap metal, stare. These lead us into the most intimate part of the locale, colored in pinks. Luminous structures, tables and chairs shaped like daisies create a completely female area, that conceals in a side-room the restaurant. Nearby, the dance floor, on which a semi-illuminated Cupid winks down at his victims from the ceiling.

Toutes les créatures nées de l'imaginaire de Fabio Novembre dessinent des métaphores à la lecture plus ou moins forte. Mystique, sociologue ou architecte de la passion, le fait est que dans l'Atlantique, apocalyptique créateur évoque la difficulté que trouvent les flèches de Cupidon pour atteindre le coeur des personnes dans le Milan 1995 a.J.-C. Le chaos de la communication est représenté dans le bleu des carrelages Bisazza comme un océan où flotte le bar circulaire, au-dessus duquel est suspendu un superbe lustre en fibre optique. C'est la zone masculine, un lounge où apparaît un net style baroque. Plus loin, la balustrade d'une passerelle construite à partir de fragments de verre, laisse se pencher de perturbantes cariatides et omenoni transmutés, faits en ferraille conduisant à la partie la plus intime du local à l'ambiance aux nuances rosées. Des structures luminescentes, des tables et des chaises en forme de marguerites contribuent à créer une aire tout à fait féminine, cachant la zone restaurant dans un coin à part. Toute proche, se trouve la zone de danse, où depuis le plafond un Cupidon à demi-lumineux cligne de l'oeil à ses victimes.

Alle Geschöpfe des phantasievollen Novembre stellen mehr oder weniger aussagekräftige Methaphern dar. Der apokalyptische Schöpfer, ein Mystiker, Soziologe und Architekt der Leidenschaft, stellt im Atlantique dar, wie schwierig es ist, daß Kupidos Pfeile im Jahre 1995 n. Chr. das Herz der Mailänder trifft. Das Kommunikationschaos wird durch das Blau des Bisazza-Fußbodens als Ozean dargestellt, in dem die kreisförmige Theke schwimmt. Darüber schwebt eine prunkvolle, aus Faseroptik hergestellte Lichtspinne. Dies ist der Männerbereich, eine Lounge im reinsten Barockstil. In der anschließenden Balaustrade mit einem aus Glasstücken gebauten Laufsteg schauen verwirrende Karyatiden und verwandelte Omenoni hervor. Diese aus Schrott angefertigten Gestalten führen zum intimsten Teil des Lokals, das in rosa Farbtönen gehalten ist. Lichtstrukturen und margeritenförmige Tische und Stühle schaffen einen rein femininen Bereich, welcher das Restaurant beherbergt. Gleich in der Nähe liegt die Tanzfläche, wo ein halbbeleuchteter Kupido seinen Opfern von der Decke aus zuzwinkert.

Mythology brought to the spaciousness of the Atlantique cathedral.
The blue flooring evokes the ocean from which life emerges metaphorically. Huge chandeliers rain down on the round bar, a kind of life-saving atoll where shipwrecked Milanese can find refuge. A walk-way displays disturbing figures that contrast with the happy area to which it leads: the kingdom of daisies.

La mythologie portée au contexte spatial de la cathédrale Atlantique. Le sol bleu évoque l'océan d'où émerge métaphoriquement la vie. Sur le bar circulaire pleuvent d'immenses lustres, tels des espèces d'atoll-secours où s'agrippent les naufragés milanais.
Une passerelle accueille d'inquiétantes silhouettes, en contraste avec l'ambiance joyeuse de l'endroit où elle aboutit : le royaume de la marguerite.

Die Mythologie bei der Raumgestaltung der Kathedrale Atlantique.
Der blaue Fußboden erinnert an einen Ozean, aus dem das Leben metaphorisch auftaucht. Über der kreisförmigen Theke hängen gewaltige Lichtspinnen herunter und bilden ein lebenrettendes Atoll für die schiffsbrüchigen Mailänder. Am Laufsteg stehen verwirrende Figuren, im Kontrast zur fröhlichen Stimmung des Zielortes: das Reich der Margeriten.

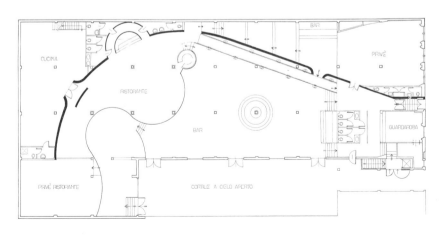

Atlantique

Psychoanalytic representation of Cupid's attempt to fire his arrows into the hearts of men and women. The theme of assimilation of space and passion appears on the steel door-frames giving on to the garden in the form of Chinese ideograms: l'amore cresce sul sesso love grows on sex.

Transposition psychanalyste des tentatives de Cupidon pour lancer ses flèches dans les coeurs des hommes et des femmes. L'assimilation entre l'espace et la passion apparaît sur les embrasures des portes en acier donnant sur le jardin, représentés par des idéogrammes chinois: l'amore cresce sul sesso love grows on sex.

Psychoanalytische Übertragung des Versuchs von Kupido, mit seinen Pfeilen die Herzen der Männer und Frauen zu treffen. Das Motto der gegenseitigen Assimilierung von Raum und Leidenschaft, in chinesischen Ideogrammen dargestellt, erscheint auf den Rahmen der Stahltüren, welche zum Garten führen: l'amore cresce sul sesso love grows on sex.

The lounge is conceived as a highly Baroque space with blue velvet curtains and sofas upholstered in the same fabric. Its overloaded lay-out is effectively seductive, and clashes with the more sugary look of the restaurant and dance floor.

Le lounge a été conçu comme un espace au style vraiment très baroque avec des rideaux en velours bleu et des canapés tapissés du même tissu. Leur disposition rechargée séduit effectivement en contraste avec un côté plus sucré du restaurant et de la zone de danse.

Die Lounge wurde in einem rein barocken Stil konzipiert, mit Vorhängen und Sofas aus blauem Samt. Die überladene Einrichtung macht einen verführerischen Eindruck, der völlig im Gegensatz zum süßlichen Aussehen des Restaurants und der Tanzfläche steht.

JAM

Leeds, United Kingdom
1998
Photography | Photo | Fotografie: James Winspear (VIEW).

An exclusive atmosphere and the absolutely latest design. These are the main features that the Norman Bar has promoted to attract customers since its opening in 1998. From the wide windows giving onto the street, it could be taken for a high-class furniture store. Shapes, colors and textures mingle in an unceasing play of impossible combinations. Sofas with ordinary proportions but rounded profiles; low tables in lively colors with smoothed edges; yellow poufs and stools with a central stem that turn them into an inverted tripod. The curving bar is lit by a strip of neon that is almost fluorescent and from outer space. At the back, an area of low tables, accompanied by seats shaped like drinking-glasses, is placed beside an imposing false white and undulating wall. This stage of grotesque contrasts provides an opportunity to sip the range of cocktails on offer in an authentic dream landscape.

Une atmosphère exclusive et un design tout à fait actuel. Ce sont les principaux atouts que Norman Bar a mis en relief pour attirer les clients depuis son ouverture en 1998. On pourrait croire que derrière ses baies vitrées il y a un magasin de mobilier exclusif. Formes, couleurs et textures s'entremêlent en un jeu incessant de combinaisons impossibles. Des canapés aux formes régulières et aux profils arrondis; des tables basses aux vives couleurs et aux coins imperceptibles; poufs et tabourets jaunes sur un tronc central qui devient un tripode inversé. Le comptoir s'allonge sinueux et éclairé par une bande de néon presque fluorescente et galactique. Au fond, une zone de tables basses entourées de sièges en forme de verres à boire s'étend tout au long d'une fausse cloison de couleur blanche et au profil ondulé. Ce scénario aux nuances grotesques permet de déguster l'offre de boissons combinées dans un paysage vraiment onirique.

Exklusive Atmosphäre und ein hochaktuelles Design. Hauptsächlich diese beiden Aspekte wurden von Norman Bar zum Gewinnen von Kunden seit der Eröffnung des Lokals im Jahre 1998 potenziert. Wenn man von der Straße aus durch die großen Fenster blickt, könnte man den Eindruck gewinnen, daß es sich hier um ein exklusives Möbelgeschäft handelt. Formen, Farben und Texturen mischen sich hier in einem unaufhörlichen Spiel mit den unmöglichsten Kombinationen. Sofas mit gleichmäßigen Formen, aber mit abgerundeten Profilen; niedrige, bunte Tische mit kaum wahrnehmbaren Ecken; gelbe Puffs und Hocker mit einem Schaft in der Mitte, der sich in ein umgekehrtes Stativ verwandelt. Die geschwungene Theke wird von einem fast fluoreszenten und galaktischen Neonstreifen beleuchtet. Hinten wurden niedrige Tische mit den dazugehörigen glasförmigen Sitzen neben einer imposanten weißen Wand mit gewelltem Profil aufgestellt. Diese Szenerie mit grotesken Nuancen ermöglicht den Gästen, das Angebot an Mixgetränken in einer echt traumhaften Atmosphäre zu genießen.

The bar is illuminated by both a row of hanging lamps and an almost fluorescent neon circuit running round its edge.

Le comptoir est éclairé par une série de lampes suspendues et par une ligne de néon presque fluorescent qui l'entoure.

Die Theke wird nicht nur von einer Reihe Hängelampen beleuchtet, sondern auch noch von einem fast fluoreszenten Neon-Stromkreis, der am Rand entlangläuft.

Norman Bar

Seen from the street, the bar looks like a furniture store with exclusive high-class design items.

Depuis la rue, le local peut paraître un magasin présentant ses meubles au design exclusif.

Steht man auf der Straße, hat man manchmal das Gefühl, daß im Lokal ein Geschäft für exklusive Design-Möbelstücke untergebracht ist

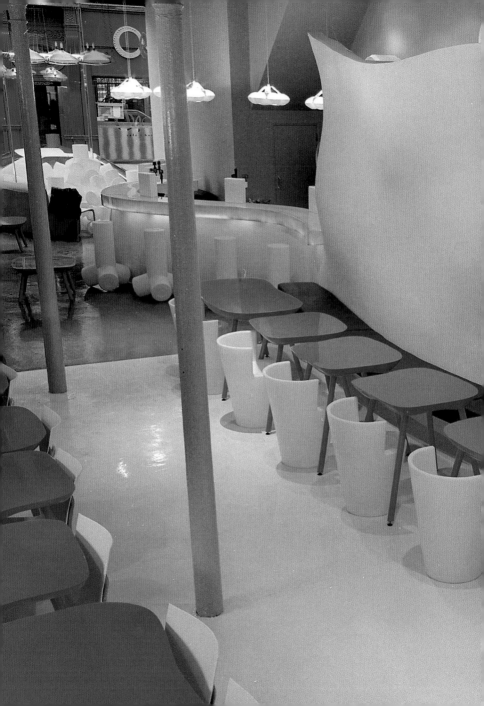

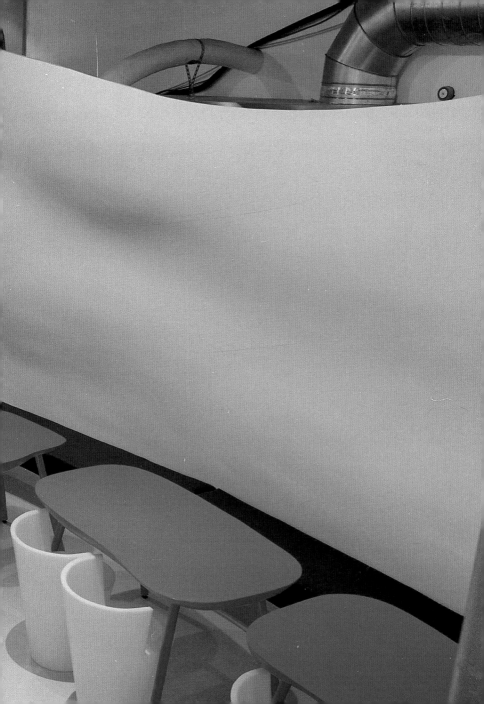

Café Larios

Tomás Alía

Madrid, España
1997
Photography | Photo | Fotografie: Uxio da Vila.

The Café Larios in Madrid combines various styles with breath-taking aesthetic coherence. Delicate design on its most New York face, it divides into a second less precious focus. You enter the Larios through a steel and glass frame split by a large marble door-way. In the main room Art Nouveau mixes with 1970s geometry and kitsch pieces. Wood, leather and parchment stand alongside cold materials and other more ethereal items, such as the feathers that dress the central column. Above the dominant white, dark brown and silver the two resin-sculptured lamps in the colors of the Larios company stand out. Other outstanding pieces are the large bar in marble and dark wood, the white leather seats and the varying lights with parchment shades. The lower floor has more of an industrial flavor and heightened colors. Its floors and columns are dressed with resins and various kinds of steel sheets. Daisy-shaped red lights hang over the two bars of gray marble.

Le madrilène Café Larios combine différents styles avec une cohérence esthétique admirable. Le fin stylisme de son côté le plus new-yorkais se dédouble en un second faisceau à effet moins précieux. On rentre dans le local à travers un entrelacement en acier et verre traversé par un grand portique en marbre. Dans la salle principale, l'Art Nouveau se mêle aux géométries des années 70 et aux pièces kitsch. Bois, cuir et parchemins cohabitent avec des matériaux froids et avec d'autres éléments éthérés comme les plumes qui revêtent la colonne centrale. Sur les blancs, marrons foncés et argents se détachent les deux lampes sculpturales en résine aux couleurs de la firme Larios. Il faut remarquer le grand comptoir en marbre et en bois sombre, les sièges en cuir blanc et les différentes lampes aux abat-jours en parchemin. L'étage inférieur montre un côté plus industriel et coloré. Ses sols et ses colonnes revêtues avec des résines et des tôles d'acier aux différentes caractéristiques. Sur les deux comptoirs réalisées en marbre gris se détachent les lampes rouges en forme de marguerites.

Im Madrider Café Larios werden unterschiedliche Stile mit einer beneidenswerten ästhetischen Kohärenz kombiniert. Feiner Stilismus nach reinster New Yorker Art ist hier neben einem zweiten, weniger geschraubten Stil vorhanden. Man gelangt in das Lokal durch ein Gerüst aus Stahl und Glas mit einem großen Marmorportikus. Im Hauptsaal vermischt sich Art Nouveau mit Formen der 70er Jahre und Gegenständen im Kitsch-Stil. Hier trifft der Gast sowohl auf Holz, Leder und Pergament als auch auf kalte Materialien und andere Stoffe wie die Federn, die die mittlere Säule schmücken. Auf den vorherrschenden weißen, dunkelbraunen und silbernen Farbtönen heben sich die beiden Skulptur-Lampen aus Harz in den Farben der Firma Larios ab. Weitere hervorzuhebende Stücke sind die große Theke aus Marmor und dunklem Holz, die Sitze aus weißem Leder und die verschiedenen Lampen mit Pergamentschirmen. Das untere Stockwerk erinnert eher an eine Fabrik, ist aber gleichzeitig farbenfroh. Fußboden und Säulen wurden mit Harz und Stahlblech verschiedener Arten verkleidet. Über den beiden Theken aus grauem Marmor heben sich die roten, margeritenförmigen Lampen ab.

Access to the Larios is through an impressive steel and glass frame split by a white marble door-way.

L'accès au local se fait à travers un impressionnant treillis en acier et en verre traversé par un portique en marbre blanc.

In das Lokal gelangt man durch ein beeindruckendes Gerüst aus Stahl und Glas mit einem großen Marmorportikus.

On the main floor there is a perfect combination of warm materials such as wood and cold ones such as steel and glass.

Les matériaux chauds comme le bois et froids comme l'acier ou le verre sont, à l'étage principale, en parfaite harmonie.

Im Hauptgeschoß findet man eine perfekte Kombination von warmen Materialien, wie Holz, und kalten Materialien, wie Stahl und Glas, vor.

Café Larios

The dominant hues are white, dark browns, silver and metal, distorted only by some intentional but fleeting item in a livelier color.

Les tons prédominants sont le blanc, les marrons foncés, les argentés et les métalliques qui ne sont rompus que par quelque élément choisi et isolé de couleur plus vive.

Die vorherrschenden Farbtöne sind weiß, dunkelbraun, silber und Metallic-Töne, nur distorsioniert von einigen wenigen Elementen in lebhafteren Farben.

The red and yellow resin sculpture-lamps on the upper floor find their equivalent in the cellar bars: red lights shaped like daisies.

Les lampes sculpture en résine rouge et jaune se détachent à l'étage supérieur et trouvent leur équivalent sur les comptoirs du sous-sol: des lampes rouges en forme de marguerites.

Die unübersehbaren Skulptur-Lampen aus rotem und gelbem Harz der oberen Etage sind an den Theken des Kellergeschosses wiederzufinden: es handelt sich um rote, margeritenförmige Lampen.

Vertigo, Tower 42

Fletcher Priest Architects

London, United Kingdom
2000
Photography | Photo | Fotografie: Chris Gascoigne (VIEW).

Enjoy marvellous views over the British capital while you savour exquisite caviar eased down by a fine glass of champagne. A dream come true in this bar on the 42nd floor of a London skyscraper. Its thirty varieties of champagne and carefully selected sea foods are its main gastronomic appeal. But the real impact and main attraction of this establishment is being able to look out from its wide windows over the city. An oval room gives you a view of London from a truly vertiginous perspective while you are sitting in a comfortable rotating arm-chair. The danger is non-existent, but the sensation is indescribable. Whether by day or night, the feeling of having the world at your feet is really impressive. After this vertiginous experience, one can just relax and chat in its comfortable and intimate inner rooms.

Jouir des merveilleuses vues sur la capitale anglaise et déguster en même temps un délicieux caviar accompagné d'un excellent verre de champagne. Un rêve qui devient réalité dans ce local situé à l'étage 42 d'un gratte-ciel de Londres. Ses trente variétés de vins mousseux et une sélection soignée de fruits de mer constitue son offre gastronomique principale. Mais le point fort, le meilleur attrait de cet établissement est la possibilité, depuis les grandes baies, de se pencher sur la ville. Une salle ovale permet de contempler Londres à partir d'une perspective vertigineuse tout en restant assis dans un confortable fauteuil tournant. Le danger est pratiquement nul mais la sensation est indescriptible. Que ce soit le jour ou la nuit, le spectacle du monde à vos pieds est vraiment fascinant. Après avoir ressenti le vertige, il ne reste plus qu'à se reposer et avoir une conversation animée dans les accueillantes et intimes salles intérieures.

Herrliche Ausblicke auf die englische Hauptstadt bei köstlichem Kaviar und einem Glas auserlesenen Champagner: Dieser Traum wird auf dem 42. Stockwerk eines Londoner Wolkenkratzers wahr. Hier werden dreißig Sorten Schaumwein und eine exquisite Auswahl von Meeresfrüchten angeboten. Das Highlight des Lokals ist jedoch die beeindruckende Aussicht auf die Stadt. Von einem ovalen Saal aus kann man aus einer schwindelerregenden Perspektive, ganz bequem in einem Drehsessel sitzend, auf London herabblicken. Es besteht so gut wie keine Gefahr, aber man hat ein ganz unbeschreibliches Gefühl. Der Eindruck, daß einem die Welt zu Füßen liegt, ist sowohl bei Tag wie auch bei Nacht überwältigend. Nach diesem schwindelerregenden Erlebnis gibt es nichts Besseres als sich in die gemütlichen und intimen Innenräume zurückzuziehen und sich angeregt zu unterhalten.

From the seats in the
glass-enclosed room,
anyone can become a privileged
spectator of the London landscape.

*Depuis les sièges de la salle aux
baies vitrées, n'importe qui peut
devenir un spectateur d'exception
de l'horizon londonien.*

Von den Sitzen des verglasten
Saales aus kann jeder Gast den
außergewöhnlichen Blick auf
London genießen.

Vertigo. Tower 42

Mohmah

Stefano Severi

Carpi, Italia
1999
Photography | Photo | Fotografie: Alberto Ferrero.

Music, fashion, art, photography. Four inspirations that are posed as protectors of the true protagonist of the space, the kitchen. This alternating context interprets too the fusion that must not be absent these days from our plates. Once dinner dates reach their end, the atmosphere gives way to club music, where its variety of functions declares its magical intentions, with emphasis on the decor added. The use of neutral colors, gray and white, on walls and ceilings poses an architectural game which opens out lines in the reconciliation of opposites. The furniture of varnished wood contrasting with stainless steel and finished in leather is placed on turquoise flooring. The result is an elegant, but not invasive universe, as Severi the architect posits. This contemporary ensemble shatters the expectations of Carpi's inhabitants when they express their doubts or inability to understand with a Mo! Mah?

Musique, mode, art, photographie. Quatre motifs d'inspiration s'érigent en protecteurs de la véritable protagoniste de l'espace, la cuisine. Cette alternance contextuelle interprète également la fusion qui ne doit jamais manquer, actuellement, dans les mets. Dès que les rendez-vous pour dîner touchent à leur fin, l'ambiance donne place à la version musique club où la multiplicité fonctionnelle déclare ses intentions magiques, soulignant la propriété appliquée. L'utilisation de couleurs neutres, le gris et le blanc, sur les murs et les plafonds propose un jeu architectonique déployant des plans en syncrétisme d'antithèse. Le mobilier en bois laqué nuancé par des appliques en acier inox et des finitions en cuir est distribué sur le sol bleu turquoise. Le résultat est un univers élégant non envahissant, comme affirme l'architecte Severi lui-même. Un ensemble contemporain qui chamboule les idées des habitants de Carpi qui lancent un Mo! Mah! pour manifester leur doute ou montrer qu'ils n'y comprennent rien.

Musik, Mode, Kunst, Fotografie. Diese vier Inspirationen sind die Beschützer der Küche, des Stars des Lokals. Diese Kontextalternanz gibt auch die Verschmelzung wieder, die heutzutage in der Gastronomie nicht fehlen darf. Wenn die Tische nach dem Dinner abserviert worden sind, verwandelt sich das Lokal in einen Music-Club, in dem die funktionale Vielfalt magisch wirkt. Die Verwendung von neutralen Farben, grau und weiß, bei Wänden und Decken stellt ein architektonisches Spiel dar, das von einem entgegengesetzten Synkretismus gekennzeichnet ist. Das Mobiliar aus lackiertem Holz mit Verzierungen aus rostfreiem Stahl und Leder steht auf einem türkisblauen Fußboden. Das Ergebnis ist eine elegante, aber nicht erdrückende Landschaft, gemäß Interpretation des Architekten Severi. Ein zeitgenössisches Ensemble, das die aus Carpi stammenden Leute verblüfft, wenn sie bei Zweifel oder Verständnislosigkeit "Mo! Mah?" ausrufen.

The lighting highlights
all the angles of the Mohmah.
Its name is a characteristic
Carpi dialect word for expressing
doubt or hesitation.

L'éclairage met en évidence
tous les angles du Mohmah.
Son nom est une expression typique
du dialecte des habitants de Carpi lorsqu'ils
manifestent un doute ou une hésitation.

Die Beleuchtung hebt alle Ecken und
Winkel des Momah hervor.
Der Name des Lokals ist ein typischer
Ausdruck des in Carpi gesprochenen
Dialektes, womit Zweifel geäußert wird.

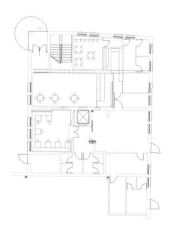

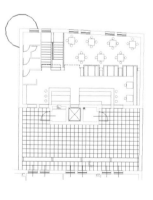

Mohmah

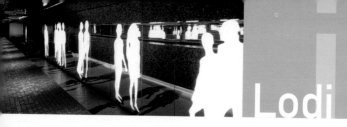

Lodi

Fabio Novembre

Milano, Italia
1998
Photography | Photo | Fotografie: Alberto Ferrero.

Among bar-coding that shows its every-day expiry date. That's how Lodi publicises itself: a piazza-salotto idea with which it makes an effort to expand a pronounced and very narrow space. An initial hall follows the design of a bar-code, idea that other Fabio Novembre creations pursue, as an allegory of the passing of time and persons. It has rounded corners and flood-lights in the floor, which prepares for the drinks area: a deep tunnel accommodating the bar on its left side. Invading this becomes enticing as you notice the shadows thrown onto the floor, effect of the silhouettes chiselled on the mirror surface that covers the entire right-hand side. Fluorescent lights behind these figures solve lighting needs and give the sensation that there are people even if the premises are empty. Once you step on Warhol's shadow, you find the tunnel has ended: another bar-code detains the forward march of time. It is the end of journey where the traveller can make him/herself comfortable.

Codes à barres comme expression d'un quotidien caduque. Le Lodi a été projeté comme un concept de piazza-salotto manifestant l'effort pour dilater un espace prononcé et très étroit. Un vestibule initial suit le dessin d'un code à barres, idée commune à d'autres créations de Fabio Novembre, comme une allégorie du temps qui passe et des gens qui se succèdent. Ses coins sont arrondis et les feux insérés dans le pavement, qui prévoit une aire pour prendre des verres: un profond tunnel accueille un comptoir côté gauche. On a envie de l'envahir en voyant les ombres qui se reflètent sur le carrelage, effet des silhouettes ciselées sur la surface de la glace qui couvre entièrement le mur côté droit. Des fluorescents installés derrière ces personnages couvrent les nécessités de lumière et donnent la sensation de la présence de personnes même si le local est vide. Dès qu'on marche sur l'ombre de Warhol on sait que c'est la fin du tunnel: un autre code à barres arrête l'avance du temps. C'est la fin du parcours et le voyageur peut s'installer.

Lodi präsentiert sich zwischen Barrencodes, die den alltäglichen Verfall ausdrücken. Bei dem als Piazza-Salotto konzipierten Lokal erkennt man die Bemühung, einen sehr engen Raum optisch zu vergrößern. Wie bei anderen Schöpfungen von Fabio Novembre ist der Vorraum vom Design eines Barrencodes abgeleitet und stellt eine Allegorie des Laufes der Zeit und der Aufeinanderfolge der Menschen dar. Merkmale des Lokals sind die abgerundeten Ecken und die Fußbodenstrahler; ein tiefer Tunnel beherbergt die Theke auf der linken Seite. Die auf dem Fußboden reflektierten Schatten weisen den Weg zur Theke hin. Diese Schatten werden von den auf dem Spiegel, welcher die ganze rechte Wand der Theke verkleidet, ziselierten Gestalten geworfen. Hinter diesen Figuren installierte Leuchtröhren sorgen dafür, daß genügend Licht vorhanden ist und lassen das Gefühl aufkommen, daß, obwohl das Lokal leer ist, Gäste da sind. Sobald man auf Warhols Schatten tritt, ist der Tunnel zu Ende: ein anderer Barrencode stoppt den Lauf der Zeit. Hier endet der Weg, der Reisende kann es sich nun bequem machen.

Conceived as the bar-coding on a book,
from the entrance-hall you can look down the deep tunnel.
The aim of making the premises look bigger is achieved
by reflecting lighted figures on the floor: following the photos of Richard
Avedon for The Factory, the other temple of Novembre in New York.
The clearly defined corridor is completely covered
with Bisazza Vetricolor material in brown tones.

Conçu comme le code à barres d'un livre,
depuis le vestibule on peut voir le profond tunnel.
L'expansion visuelle est réelle dès que les silhouettes illuminées
se reflètent sur le carrelage du sol: selon les photographies de Richard Avedon
pour The Factory, l'autre temple de Fabio Novembre à New York.
Le couloir prononcé est couvert par le matériau Bisazza Vetricolor
dans les tons marron.

Das Lokal ist als Barrencode eines Buches konzipiert, vom Vorraum aus sieht
man den tiefen Tunnel. Die optische Vergrößerung wird durch Reflektierung
der beleuchteten Figuren auf den Fußboden erreicht –anhand Richard
Avedons Fotografien für The Factory, der andere New Yorker Tempel von
Novembre. Der enge Flur ist völlig mit Bisazza-Vetricolor-Material in braunen
Farbtönen verkleidet.

When you reach the end of the tunnel, a new cabin of bar-codes, a snapshot parallel to the one in the hall, welcomes groups of Chipre de Amat tables and R3 stools by Costantino, designed by Carlo Mollino. The wall that closes the "Lodi nave" is made from strips of mirror that double the total space of the premises.

Lorsqu'on arrive à la fin du tunnel, une nouvelle cabine de codes à barres, instantanée parallèle à celle du vestibule, accueille les groupes de tables modèle Chipre de Amat, et des tabourets modèle R3 de Constantino, design de Carlon Mollino. Le mur fermant la "nef Lodi" est fait à partir des plaques de miroirs qui doublent tout l'espace du local.

Am Ende des Tunnels kommt man zu einer weiteren Barrencode-Kabine, die parallel zu derjenigen des Vorraums liegt und in der Tischgruppen des Modells Chipre von Amat, sowie Hocker des Modells R3 von Costantino, entworfen von Carlo Mollino, stehen. Die Wand, welche die "Lodi-Halle" abschließt, ist aus Spiegelplatten hergestellt, die den gesamten Raum des Lokals verdoppeln.

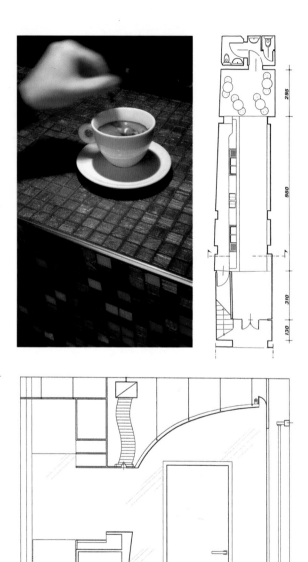

Lodi

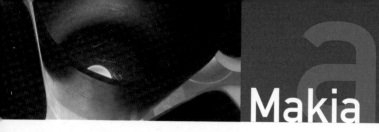

Makia

Laura Tirassa

Milano, Italia
1998
Photography | Photo | Fotografie: Paola D'Amico.

The objective of Laura Tirassa, designer and proprietor of the Makia, was to make transparency and visibility the starting-points of her project. The original bar from the 1930s was painted white to fit in with the glass and mirrors, preferred materials in the Makia. The rest of the establishment uses very few elements so as to emphasise its functional nature, which highlights the secure and graceful movements of the bar-tenders preparing their cocktails behind the bar. The decor of the rooms consists of both original furniture, such as the tables, and 1970s items found in antique shops, such as the Cassina chairs, originally from a Paris office. The result is an establishment that is one of the new wave of Milanese fashion bars. Its relaxed atmosphere and soft melodies make the Makia a perfect enclave for an elegant and sophisticated after-dinner pre-disco drink.

L'idée de Laura Tirassa, dessinatrice et propriétaire du Makia a été de réaliser une ambiance où la transparence et la visibilité seraient le point de départ du projet. Le comptoir original des années 30 a été peint en blanc, en accord avec le verre et les miroirs, matériaux privilégiés dans le Makia. Le reste de l'établissement se compose de très peu d'éléments, pour renforcer une fonctionnalité qui a comme finalité d'embellir les mouvements assurés et graciles des garçons qui préparent leurs cocktails derrière le comptoir. La décoration des salles est faite de meubles inventés -c'est le cas des tables- et de meubles des années soixante dix récupérés chez les antiquaires -c'est le cas des chaises de Cassina qui proviennent d'un bureau parisien. Le résultat est un établissement qui s'inscrit dans le déferlement milanais des locaux à tendance. Son atmosphère relax et les mélodies soft font du Makia un parfaite enclave pour un après dîner pré-disco drink élégant et sophistiqué.

Laura Tirassa, Designerin und Inhaberin des Makia, wollte ein Ambiente schaffen, bei dem Transparenz und Übersichtlichkeit die Ausgangspunkte des Projektes sein sollten. Die aus den 30er Jahren stammende Theke wurde weiß gestrichen, im Einklang mit dem Glas und den Spiegeln, den bevorzugten Materialien des Makia. Der Rest des Lokals besteht aus sehr wenigen Elementen zur Betonung einer Funktionalität, welche die sicheren und leichten Bewegungen der Kellner, die hinter der Theke die Cocktails mixen, schöner wirken lassen. Die Dekoration der Räume besteht aus Phantasiemöbeln, wie zum Beispiel die Tische, und aus von Antiquaren restaurierten Möbeln der siebziger Jahre, wie die Stühle von Cassina, welche aus einem Pariser Büro stammen. Das Ergebnis ist eines der zahlreichen Trend-Lokale, die in der letzten Zeit in Mailand eröffnet worden sind. Die entspannte Atmosphäre und die Soft-Melodien machen das Makia zu einem perfekten Ort für einen eleganten und exquisiten after-dinner pre-disco Drink.

The outstanding features of the Makia are its elegant and modern atmosphere, thanks to its abundant use of glass and mirrors, which spread colored light over the walls.

Le Makia est caractérisé par son ambiance élégante et moderne, grâce à l'utilisation abondante des miroirs ou du verre qui diffuse une lumière de couleurs sur les murs.

Das Makia besticht wegen seines eleganten und modernen Ambientes, dank des großzügigen Gebrauchs von Materialien wie Spiegeln und Glas, welche buntes Licht auf die Wände werfen.

Makia

Original pieces of furniture adorn the Makia, such as the tables
with a tubular base and a circular glass top that favours social
contact between customers. The Cassini chairs, like the rest
of the furniture, were found in second-hand shops. The lamps show
off the art of Archimede Seguso, a famous Venetian glass master.

*Les meubles du Makia sont des pièces inventées, comme c'est le cas
des tables, qui ont une base en tube et un plan circulaire en verre
qui favorise la convivialité entre les clients. Les chaises sont signées
Cassina et comme le reste du mobilier elles ont été récupérées chez
les antiquaires. Les lampes sont le reflet de l'art d'Archimède Seguso,
un célèbre maître verrier vénitien.*

Die Möbel des Makia sind Phantasie-Stücke, ebenso die Tische, deren runde
Glasplatten auf Rohren aufliegen, was die Kommunikation zwischen den
Kunden fördert. Die Stühle von Cassina, wie auch das restliche Mobiliar,
wurden von Antiquaren restauriert. Die Lampen zeugen von der Kunst des
berühmten Meisters des venezianischen Glases Archimede Seguso.

Julien Launge Bar

Marcello Zerbini, Maria Cristina Bottoni, Clara Villani

Milano, Italia
2001
Photography | Photo | Fotografie: Paola D'Amico.

The pleasure of giving yourself over to 1960s originals. Letting your imagination fly among murals that recreate pop colors and shapes can be a complete dream trip. The relationship between the fabric-covered walls, the sofa area and the leaning wall forms a peaceful bar in which red, orange and white are the three principles governing the space. The decorated walls and the sofa area are placed right by the entrance, where you will also find the bar, acting as a kind of nexus with the outside world. The architects created a wider area at the back of the bar where a livelier atmosphere rules. As such, the wall leaning inwards balances the more enclosed inner room and the entrance area open to the street window. The plastic on the walls, later varnished, the orange resin flooring and the glamorous sofa also covered with red plastic are all identifying features of a 1960s past, recovered so to make you feel at home.

Le plaisir de se complaire dans les prototypes des années soixante. Laisser l'imagination s'envoler parmi les graphismes muraux qui font revivre les couleurs et les formes pop peut devenir un voyage de rêve. La relation entre les murs tapissés, la zone des divans et le mur incliné décrit un local pacifique où le rouge, l'orange et le blanc sont les trois bases pour ordonner l'espace. Les murs décorés et la zone des divans ont été disposés juste à l'entrée où se trouve également le comptoir qui fait le lien avec l'extérieur. Les architectes ont voulu créer une zone plus étendue au fond du local pour obtenir une atmosphère plus vivante. Pour cela, le plan incliné équilibre à nouveau la salle intérieure, plus réservée et la zone d'entrée ouverte sur la vitrine. Le plastique des murs qui ont été vernis ensuite, le pavement en résine orange ou le divan glamoureux recouvert également en toile plastique rouge sont les signes caractérisant un passé, la période des années soixante, qui a été récupéré pour se sentir comme chez soi.

Die Prototypen der 60er Jahre genießen. Der Phantasie freien Lauf lassen unter Wandgraphiken, welche die Farben und Formen des Pop-Stils zu neuem Leben erwecken, kann eine traumhafte Reise sein. Die Beziehung der mit Stoff verkleideten Wänden, des Bereiches der Sofas und der schrägen Wand zueinander ergibt ein ruhiges Lokal, in dem die drei Farben Rot, Orange und Weiß den Raum beherrschen. Die dekorierten Wände und der Bereich der Sofas wurden genau an den Eingang platziert, wo sich auch die Theke befindet, als Verbindung zur Außenwelt. Die Architekten wollten einen geräumigeren Bereich im hinteren Teil des Lokals schaffen, um dort eine lebhaftere Atmosphäre gestalten zu können. Deshalb gleicht die schiefe Ebene den intimeren Innenraum und den offenen Eingangsbereich über dem Schaufenster wieder aus. Die mit Kunststoff verkleideten und nachträglich lackierten Wände, der Fußboden aus orangem Harz, oder das glamouröse, ebenfalls mit rotem Kunststoff bezogene Sofa sind Merkmale der Mode der 60er Jahre, auf die wieder zurückgegriffen wurde, damit der Gast sich wie zu Hause fühlt.

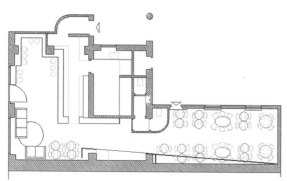

Conceived round the theme of welcome, the choice of furniture confirms the evocation of the items you would find in a home. The white plastic chairs are manufactured by Knoll, from a design by A. Jacobsen. The Minotti sofas, lined in red plastic, are designed by R. Dordoni. However, it is the graphics reproduced on the wall fabric which makes the fantasy of other times take off. They are by the Peri Tessuti company, following the architects' own design.

Conçu autour du thème de l'accueil, le choix du mobilier confirme une évocation voulue des éléments disposés comme chez soi. Les chaises en plastique blanc sont produites par Knoll, d'après un design de Al Jacobsen. Les canapés de Minotti, revêtus de plastique rouge ont été dessinés par R. Dordoni. Mais c'est le graphisme reproduit sur le revêtement tissu des murs qui souligne la fantaisie d'autrefois. Selon le dessin des architectes, il a été réalisé par l'entreprise Peri Tessuti.

Bei der Auswahl des Mobiliars wurde an die Gemütlichkeit gedacht, was die Absicht, an die in einer Wohnung aufgestellten Elemente zu erinnern, bestätigt. Die weißen Stühle aus Kunststoff wurden von Knoll hergestellt, nach einem Entwurf von A. Jacobsen. Die mit rotem Kunststoff bezogenen Sofas von Minotti wurden von R. Dordoni entworfen. Die auf dem Stoff der Wände reproduzierte Graphik ist es jedoch, was die Phantasie vergangener Zeiten ehrt. Von den Architekten selbst entworfen, wurde sie von der Firma Peri Tessuti angefertigt.

Julien Launge Bar

An idea of uniformity glides over the walls conceived as a container.
A white wall, leaning inwards at the back of the bar, leads those looking for
a bolder climax towards the magnet of the orange circle on the back wall.
Magnificent, the low tables in the style of the Scandinavian chairs of
Saarineen: by placing one base on another, a surface of great size is created.

*Une idée d'uniformité plane sur les murs traités comme un container. Un mur
blanc, à demi incliné au fond du local, conduit ceux qui désirent un climax plus
audacieux: le cercle orange sur le mur est l'aimant que cette ambiance réclame.
De superbes tables basses qui reprennent le style des chaises scandinaves de
Saarineen: à partir d'une base disposée sur une autre, on a placé un dessus,
surface aux dimensions considérables.*

Über den als Behälter konzipierten Wänden schwebt die Idee der
Uniformität. Eine weiße, halbschräge Wand im hinteren Teil des Lokals dient
als Wegweiser für diejenigen Leute, die eine gewagtere Klimax suchen: der
orangene Kreis auf der Wand ist der Magnet, der diese Atmosphäre anzieht.
Großartig sind die niedrigen Tische im Stil der skandinavischen Stühle von
Saarineen: Auf eines der beiden Stützelementen wurde eine Platte von
beachtlicher Größe aufgelegt.

Le Trabendo

Graphics | Graphisme | Werbegraphik: Futura 2000
Paris, France
2000
Photography | Photo | Fotografie: Fabrice Guyot.

Le Trabendo is located in La Villette park, the largest green space in Paris. Heir of the legendary club Hot Brass, the current establishment was born of the amazing work of a team consisting of the architect-designer Kristian Gavoille and the painter-graphic artist known by the name of Futura 2000. Aiming to create a space in the style of a "modern cabaret" that would house the most eclectic shows, this night club displays an aesthetic which is not at all aseptic. Its dark, lugubrious interior, as if it were the inside of a rusty tank, contrasts with the characters that decorate the walls. A resin floor that looks like a mirror of water and a twelve meter-long glass bar that glows and fills the space, absorbing the spectator's gaze, stand out in this atmosphere of "rust".

Le Trabendo est situé dans le parc de la Villette, le plus grand espace vert de Paris. Héritier du mythique club Hot Brass, l'établissement actuel est né du travail de génie d'une équipe composée par l'architecte dessinateur Kristian Gavoille et le peintre graphiste qui se présente sous le nom de Futura 2000. Avec l'intention de créer un espace comme une sorte de "cabaret moderne" pour accueillir les spectacles les plus éclectiques, ce club nocturne est présenté avec une esthétique très peu aseptique. Son intérieur est sombre, lugubre, comme l'intérieur d'une citerne corrodée et contraste avec les personnages qui décorent les murs. Dans cette ambiance "d'oxyde" on remarque un pavement de résine semblable à un miroir d'eau, et un comptoir en verre long de douze mètres reluit et dilate l'espace, absorbant le spectateur.

Le Trabendo befindet sich im Park La Villette, der größten Pariser Grünanlage. Nachfolger des legendären Clubs Hot Brass, ist das Lokal ein geniales Werk des Architekten und Designers Kristian Gavoille und des Malers und Graphikers, der sich unter dem Namen Futura 2000 verbirgt. Die kaum als aseptisch zu bezeichnende Ästhetik dieses Nachtclubs verfolgt das Ziel, ein "modernes Kabarett" zu schaffen, in dem die eklektischsten Shows vorgeführt werden. Das dunkle, düstere Innere des Lokals, das wie das Innere einer zerfallenen Zisterne anmutet, steht im krassen Gegensatz zu den auf den Wänden abgebildeten Gestalten. In diesem "rostigen" Ambiente sticht der Harzfußboden, der wie ein Spiegel aus Wasser aussieht, sowie auch die zwölf Meter lange Theke aus Glas, die glitzert und den Raum optisch vergrößert, hervor, und lenkt dabei die Aufmerksamkeit der Zuschauer auf sich.

Conceived as a kind of "modern cabaret", Le Trabendo is a favorite locale of the Paris night thanks to its commitment to putting on gigs of the top music groups.

Conçu comme une sorte de "cabaret moderne", Le Trabendo est un des locaux préférés des nuits parisiennes grâce à son travail de présentation des concerts des groupes musicaux les plus remarquables.

Als eine Art "modernen Kabaretts" konzipiert, ist Le Trabendo eines der bevorzugten Lokale des Pariser Nachtlebens, da hier stets die besten Musikgruppen auftreten.

A resin floor that looks like a mirror of water and a glass bar that glows and fills the space, absorbing the spectator's gaze, stand out in this rusted, lugubrious environment.

Dans une ambiance oxydée et lugubre, on remarque un pavement en résine qui semble être un miroir d'eau et un comptoir en verre reluit et dilate l'espace en absorbant le spectateur.

In einem rostigen und düsteren Ambiente fallen der wie ein Spiegel aus Wasser anmutende Harzfußboden und die glitzernde Theke aus Glas, die den Raum optisch vergrößert, auf, wodurch die Aufmerksamkeit der Zuschauer erregt wird.

Le Trabendo

The walls of Le Trabendo are home to the powerfully expressive characters of the graphic artist Futura 2000. These wild maniacs stare and grin, provoke and outrage the audience of the locale.

Les murs du Trabendo hébergent des personnages à forte expression, oeuvre du graphiste Futura 2000. Ces énergumènes si drôles regardent et sourient, provoquent et font violence au public du local.

Von den Wänden des Le Trabendo schauen die ausdrucksstarken, vom Graphiker Futura 2000 geschaffenen Gestalten. Das Publikum wird von diesen lustigen Rüpeln angeblickt und angelächelt, provoziert und gereizt.

LE TRABENDO
paris la villette

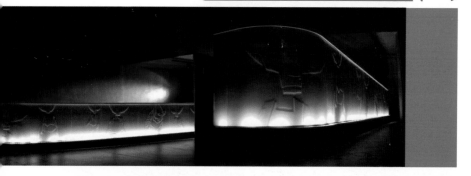

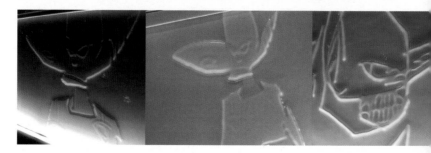

Light Bar

Philippe Starck

London, United Kingdom
1999
Photography | Photo | Fotografie: Chas Wilshere.

St. Martin's Lane is one of the magical hotels owned by the iconoclast Ian Schrager, located right in the middle of Covent Garden. Conceived for a new jet set of nomads who roam the world in search of new experience, this hotel is the most intimate collaboration undertaken by Schrager and the renowned designer Philippe Starck. The outcome is a subversive collision of influences that is magical, amusing and exuberant. The Light Bar is one of the establishments open inside the hotel. The basis for its sophisticated atmosphere is the complex lighting system created on the neutral background of slate floors and walls of grey stone. Four zones are defined with purple, green and yellow lights: on their high walls are projected the faces of young people making funny faces. As customers pass by each face, they will see how their cocktails pick up extraordinarily captivating nuances.

St Martins Lane est un des hôtels magiques propriété du transgresseur Ian Schrager, situé en plein centre de Covent Garden. Conçu pour une nouvelle jet set de nomades qui parcourent le monde à la recherche de nouvelles expériences, cet hôtel constitue le travail conjoint le plus personnel réalisé par Schrager et le dessinateur de renom Philippe Starck. Le résultat est une collision subversive d'influences au résultat magique, drôle et exubérant. Le Light Bar est un de ses établissements. La base de son atmosphère sophistiquée est le système d'éclairage complexe créé sur la base neutre des sols en ardoise noire et les murs en pierre grise. Des lampes pourpres, vertes et jaunes délimitent les quatre zones. Sur les murs sont projetés les visages de jeunes garçons qui font de drôles grimaces. Les clients verront, en passant par chacune de ces zones, que leurs cocktails reflètent des nuances étrangement captivantes.

Mitten im Herzen von Covent Garden liegend, ist St Martins Lane eines der zauberhaften Hotels, dessen Eigentümer der Provokateur Ian Schrager ist. Das für den neuen Jet-set, deren Mitglieder auf der Suche nach neuen Erfahrungen ständig durch die Welt reisen, gedachte Lokal ist das von der Zusammenarbeit Schagers und des renommierten Designers Philippe Starck am meisten geprägte Werk. Das Ergebnis ist ein subversives Aufeinanderprallen von Einflüssen, das magisch, belustigend und überschwenglich wirkt. Die Light Bar ist eines der öffentlichen Lokale innerhalb dieses Hotels. Grundlage ihrer exquisiten Atmosphäre ist die komplexe Beleuchtungsanlage, welche auf der neutralen Oberfläche der Fußböden aus schwarzen Schieferplatten und der Wände aus grauem Stein installiert ist. Mit purpurfarbenen, grünen und gelben Lichtern wurden vier Bereiche abgegrenzt, auf deren hohen Wände Gesichter von jungen Leuten lustige Grimassen schneiden. Wenn die Gäste an den Gesichtern vorbeigehen, werden sie feststellen, daß sich in ihren Cocktails seltsame Formen widerspiegeln.

The eclectic range of furniture and fittings includes collectors' items such as the wine-glasses on exhibit in a cabinet of the same material: a sample of the combination of aesthetic influences in this bar.

L'éclectique sélection du mobilier et la présence de pièces de collection, comme les verres en cristal présentés dans une vitrine sont un exemple de la combinaison esthétique appliquée à ce local.

Das eklektische Mobiliar und die Kollektionsstücke, wie die in einer Glasvitrine ausgestellten Kristallgläser, sind ein Beispiel der Verbindung verschiedener ästethischer Einflüsse, die im Lokal zu finden ist.

Light Bar

Fuse

Àngels Hidalgo de la Torre

Barcelona, España
2001
Photography | Photo | Fotografie: David Manchón.

This locale in Barcelona's central Eixample area breaks with traditional rules. In just one year it has become an essential point of reference for the city's fashion vanguard. Split into two distinct rooms, Fuse opts for a combination of colors, textures and varied materials, from the most rustic to the most sophisticated, though always fresh and dynamic in its setting. The first room has a bar with cloakroom, in front of which amateur cybernauts can consult their e-mail or lose themselves on the Web using the computer terminals lined up on the illuminated ledge running along the main wall. The second room, at the back of the locale, has the dance floor, surrounded by easy-to-move chairs and tables for dining or just having a drink.

Le local situé en plein Eixample barcelonais rompt avec les normes de la tradition. En un an il est devenu la référence claire pour l'avancée "fashion" de la ville. Divisé en deux salles bien différenciées, Fuse a misé sur une combinaison de couleurs, textures et matériaux divers; du plus rustique au plus sophistiqué, sans jamais abandonner la fraîcheur et le dynamisme de son ambiance. La première salle accueille le comptoir avec garde-robe. Face à celui-ci tout amateur cibernaute peut lire son courrier électronique ou se perdre sur la Toile en utilisant les ordinateurs alignés sur un plan de travail tout au long du mur principal. Dans la seconde salle, au fond du local, la piste de danse est entourée de tables et de chaises, facilement transportables, où l'on peut dîner ou prendre un verre.

Dieses inmitten des Eixample von Barcelona gelegene Lokal bricht alle Normen der Tradition. Für die Vorreiter der "Fashion" ist es in nur einem Jahr zu einem Begriff geworden. In dem in zwei von einander unabhängige Säle gegliederte Fuse werden unterschiedliche Farben, Texturen und Materialien kombiniert, vom äußerst Rustikalen bis hin zum Exquisitesten, wobei es auch nicht an Gewagtheit und Dynamismus fehlt. Im ersten Saal befindet sich eine Theke mit Garderoben-Service, gegenüber davon können Internet-Fans an den auf einem beleuchteten Bord aufgereihten Computern E-mails lesen und schreiben oder im Netz surfen. Im hinteren Teil des zweiten Saales erstreckt sich die Tanzfläche, welche von leicht wegzuräumenden Tischen und Stühlen umgeben ist. Dort kann man zu Abend essen oder auch nur etwas trinken.

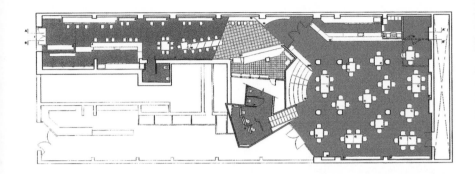

White is the unifying color
of the spaces, present in both
the basic structural elements
and most of the furniture.

*Le blanc est la couleur choisie pour
unir les espaces: on le trouve dans les
éléments structurels de base et dans
la plus grande partie du mobilier.*

Weiß ist die vereinheitlichende Farbe
der Räume und ist sowohl bei den
Grundelementen wie auch bei dem
größten Teil der Möbel vorhanden.

Fuse

The lighting system highlights certain structures and is also itself an essential item of decoration.

Le système d'éclairage est pensé pour rehausser certaines structures et comme instruments décoratif fondamental.

Das Beleuchtungssystem dient zum Hervorheben einiger Strukturen und außerdem als wesentliches Dekorationsmittel.

Kaiku

Roberto Ercilla y Luis Zufiaur

Vitoria, España

1994

Photography | Photo | Fotografie: César San Millán.

Located in Vitoria's Cuesta de San Francisco, Kaiku revolves round two central ideas. First, the existence of a basement has made it possible to locate a wine-cellar well communicated with the main bar. This emerges from below as the most distinctive element of Kaiku. Second, the open area at the back is used to suggest visual extension of the interior space. Textures, colors and shapes become here the authentic protagonists of the communication with the clientèle that is being aimed for. Reinforced concrete in the bar, benches and tables, elemental volumes of a suggestive and simple plastic geometry; the wooden platform that runs right through the locale as continuous tiling; and the ceiling-to-floor double pane of glass that faces the back-patios are just a few examples of this carefully thought-out stage set.

Situé dans la Cuesta de San Francisco à Vitoria, Kaiku a été conçu autour de deux idées centrales. D'une part, la présence d'un sous-sol au centre du local a permis la création d'une cave bien communiquée avec le comptoir central du bar, qui émerge depuis le sous-sol comme l'élément le plus remarquable. D'autre part, l'existence d'une zone arrière ouverte est comme le prolongement visuel de l'espace intérieur. Les textures, les couleurs et les formes deviennent ici les authentiques protagonistes de la communication que l'on veut établir avec les clients. Du béton armé pour le comptoir, les bancs et les tables, conformant des volumes élémentaires à la géométrie plastique suggestive et simple; le parquet en bois s'étend en un plancher continu; et la double baie vitrée s'élève du sol au plafond enfermant le patio. Ce sont des éléments remarquables de cette scène très étudiée.

Kaiku, in der Cuesta de San Francisco in Vitoria gelegen, wird von zwei Grundideen beherrscht. Einerseits hat das Vorhandensein eines Kellers in der Mitte des Lokals ermöglicht, eine Weinkellerei einzurichten, welche mit der mittig angeordneten Theke gut verbunden ist. Diese tritt aus dem Kellergeschoß hervor und ist aus diesem Grunde das repräsentativste Element der Bar. Andererseits wurde der Hinterhof zur optischen Vergrößerung des Innenraumes ausgenutzt. Die Texturen, Farben und Formen spielen nun die Hauptrolle bei der Kommunikation, die man mit den Gästen aufzunehmen versucht. Die Theke, Bänke und Tische aus Stahlbeton stellen Grundkörper einer sowohl suggestiven als auch einfachen plastischen Geometrie dar; das Holzpodium, das sich über das ganze Lokal wie ein durchlaufender Boden erstreckt, und die Doppelglaswand, die Hinterhof und Lokal voneinander trennt, sind nur einige Beispiele dieses durchdachten Szenario.

The double pane of glass that gives on to the back-yard
recalls oriental-style scenes. The effect is to extend visually
the indoor space.

La double baie vitrée donnant sur le patio rappelle
certains lieux proches des ambiances orientales.
L'effet en est un prolongement visuel de l'espace intérieur.

Die Doppelglaswand zum Hinterhof erinnert an fast
orientalisch anmutende Szenarios.
Dadurch wird eine optische Vergrößerung des Innenraumes
erzielt.

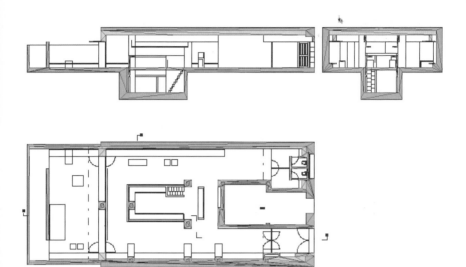

Structured as a box of light in which masses take on geometric form, the bar's true protagonists are its basically gray and green textures and colors.

Structuré comme une caisse diaphane dans laquelle les volumes prennent une forme géométrique, les véritables protagonistes sont les textures et les couleurs employées, gris et vert surtout.

Das Lokal ist wie ein diaphaner Kasten strukturiert, in dem die Elemente einen geometrischen Charakter annehmen, und die verwandten Texturen und Farben, hauptsächlich graue und grüne Farbtöne, die Hauptrolle spielen.

Kaiku

The wooden platform that runs across the entire floor unifies the interiors. The ubiquitous reinforced concrete used in benches, tables and the bar gives off a cold plastic feeling throughout the bar.

Le parquet en bois s'étend en un seul plancher et unifie les intérieurs. Le béton armé omniprésent forme les bancs, les tables et le comptoir confèrent une froide plasticité à tout l'intérieur.

Das sich über den ganzen Boden erstreckende Holzpodium vereinheitlicht die Innenräume. Der allgegenwärtige Stahlbeton, der bei Bänken, Tischen und auch bei der Theke verwandt wurde, suggeriert eine kalte Plastizität im ganzen Lokal.

No Rio Dour

Guilherme Couto y António Costa Leite
Porto, Portugal
1997
Photography | Photo | Fotografie: Nuno Borges de Araujo.

This bar-restaurant seems to wander with its feet off the ground over the waters of the Duero river on its passage through the bohemian Portuguese city of Oporto, like a boat adrift, at times immobile, at times oscillating. Its privileged location turns this horizontal structure, made mainly of wood and steel, into a magnificent veranda over the river-scape. One wall joins its body to the land whilst its interior opens out to the river. What could very well be the hold of this improvised ship is occupied by the kitchen and restaurant services. The diners eat on the main floor, which has one internal space of about 75 square meters and an outside space of about 125 square meters. However, the limits between the two areas are blurred because of the glass elements used to divide the spaces. In contrast with this transparency, the furniture is based on teak, iron, copper and fiber-cement.

Hors de la terre ferme ce bar-restaurant semble voguer sur les eaux du Duero à son passage par la ville un peu bohème de Porto. Comme un bac, immobile ou oscillant, partant à la dérive. Sa situation privilégiée fait que cette structure horizontale en bois où prédomine l'acier se transforme en un balcon extraordinaire sur le paysage fluvial. Un mur unit le corps à la terre pendant que ses espaces s'ouvrent sur le fleuve. Ce qui pourrait bien être la cale de ce navire improvisé est occupé par la cuisine et par les services du restaurant. Les commensaux se placent au niveau principal divisé en un espace intérieur, mesurant 75 mètres carrés et un espace extérieur mesurant 125 mètres carrés. Cependant les limites entre les deux zones sont diffuses grâce à des éléments de séparation en verre. Le mobilier en bois de kambala, fer et cuivre et fibro-ciment contraste avec la transparence.

Ein der lebensfrohen portugiesischen Stadt Porto gelegen, läßt sich dieses Bar-Restaurant wie ein manchmal stillstehender und manchmal schaukelnder Prahm auf dem Fluß Douro treiben. Dank dieser privilegierten Lage wird die vorwiegend aus Holz und Stahl bestehende horizontale Struktur zu einem einzigartigen Balkon über der Flußlandschaft. Eine Wand verbindet diesen Teil des Gebäudes mit dem Boden, wogegen der Raum selbst nach dem Fluß geht. Was hier sehr gut die Ladeluke des improvisierten Schiffes sein könnte beherbergt die Küche und die Dienstbereiche des Restaurants. Die Gäste werden im Hauptgeschoß, das in einen etwa 75 m2 großen Innenraum und einen 125 m2 großen Außenbereich gegliedert ist, empfangen. Durch den Gebrauch von Glaselementen wirkt jedoch die Abgrenzung zwischen beiden Bereichen verschwommen. Das Mobiliar aus Kambala-Holz, Eisen, Kupfer und Faserzement kontrastiert mit der Durchsichtigkeit.

The main floor, looking like
a jetty over the river, shares
the horizontal lines of the
service area.

*Le niveau principal, à mode
d'embarcadère sur les eaux du
fleuve, s'unit à la zone des services
en horizontalité de toutes les lignes.*

Das als Anlegestelle entworfene
Hauptgeschoß weist, wie auch die
Dienstbereiche, horizontale
Linien auf.

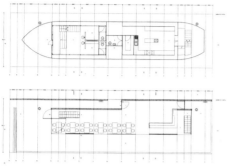

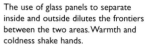

The use of glass panels to separate inside and outside dilutes the frontiers between the two areas. Warmth and coldness shake hands.

L'utilisation de panneaux en verre pour séparer l'intérieur de l'extérieur fait que, par moments, les limites entre les deux zones du local s'estompent. Accueil et froideur se donnent la main.

Durch Verwendung abtrennender Glasplatten zwischen Außen- und Innenbereich ist der Übergang zwischen den beiden Bereichen fließend. Wärme und Kälte reichen sich hier die Hand.

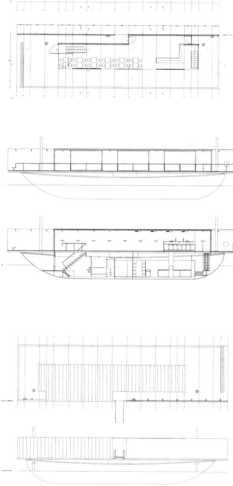

No Rio Douro

The views of the city from the terrace and the
inside of the restaurant make up its main attractions.
The frontier between land and water
is sometimes blurred.

Les vues sur la ville depuis la terrasse et l'intérieur
du restaurant constituent un de ses meilleurs atouts.
Il arrive que les limites entre terre et eau s'estompent.

Einer der hauptsächlichen Anziehungspunkte dieses
Lokals ist der Ausblick auf die Stadt, den man von der
Terrasse und dem Restaurant aus hat.
Die Grenze zwischen Erde und Wasser wirkt hier
manchmal wie verschwommen.

Fonfone

Alfonso de la Fuente Rey (Pichiglas)
Barcelona, España
2000
Photography | Photo | Fotografie: Martí Llorens.

Fonfone pops up in Barcelona's Old Quarter as a Yin and Yang encounter conceived as pure geometry. This universe of mould-breaking design has two opposite poles posed as technical solution to the excessive length of the original premises. The front area of the room, used as a reception area, is the cold North, dominated by greens and blues. At the back, like a flame of attractive flashes call people forward, lies the South, warm and ardent, dominated by reds, yellows and oranges. As an element common to both hemispheres, we find the dominant material, plastic, used on floors, walls and lamps. The bar, stretching throughout the locale, is divided into two by the lighting tones created by lamps of Logo pieces of different colors and integrated circuits.

Fonfone émerge en pleine vieille ville de Barcelone comme lieu de réunion yin yan conçu à partir d'un schéma purement géométrique. Cet univers de design en transgression possède deux pôles opposés comme solution à la longueur excessive du local original. La partie avant de la salle, qui sert de réception, est le nord froid, dominé par des verts et des bleus. Au fond, comme une flamme aux scintillements attrayants invite les gens à s'approcher: c'est le pole sud, chaud et ardent. Les nuances des rouges, des jaunes et des orangés y dominent. Comme élément commun aux deux hémisphères domine la matière plastique appliquée sur les sols, les murs et les lampes. Le comptoir qui s'étend tout au long du local est divisé en deux au moyen de l'intensité de l'éclairage qui provient des lampes qui ont été confectionnées avec des pièces de Lego aux différentes couleurs et circuits intégrés.

Im mitten in der Altstadt von Barcelona gelegenen Fonfone treffen das Yin und das Yang, beide rein geometrisch konzipiert, aufeinander. In diesem Universum, das mit den Gesetzen des Designs bricht, sind zur Lösung der ursprünglich übermäßigen Länge des Lokals zwei gegensätzliche Pole vorhanden. Der zum Empfang der Gäste dienende Vorraum stellt den kalten Norden dar und wird von grünen und blauen Farbtönen beherrscht. Hinten befindet sich, wie eine flackernde Flamme, die die Leute anlocken soll, der heiße und feurige Südpol. Hier herrschen rote, gelbe und orange Farbtöne vor. Gemeinsam haben beide Hemisphären die Verwendung von Kunststoff –dem im Lokal vorherrschende Material– an Fußböden, Wänden und Lampen. Aus verschiedenfarbigen Logo-Teilen und aus integralen Schaltkreisen bestehende Lampen beleuchten die sich am ganzen Lokal lang erstreckende Theke und teilen sie in zwei Hälften.

Lighting in different colors marks
the exact division between the two areas
of the bar, hot and cold.

*Les ressources de l'éclairage aux différentes
couleurs marquent les limites précises entre les
deux zones chaude et froide du local.*

Dank der verschiedenfarbigen Beleuchtung
werden die beiden Bereiche des Lokals, heiß
und kalt, genau abgegrenzt.

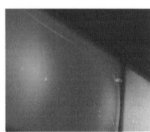
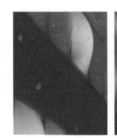

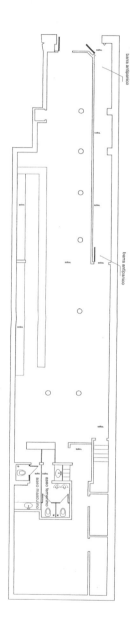

SALIDA DE EMERGENCIA
barra antipanico

barra antipanico

The furniture in white –stools lining the bar and sofas along the wall –break up the dominating color duality.

Le mobilier est blanc: tabourets alignés le long du comptoir et canapés le long du mur sont en rupture avec la dualité chromatique générale.

Die weißen Möbelstücke –vor der Theke aufgereihte Hocker und an der Wand stehende Sofas– brechen die vorherrschende Farbendualität.

Fonfone

The division into two different areas has resolved the feeling of excessive length the original premises had.

Le dédoublement en deux zones a résolu l'excessive longueur du local original.

Die Teilung des Raums in zwei verschiedene Bereiche hat das Problem der übermäßigen Länge, das beim ursprünglichen Lokal vorhanden war, gelöst.

Magritte

Marcello Panza, Claudio Giunnelli

Caserta, Italia
1997
Photography | Photo | Fotografie:Matteo Piazza.

Where the Magritte now stands used to be a theatre that became a cinema and then a fashion workshop. However, in its current restructuring, the stage and the two levels are the only elements that have been recovered. Internal space has been resolved as a modernised version of an old café, converted into restaurant, American-style bar and disco area at the same time. Marcello Panza has used the personal style of the famous Belgian painter to investigate formal and aesthetic questions close to Surrealism. The use of three-dimensional works or of details of paintings converts the place into a mixture of Surrealism and Pop Art. The result has become a small world that pays homage to artists such as Magritte, Dalí and Man Ray. As such, he achieves a suggestive spectacle of evasion whilst sheltering behind allusive, ironic and cultured decoration.

Le Magritte occupe un espace qui était autrefois un théâtre, ensuite une salle de cinéma, puis un atelier de confection de mode. La restructuration actuelle n'a pu récupérer que la scène et les deux niveaux. La solution spatiale interne est une version modernisée d'un vieux café, devenu restaurant, bar américain et zone de discothèque en même temps. Marcello Panza se sert du style du célèbre peintre belge pour fouiller dans les aspects formels et esthétiques propres au surréalisme. L'utilisation d'oeuvres tridimensionnelles ou de détails de tableaux fait que le style de l'établissement soit à mi-chemin entre le surréalisme et le pop art. Le résultat est un petit cosmos qui est un sincère hommage aux génies comme Magritte, Dalí ou Man Ray. Ce qui donne un suggestif spectacle d'évasion dans un décor ironique et cultivé, plein d'allusions.

Der Raum, den Magritte einnimmt, war ursprünglich ein Theater, das erst zu einem Kino, und dann zu einem Modeatelier umfunktioniert wurde. Die Bühne und die beiden verschiedenen Ebenen sind jedoch die einzigen Elemente, die aus der ersten Epoche des Lokals stammen und restauriert werden konnten. Das Ergebnis der Umstrukturierung ist eine modernisierte Version eines alten Cafés, das zugleich Restaurant, American Bar und Diskothek ist. Marcello Panza bedient sich des persönlichen Stils des berühmten belgischen Malers, um nach neuen, dem Surrealismus ähnlichen förmlichen und ästhetischen Aspekten zu suchen. Die Verwendung von dreidimensionalen Werken oder Gemäldedetails gibt dem Lokal das Gepräge einer Mischung von Surrealismus und Pop Art. Dies ergibt ein kleines Kosmos, das Persönlichkeiten wie Magritte, Dalí oder Man Ray alle Ehre antut. Folglich kann dem Gast mit einer andeutenden, ironischen und gepflegten Dekoration ein suggestives Schauspiel dargeboten werden.

Marcello Panza uses a bar shaped like a *baguette* and tables dressed in shoes to recreate the formal symbolism of Dalí.

Marcello Panza utilise le comptoir du bar en forme de baguette et des tables à souliers en une recréation des formes symboliques chères à Dalí.

Marcello Panza verwendet eine baguetteförmige Theke und Tische mit Schuhen, was Dalís förmliche Symbolik wiedergibt.

Magritte

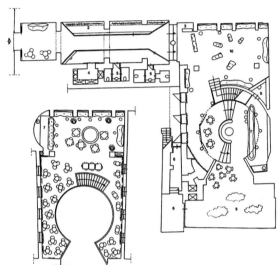

The lips of Man Ray appear on a bright blue sky in Magritte's style. Some red easy chairs and a table shaped like a fried egg are a variation on Dino Gavina's Magritte chair.

Sur un ciel bleu propre à Magritte, les lèvres de Man Ray apparaissent. Des divans rouges et une petite table en forme d'oeuf sur le plat sont un retour à la chaise Magritte de Dino Gavina.

Auf dem im Stil von Magritte gemalten blauen Himmel erscheinen die Lippen von Man Ray. Rote Lehnstühle und ein als Spiegelei geformter kleiner Tisch sind ein Remake des Magritte-Stuhles von Dino Gavina.

The Magritte is a space that renders homage to escape, dream and fantasy. Its decor is a constant and delicious meeting with the modern artistic tradition, loaded with startling ironies.

Le Magritte fait hommage à l'évasion, au rêve, à la fantaisie. Sa décoration est un rendez-vous continuel avec une tradition créative moderne, exquise, chargée d'une étonnante ironie.

Das Magritte tut der Flucht aus dem Alltag, dem Träumen und der Phantasie alle Ehre an. Seine Dekoration ist eine ständige und exquisite Begegnung mit der modernen kreativen Tradition, voller erstaunlicher Ironie.

Lore

Annette Axthelm (Architekturbüro Axthelm Frinken)
Berlin, Deutschland
1999
Photography | Photo | Fotografie: Pablo Castagnola.

Over 300 square meters of an old factory turned into a trend-setting bar, Lore has a huge main room presided over by an enormous bar about thirty meters long, at which every kind of cocktail and delicious combinations can be savored. At the bar rotating stools in white upholstery line up. White is repeated in the chairs that go with the wood and metal tables, in the sofas and in the seats covered in black leather. A steel bridge leads to the second room in which the temperature seems to rise to the maximum because of the burning furnaces that have been preserved. It is not for nothing that the name of the bar alludes to the barrows that carried the coal that fed the furnaces. The industrial aesthetic is predominant on this second storey turned into a dance floor.

Plus de 300 mètres carrés d'une ancienne fabrique, conçu comme un local à tendance, permet au Lore de compter avec une grande salle principale présidée par un énorme comptoir d'environ trente mètres, pour déguster toute sorte de cocktails et des combinés exquis. Des tabourets tournants sont alignés en face, ils sont tapissés en blanc, couleur reprise sur les chaises qui se trouvent autour des tables en bois sur des structures métalliques; les canapés et les sièges sont tapissés en cuir noir. On accède par un pont en acier à la deuxième salle dans laquelle la température semble monter à cause de la combustion des anciens fours qui sont restés. Ce n'est pas sans raison que le nom du local fait allusion aux brouettes qui transportaient le charbon pour alimenter ces fours. L'esthétique industrielle domine dans ce second niveau qui sert de piste de danse.

Mehr als 300 m2 einer ehemaligen Fabrik wurden zu einem Trendlokal. Lore verfügt über einen geräumigen Hauptsaal, der von einer enormen, etwa 30 m langen Theke beherrscht wird, wo jede Art von Cocktails und exquisite Mixgetränke angeboten werden. Davor stehen weiß gepolsterte Drehhocker. Ebenfalls weiß sind die Stühle, die bei den Holztischen mit Metallstruktur und den schwarzen Ledersofas und Sitzen stehen. Über eine Stahlbrücke gelangt man in einen zweiten Raum, wo wegen der erhalten gebliebenen und in Betrieb befindlichen Öfen, die Temperatur stark anzusteigen scheint. Nicht umsonst weist der Name des Lokals auf die Loren hin, mit welchen die Kohle zur Speisung der Öfen transportiert wurde. Die Industrie-Ästhetik beherrscht die als Tanzfläche hergerichtete zweite Etage.

All the fittings and furniture that grace the bar's spaces are designed by Motor Berlin.

Tous les éléments du mobilier décorant les différents espaces appartiennent au design de Motor Barlin.

Alle Möbelstücke der verschiedenen Räume des Lokals wurden von Motor Berlin entworfen.

Lore

The industrial aesthetic of the dance floor is even seen in the toilets, dominated by metal and concrete.

L'esthétique industrielle de la salle de danse est présente même dans les zones des toilettes où prédominent le métal et le béton.

Die Industrie-Ästhetik der Tanzfläche ist auch in den Waschräumen vorhanden, wobei Metall und Beton die vorherrschenden Materialien sind.

Café Zurich

Federico Correa Ruiz, Alfonso Milà Sagnier

Barcelona, España
Reform | Réforme | Erneuerung:1998
Photography | Photo | Fotografie: Martí Llorens.

Survivor of every epoch and fashion, the Café Zurich is the meeting point par excellence of Barcelona. Its privileged location on the Plaça de Catalunya makes it one of the reference points for urban leisure. Closed for years, the café has taken on new life since its reopening as an integral part of the new shopping complex known as the Golden Triangle. The main aim of the new project was to respect the image that the Zurich had had since 1925. A wide ground floor, an upstairs section and a small cellar make up the premises. Its renovation employed both traditional and modern materials: partition walls of hollow brick; walls adorned with Pladur plaster sheets; granite paving on the main floor, parquet upstairs, and non-slip tiling in the toilets. Under its arches, customers can once more enjoy their coffee while they watch the city glide by beyond the windows.

Ayant survécu à plusieurs époques et à toutes les modes, le Zurich est le point de rencontre par excellence de la ville de Barcelone. Sa situation privilégiée sur la Place de Catalunya en fait une des références pour les loisirs urbains. Il a été fermé pendant des années et il a repris une nouvelle vie depuis sa réouverture dans le nouvel édifice commercial Triangle d'Or. Le nouveau projet avait comme objectif principal le respect de l'image appartenant au local depuis 1925. Un grand rez-de-chaussée, une mezzanine et un petit sous-sol forment l'ensemble actuel. Sa rénovation a été faite au moyen d'un choix de matériaux traditionnels et modernes: des cloisons en céramique creuse, des renforts de murs en plâtre Pladur, pavements en granite à l'étage principal, du parquet dans la mezzanine et le sol en céramique non glissante dans les toilettes. Sous ses arcs, les clients profitent à nouveau d'un café tout en observant les passants à travers les baies vitrées.

Dieses Lokal hat alle Epochen und Moden überlebt. Das Café Zurich ist der beliebteste Treffpunkt Barcelonas. Seine privilegierte Lage, am Plaza de Catalunya, macht es zu einem Begriff der Freizeitgestaltung. Das während einiger Jahre geschlossene Lokal hat seit seiner Wiedereröffnung im Einkaufszentrum Triángulo de Oro einen neuen Impuls bekommen. Hauptziel des neuen Projekts war die Erhaltung des seit 1925 bestehenden Bildes des Lokals. Ein geräumiges Erdgeschoß, ein Zwischengeschoß und ein kleiner Keller bilden das jetzige Café. Bei der Renovierung wurden sowohl traditionelle als auch moderne Materialien verwandt: Zwischenwände aus Hohlkeramik; mit Pladur-Gipsplatten verstärkte Mauern; Granitfußböden im Erdgeschoß, Parkettfußböden im Zwischengeschoß und rutschfeste Keramikböden in den Waschräumen. Unter seinen Bögen können die Gäste wieder eine Tasse Kaffee trinken, während sie das pulsierende Stadtleben durch die großen Fenster beobachten.

Tables and chairs in a traditional style placed beside the pillars and under the arches make up a typical picture of an old-fashioned cafeteria.

Les tables et les chaises de style traditionnel disposées autour des colonnes et sous les arcs contribuent à l'ambiance typique des anciens cafés.

Die neben den Säulen und unter den Bögen stehenden Tische und Stühle geben dem Lokal das Flair der typischen alten Cafés.

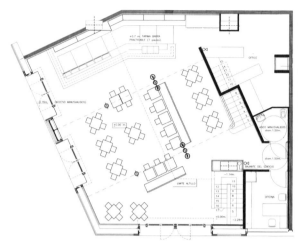

Despite the major overhaul of the premises, the Zurich retains its bohemian spirit and the elements that make it so characteristic.

Malgré les importants travaux de rénovation, le local garde tout l'esprit bohème et tous les éléments qui le rendent si caractéristique.

Trotz der tiefgreifenden Renovierung sind der Geist der Boheme und die charakteristischen Merkmale des Lokals nicht verlorengegangen.

Café Zurich

Palais de la Bière

Architectures Jean Nouvel
Strasbourg, France
1999
Photography | Photo | Fotografie: Philippe Ruault.

A homage to beer as its leitmotiv and a play of mirrors and lights. What is known as the Grande Brasserie de la Patrie Schutzenberger Sa takes its name from the French Revolution. The project was born in the desire to refit the Palais de la Bière, place linked to the history of Strasbourg, and make it a meeting place for eating out and having a drink, in line with the Alsatian tradition of combining the modern with celebration. The locale is some 40 meters long and its narrowness helps the device of a wall with continuous references to beer brands, subliminal images suggested as in a camera cut. A monumental 1930s chandelier hangs from the ceiling above the central bar. Made from small round glass cobbles, its motion creates virtual effects on the wall. Unlike the veins that flower in the wood, the main material of the brasserie, the fabrics hanging from the ceiling create orange and black moirés that darken the scene still further.

Un hommage à la bière comme leitmotiv et un jeu d'effets des miroirs et des lampes. Ce qui est connu comme la Grande Brasserie de la Patrie Schutzenberger Sa tient son nom de la Révolution Française. Un projet de réhabilitation du Palais de la Bière, lieu lié à l'histoire même de la ville de Strasbourg veut en faire un lieu de réunion pour prendre un repas ou un verre, selon la tradition alsacienne qui allie la modernité et la fête. Le local étroit s'étend au long de 40 mètres ce qui facilite le jeu du mur sur lequel se reflètent de nombreuses références à des marques de bière, et des images subliminales qui sont suggérées comme dans un fondu audiovisuel. Sur le plafond, monumental sur le bar central, une verrière année trente, construite à partir de petites pièces de verre rond. Son reflet sur le mur produit des récréations virtuelles. En contraste avec les veines apparentes du bois, matière régnant dans la brasserie, les tentures partant du plafond, créent des moirés oranges et noirs, rendant encore plus opaque la scène.

Eine Huldigung des Bieres als Leitmotiv und ein Zusammenspiel von Spiegeln und Lichtern. Die sogenannte Grande Brasserie de la Patrie Schutzenberger Sa wurde nach der Französischen Revolution benannt. Dieses Projekt entstand, als man das Palais de la Bière, ein mit der Geschichte Straßburgs eng verbundener Ort, sanieren und zu einem Treffpunkt machen wollte, wo man zum Essen und Trinken zusammenkommt, und dabei wurden nach elsässischer Tradition Modernität und festliche Stimmung verbunden. Auf die Wand des 40 m langen, engen Lokals können Bilder projiziert werden, die Biermarken unterschwellig andeuten. An der prächtigen Decke, über der in der Mitte stehenden Theke, eine aus kleinen, runden Glasbausteinen gefertigte Verglasung aus den 30er Jahren, die virtuelle Gestalten auf die Wand wirft. Im Gegensatz zu den Maserungen des Holzes, des Starmaterials der Brasserie, bilden die von der Decke herabhängenden Stoffstreifen orange und schwarze Moirés, wodurch das Lokal etwas schummerig erscheint.

On the luminous wall of beer bottle bottoms in yellows and whites, fitted into the cement, are reflected the chandelier, the video images filming the street, the spire of the cathedral of Strasbourg and the entrance to the brasserie.

Sur le mur coloré, des fonds de bouteilles de bière aux couleurs jaunes et blanches, emboîtées dans le béton, se réfléchit la verrière, les images vidéo qui filment la rue, la flèche de la cathédrale de Strasbourg et l'entrée de la brasserie.

Auf der Lichtwand, die aus in Beton eingesetzten gelben und weißen Bierflaschenstücken besteht, werden die Verglasung und die Videoaufnahmen von der Straße, der Kirchturmspitze des Straßburger Münsters und des Eingangs der Brasserie reflektiert.

Palais de la Bière

The painting on the walls, a
symbiosis of black to orange, is by
Alain Bony. The surfaces of the
tables are in stainless steel treated
as if it were tin, zinc or some other
material.

*Le travail de peinture sur les murs est
l'oeuvre de Alain Bony, une symbiose
entre le noir et l'orange. Las surfaces
des tables sont en acier inox, traité
comme de l'étain, du zinc ou autres
matériaux.*

Die an den Wänden zu sehende
Malereiarbeit stammt von Alain Bony,
eine Symbiose vom schwarzen
Farbton bis zum orangen hin. Die
Tischplatten sind aus rostfreiem
Stahl, behandelt wie Zinn, Zink oder
anderes Material.

Living

Elisabeth Cristià Margenat
Barcelona, España
2001
Photography | Photo | Fotografie: David Manchón.

Located in a xixth-century building, this Barcelona bar was originally a hardware store. In fact, a forge divided the premises into two levels and split the singular stone pillars, which were recovered, along with the escutcheon on the front wall, from the demolition of the offices of the Poblet Monastery. Today, its rectangular surface is structured on the basis of the line marked by the pillars beside the bar. Next to them, a red wall resolves the design of the bar and the cabin of the disc-jockey. In addition, the closeness of the columns to this monotone background makes them stand out still more from the other elements of the room. The finished details employ economic and simple items such as white-tiled kitchen sinks hung on the wall, with two angles serving as basins.

Situé dans un bâtiment du xixe siècle, ce local barcelonais était autrefois une quincaillerie. En fait, un faux plancher divisait le local en deux étages et les singulières colonnes à mi-hauteur. Elles ont été récupérées, comme l'écusson visible sur la façade qui appartenait au siège du monastère de Poblet. Actuellement, sa surface rectangulaire est structurée autour des colonnes disposée près du comptoir. Près d'elles on a disposé un plan couleur rouge qui résout le design du comptoir et de la cabine du disc-jockey. D'ailleurs, la proximité des colonnes de ce fond monochrome les soulignent par rapport au reste de la salle. Pour les finitions on a choisi des éléments aussi économiques que simples tels que les éviers de cuisine en céramique blanche, accrochés au mur qui servent de lavemains.

Dieses Lokal, das ehemals eine Eisenwarenhandlung war, ist in einem im 19. Jahrhundert in Barcelona errichteten Gebäude untergebracht. Eine Zwischendecke gliederte das Lokal in zwei Ebenen und teilte die einzigartigen Steinsäulen, die, wie auch das an der Fassade befindliche Wappen, aus dem Kloster von Poblet stammen. Heute wird der rechteckige Raum von den neben der Theke stehenden Säulen strukturiert. Mit der daneben befindlichen roten Fläche wurde das Design der Theke sowie der DJ-Kabine herausgestellt. Außerdem werden die Säulen durch ihre nahe Lage an diesem einfarbigen Hintergrund noch mehr hervorgehoben. Zur Dekoration wurden ganz billige und einfache Elemente, nämlich an der Wand hängende Spülbecken aus weißer Keramik, zum Händewaschen, ausgewählt.

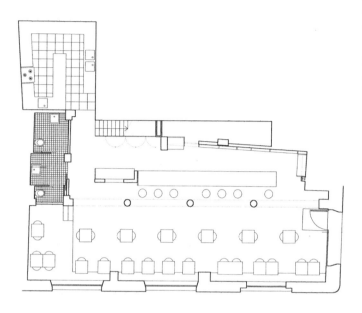

Soft tones predominate in nearly all the items of decoration.

Les nuances douces dominent dans presque tous les éléments composant la décoration du local.

Sanfte Farben herrschen bei fast allen Dekorationselementen des Lokals vor.

Living

Santé Café

160 BIS Arquitectura

Barcelona, España
2000
Photography | Photo | Fotografie: Pep Escoda.

Cafeteria by day, reading room in the afternoon, and a place to drink when night falls. Santé Café is an ambivalent place, feature taken as the main argument by its creators when positing its design and setting. The flooring and walls in warm but striking colors are transformed by a carefully worked out lighting system that lets you glide from one environment to another almost imperceptibly. Most of the basic furnishing is fashioned from oak and combines with pieces by illustrious designers such as Philippe Starck. But if there is one element that defines this bar of scarcely fifty square meters, it is that it looks like an enormous shop-window in which the customers themselves are the objects on display and, in their turn, voyeurs of the street, an idea recovered from 1960s and '70s shop-windows in the city of Amsterdam.

Cafétéria pendant journée, lieu de lecture l'après-midi et le soir local nocturne. Santé Café est un lieu ambivalent, c'est la caractéristique principale que les dessinateurs ont retenu dans leur projet. Le sol et les murs aux couleurs chaudes et vives, se transforment par un système d'éclairage fait que l'on passe imperceptiblement d'une ambiance à une autre. La plupart du mobilier est en bois de chêne et se combine avec des pièces d'artistes aussi illustres que Philippe Starck. Mais l'élément définissant le mieux ce local de cinquante mètres carrés à peine, est sa ressemblance avec une grande vitrine où les clients eux mêmes sont les objets exposés et tout en étant également les voyeurs de tout ce qui se passe dans la rue. Idée prise de modèles précédents des années soixante et soixante-dix et des vitrines de la ville d'Amsterdam.

Tagsüber Cafeteria, am Nachmittag Leseraum und am Abend Pub. Santé Café ist ein ambivalentes Lokal, was die Designer beim Entwurf und der Ambientierung häuptsächlich bedacht haben. Die warmen, auffallenden Farben des Fußbodens und der Wände verwandeln sich dank eines durchdachten Beleuchtungssystems, so daß der Übergang von einem Ambiente zum anderen kaum bemerkt wird. Der größte Teil des Grundmobiliars wurde aus Eichenholz gefertigt und wird mit Möbelstücken von berühmten Designern wie Philippe Starck kombiniert. Das Hauptmerkmal des kaum 50 m2 großen Lokals ist jedoch die Gestaltung als großes Schaufenster, in dem die Gäste selbst die ausgestellten Objekte und gleichzeitig die Voyeurs, die beobachten, was sich auf der Straße abspielt, sind. Die Idee stammt von Vorbildern der 60er und 70er Jahre und von den Schaufenstern Amsterdams.

The space's versatility allows the locale to be transformed, as the day progresses, from cafeteria to drinks bar.

La versatilité de l'espace permet que le local se transforme, à mesure que le jour avance, de cafétéria en local nocturne où boire un verre.

Die Vielseitigkeit des Raumes gestattet, daß sich das Lokal im Laufe des Tages von einer Cafeteria in ein Pub verwandelt.

Most of the basic furnishing is fashioned from oak and combines with various designer pieces.

La plupart du mobilier est en bois de chêne et s'allie aux différents éléments de design.

Der größte Teil des Grundmobiliars wurde aus Eichenholz gefertigt und mit verschiedenen Designer-Möbelstücken kombiniert.

Santé Café

Light

GiovanniMaria Torno

Milano, Italia
2001
Photography | Photo | Fotografie: Paola D'Amico.

Light, located at the heart of the Milan that admires cutting-edge design, is a loft in a building dating from the late XIXth century. The element that makes Light a place overflowing with personality is that all the items of decor have been specially designed and constructed for the locale. Thanks to an imaginative effort to seek innovative materials, elements and colors, in this bar past and future jump into the present. Under the very high ceilings of bare brick, arches and chimneys balance against the wood parquet flooring, bars coated with alabaster, immaculately colored cloth, bright poufs and small leather sofas. The small neon lights and an infinite number of candles fill the locale. The taste for the antique and the most modern minimalism turn Light into a harmonious dance arising from the interplay of varied elements.

Le Light, dans le coeur du Milan du design d'avant-garde, est un loft situé dans un édifice datant de la fin du XIXe siècle. Ce qui donne sa personnalité au Light est le fait que tous les compléments de la décoration ont été conçus et réalisés spécialement pour cet établissement. Grâce à un effort fantaisiste pour innover dans les matériaux, les éléments et les couleurs, le passé et le futur, se retrouvent dans le présent. Sous les plafonds très élevés en maçonnerie, les arcs et les cheminées sont en opposition au parquet en bois, les comptoirs du bar sont revêtus d'albâtre, de tissus aux couleurs impeccables, les poufs en couleurs et les petits fauteuils en cuir. Les rares lampes néon et une infinité de bougies disséminées dans l'ensemble du local. Le goût du l'ancien et le minimalisme le plus moderne transforment le Light en une sorte de danse harmonieuse produite à partir du contraste des différents éléments.

Light liegt mitten im Herzen von Mailand, der Stadt des avantgardistischen Designs. Es handelt sich um einen in einem Gebäude aus dem Ende des 19. Jahrhunderts untergebrachten Loft. Was diesem Lokal Persönlichkeit verleiht ist die Tatsache, daß alle Dekorationselemente eigens dafür entworfen und angefertigt wurden. Dank der phantasievollen Bemühung, bei Materialien, Elementen und Farben Innovationen vorzunehmen, werden im Lokal Vergangenheit und Zukunft in die Gegenwart versetzt. Unter den überaus hohen, unverputzten Decken kontrastieren Bögen und Kamine mit dem Holzparkettfußboden, den mit Alabaster verkleideten Theken, dem makellosen Stoff der Vorhänge, den farbenfrohen Puffs und den kleinen Ledersofas. Wenige Neonlichter und unzählige Kerzen, die überall im Lokal zu finden sind. Die Vorliebe für das Antike und der modernste Minimalismus machen Light zu einem harmonischen, aus dem Kontrast verschiedener Elemente entstandenen Tanz.

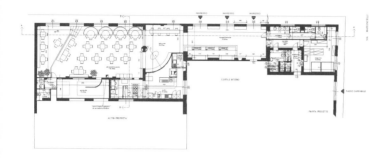

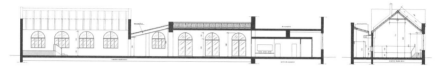

The 400 square meters of Light are divided into three areas: the bar, the lounge and the restaurant.

Sur un étage de 400 mètres carrés, le Light se divise en trois zones: le bar, le lounge et le restaurant.

Light, mit einer Fläche von 400 m², besteht aus drei Bereichen: der Bar, der Lounge und dem Restaurant.

Light

The toilets at Light are in Duravit from the Starck Edition 1 line. The colored fluoride that covers the walls, however, gives them a new look.

Les toilettes du Light appartiennent à la ligne Starck Edition 1 de Duravit. Les couleurs fluor du revêtement des murs leur donne cependant un nouveau look.

Die Ausstattung der Waschräume stammt aus der Produktlinie Starck Edition 1 von Duravit. Die schillernden Farben der Wände verleihen ihnen jedoch einen neuen Look.

Lot 61

Rafael Viñoly

New York, USA
1998
Photography | Photo | Fotografie: Alberto Ferrero.

Art for art's sake. This was the premise for Lot 61, located on 21st street, between New York's Tenth and Eleventh Avenues. Work and design by Damien Hirst, Jim Hodges and Jorge Pardo, among others, decorate the locale, in which the art lies both in the work exhibited on its walls and in the delicious dishes and cocktails that are served. An avant-garde atmosphere for people at the cutting-edge of style. Intellectuals, bourgeois bohemians and design addicts are its habitual clientèle, along with various trend fans. The two-tone red and black employed in most of the items is disconcerting. The rubber benches and arm-chairs in these colors surround the tables on which there is always a candle lit. 1950s-style stools in stunning red line up along the dark curving bar.

L'art pour l'art. Sous cette prémisse fût conçu le Lot 61, situé dans la rue 21, entre la dixième et la onzième avenue new-yorkaise. Oeuvres et design de Damien Hirst, Jim Hodges ou Jorge Pardo, entre autres, décorent le local où l'art est présent tant sur les murs que dans les délicieux plats et cocktails qui sont servis. Une atmosphère d'avant-garde pour des gens à la page. Des intellectuels, des bourgeois bohèmes et des habitués ferrus du design sont sa clientèle habituelle, et quelque amateur des nouvelles tendances. L'alliance du rouge et du noir employée dans la plupart des éléments est déconcertante et dynamique. Les bancs et les fauteuils en caoutchouc entourent les tables sur lesquelles est allumée une bougie et près du comptoir noir aux formes sinueuses s'alignent les tabourets au style des années 50 d'un rouge criant.

L'art pour l'art. Unter dieser Prämisse wurde Lot 61, in der 21. Straße, zwischen der 10. und 11. Avenue, in New York gelegen, entworfen. Werke und Designs von Damien Hirst, Jim Hodges und Jorge Pardo, unter anderen, dekorieren das Lokal, in dem die Kunst sowohl in den an den Wänden ausgestellten Werken als auch bei den köstlichen Speisen und Cocktails vorhanden ist. Eine avantgardistische Atmosphäre für Leute, die "in" sind. Intelektuelle, Bohemian bourgeoises und Designbesessene, sowie auch manche Anhänger der neuen Trends gehören zu den Stammgästen des Lokals. Die bei den meisten Elementen vorzufindende rot-schwarze Dynamik ist verwirrend. Die roten und schwarzen Bänke und Sessel aus Kunststoff stehen um den Tische herum, auf denen immer eine Kerze brennt. Bei der ebenfalls dunklen und geschwungenen Theke stehen knallrote, im Stil der 50er Jahre gehaltene Hocker.

The latest trends do not mean you can't be comfortable. The rubber chairs and arm-chairs chosen can turn a drink into an animated and relaxing chat in the half-light.

Le confort n'est pas opposé aux dernières tendances. Les fauteuils et les canapés en caoutchouc font que prendre un verre peut dériver vers une conversation animée et reposante dans la pénombre.

Hier sind Komfort und neueste Trends eng miteinander verbunden. Dank der ausgewählten Sessel und Lehnstühle aus Kunststoff kann ein Drink zu einer angeregten und entspannenden Unterhaltung im Halbschatten werden.

Dynamic red and black only combines with certain specific white items on the surface of the bar and on the glass separating screens.

L'alliance entre le rouge et le noir est rompue par quelques éléments blancs à la surface du comptoir et par les vitres de séparation.

Die rot-schwarze Dynamik paßt nur zu einigen bestimmten weißen Elementen auf der Thekenoberfläche und an den Glastrennwänden.

Lot 61

Club 22

Rafael Tamborero y José Luis López

Barcelona, España
1999
Photography | Photo | Fotografie: David Manchón.

The four sauces in the Salsitas cocktail are decor, cuisine, staff and music. This wide eclectic spirit, characteristic of this Barcelona restaurant, crosses the threshold of the evening to enter the night changed into Club 22, a locale in the latest style dominated by house garage sounds. A bar about 25 meters long receives us at the entrance with dominant whites. Inside, the dining area converted into an improvised dance floor, another bar in the centre and such striking structures as the columns in the form of a palm tree and the giant pineapple created with thixotropic cement and plaster await us. Other innovative materials are the laser-perforated iron sheets used in the supports or the polyester and fiberglass resin on the domes of the ventilators. Styles are mixed without clashes, creating a curious jungle of shapes and tendencies: colonial on the cornices, arches and folding louvres; Art Nouveau in the fittings, lattices and the metal on the bars; and Deco in everything organic and theatrical in its design.

Les quatre sauces du cocktail Salsitas sont décoration, cuisine, personnel et musique. Cet esprit large et éclectique caractérise ce restaurant barcelonais qui surpasse l'-horaire du soir pour se plonger dans la nuit transformé en Club 22, un local dernier cri où règnent les sons house garage. Un comptoir de quelques 25 mètres où domine le blanc, nous accueille à l'entrée. La zone de la salle à manger nous attend à l'intérieur, transformée en piste de danse, un comptoir au centre et des structures très voyantes comme les colonnes en forme de palmier et l'ananas géant en ciment et en plâtre. D'autres matériaux innovateurs sont le fer en tôles percées au laser employées pour les plinthes ou la résine de polyester et fibre de verre employée sur les coupoles des ventilateurs. Les styles s'entremêlent sans stridence en créant une curieuse jungles aux formes et styles variés: colonial pour les corniches, les arcs et les stores; moderniste pour le mobilier, les jalousies et le métal des comptoirs; et art déco pour toute l'esthétique organique et théâtrale.

Zur Zubereitung des Salsitas-Cocktail werden Dekoration, Cuisine, Bedienung und Musik gemixt. Diese umfassende, eklektische Philosophie, die das Barceloner Restaurant charakterisiert, ist nicht nur am Abend, sondern bis spät in die Nacht hinein, wenn es sich in Club 22 verwandelt, zu spüren. Im Trendlokal sind die House-Garage-Sounds vorherrschend. Am Eingang empfängt eine 25 Meter lange, fast völlig in Weiß gehaltene Theke die Gäste. Dann gelangt man zum im improvisierte Tanzfläche umgewandelten Speiseraum, zur anderen, in der Mitte stehenden Theke und zu außergewöhnlichen Strukturen, wie die palmenförmigen Säulen und die riesige Ananas, beides aus thixotropischem Zement und Gips angefertigt. Weitere innovative Materialien sind hier lasergeschnittene Eisenbleche, die bei den Stuhllehnen verwandt, sowie Polyesterharz und Glasfaser, die bei den Ventilatorhauben benutzt wurden. Die verschiedenen Stile vermischen sich, ohne daß es unangenehm empfunden wird, und schaffen eine eigenartige Landschaft aus Formen und Stilen: Verzierungsblenden, Arkaden und Bastjalousien im Kolonialstil; das Mobiliar, die Vergitterungen und das Metall der Theken sind modernistisch; und alle nichtfunktionellen und protzigen Elemente im Art-Déco-Stil.

Elements inspired in Art Nouveau, colonial and Deco styles combine coherently throughout the locale.

Les éléments inspirés dans les styles moderniste, colonial et art déco s'allient de façon cohérente dans l'ensemble du local.

Die im Modernismus, Kolonial- und Art-Déco-Stil inspirierten Elemente werden auf kohärente Art und Weise überall im Lokal kombiniert.

Club 22

White hues dominate all the areas
of the room almost totally, and are
only nuanced by the plays of lights
or occasional decorative details.

*Les tons blancs dominant dans
toutes les zones de la salle sont nuancés
par les jeux de lumière et des éléments
décoratifs ponctuels.*

Die weißen Farbtöne herrschen in allen
Bereichen des Saales vor und werden
lediglich durch die an ganz bestimmten
Stellen vorhandenen Spiele mit dem Licht
und Dekorationselemente nuanciert.

Mamamia

Gilberto Mancini
Senigallia, Italia
1999
Photography | Photo | Fotografie: Alberto Ferrero.

Conceptual and Surrealist art in authentic science-fiction surroundings. Mamamia astounds from start to finish, as each of its areas provides an unprecedented aesthetic experience. Its Futurist-style front only lets you glimpse a part of its secrets. The large room holding the dance floor is designed on criteria of straight lines. The yellow of the walls and furnishings contributes to the uniformity of the atmosphere. The rest rooms are also a genuine work of art. The black and white of its tiles gives way to disturbing shapes and mosaic drawings. The logo of the locale appears on its wood and steel doors. The dining-room has a dynamic of oval shapes on the main tables and across the false ceiling, which is finished off by a wooden panel. The furniture's whites and yellows contrast with the warm wood of the panels and floor.

Art conceptuel et surréaliste dans un environnement de science fiction. Mamamia surprend du début à la fin car chaque ambiance constitue une expérience esthétique sans précédents. La façade, au style futuriste, ne laisse entrevoir que quelques secrets de l'intérieur. La grande salle où se trouve la piste de danse a été conçue à partir de lignes très régulières et la couleur jaune des murs et du mobilier contribue à uniformiser le tout. Les toilettes sont également une authentique oeuvre d'art. Le noir ou blanc des carrelages est la base pour d'inquiétantes formes et dessins du mosaïque. Le logo du local apparaît sur les portes en bois ou en acier. La salle à manger présente une dynamique de formes ovales appliquées au faux-plafond couronné d'un panneau en bois ainsi qu'aux tables principales. Le blanc et le jaune du mobilier fait contraste avec la chaleur du bois des panneaux et du parquet.

Konzeptkunst und Surrealismus in einer echt galaktischen Atmosphäre. Mamamia überrascht den Gast vom Anfang bis zum Ende, denn jedes Ambiente ist ein ästhetisches Erlebnis ohnegleichen. Die futuristische Fasade läßt nur einen Teil seines geheimnisvollen Inhalts erahnen. Der geräumige Saal, in dem die Tanzfläche liegt, weist eine sehr regelmäßige Geometrie auf. Die gelbe, futuristisch anmutende Farbe der Wände und Möbel trägt zur Vereinheitlichung des Ambiente bei. Die Toiletten sind ebenfalls ein echtes Kunstwerk. Das Schwarz und Weiß der Fliesen zeichnet beunruhigende Formen und Mosaikbilder. Das Logo des Lokals erscheint auf den Holz- und Stahltüren. Ovale Formen charakterisieren die mit einem Holzpaneel versehene abgehängte Decke und die größeren Tische. Die weißen und gelben Farbtöne des Mobiliars kontrastieren mit dem Holz der Paneele und des Fußbodens.

Wood is one of the noble materials used to cover the floor, the separating panels and on some pieces of specially designed furniture.

Le bois est l'un des matériaux nobles revêtant le sol, les panneaux de séparation et quelques uns des éléments du mobilier au design unique.

Holz ist eines der edlen Materialien, das als Fußbelag, bei den Trennwänden und bei einigen Designer-Möbelstücken verwendet wurde.

Mamamia

The futuristic aesthetic of its outside wall is repeated in the main room, in which the color yellow is the unifying theme.

L'esthétique futuriste de ses extérieurs est repris dans la salle principale où le jaune constitue l'unité d'ensemble.

Die futuristische Ästhetik der Fassade ist im Hauptsaal wiederzufinden, wo das Gelb kohäsionierend wirkt.

Rita Blue

Xefo Guasch

Barcelona, España
1999
Photography | Photo | Fotografie: Pep Escoda.

Rita Blue is one of a new wave of night-owl, sophisticated and avant-garde bars gambling on the face-lift of Barcelona's Raval quarter, no longer the subterranean area it used to be. Both in its decor and its cuisine, Rita is a kindly wink towards its older sister, the famous Margarita Blue. The decor of Rita, half-restaurant and half-bar, looks for functional solutions without losing the happy and colorful touch of its Mexican aesthetic. The resistant and economic furniture is by Amat, and the lighting by Santa & Cole, always effective resources that are intercalated with certain fantasy items such as the original Agatha Ruiz de la Prada stools or the Lucelino lamps by Ingo Maurer. The Rita Blue also has a cellar that provides an ideal space for customers to pace out their first after-dinner dance steps.

Le Rita Bleu fait partie d'une nouvelle vague de locaux qui parient sur une rénovation de la physionomie noctambule, d'avant-garde et sophistiquée du quartier du Raval de Barcelone, loin de son antérieur look underground. Tant par sa décoration que par sa cuisine, le Rita est un sympathique clin d'oeil à son aîné, le célèbre Margarita Blue.

La décoration de l'établissement à mi chemin entre restaurant et bar, recherche des solutions fonctionnelles sans perdre la touche coloriste et joyeuse de l'esthétique mexicaine. Le mobilier résistant et bon marché est de Amat et l'éclairage de Santa & Cole, ressource toujours efficace qui s'intercale avec quelques meubles capricieux comme les tabourets originaux de Agatha Ruiz de la Prada où les lampes de Lucelino de Ingo Maurer. De plus, le Rita Blue dispose d'un soussol qui est l'espace idéal pour que les clients, après le dîner, puissent faire les premiers pas de danse.

Rita Blue ist eines der vielen neuen Lokale des ehemals mit Underground-Look behafteten Raval-Viertels, die auf ein neues, avantgardistisches Aussehen setzen. Rita erinnert sowohl hinsichtlich der Dekoration wie auch der Küche an seinen legendären älteren Bruder Margarita Blue. Die farbenfrohe, mexikanisch angehauchte Dekoration der Bar-Restaurant soll jedoch auch funktional sein. Das stabile und einfache Mobiliar von Amat und die Beleuchtung von Santa & Cole werden mit einigen Designer-Möbelstücken, wie die originellen Hocker von Agatha Ruiz de la Prada, und den Lucelino-Lampen von Ingo Maurer untersetzt. Rita Blue verfügt ebenfalls über einen Kellerraum, wo die Gäste nach dem Dinner das Tanzbein schwingen können.

The Rita Blue takes its name from St. Rita,
image from the nearby church of St. Agustí.
The Blue is a sincere homage to the Margarita
Blue, its older sister.

Le Rita Blue prend son nom de Sainte Rita
qui a sa statue dans l'église voisine de Sant Agustí.
Le Blue est le sincère hommage au Margarita Blue,
son aîné.

Rita Blue wird nach dem Bild der Heiligen Rita,
das die in der Nähe liegende Kirche Sant Agustí
beherbergt, benannt.
Die Bezeichnung Blue wurde dem Lokal zu Ehren
des älteren Bruders Margarita Blue gegeben.

Rita Blue

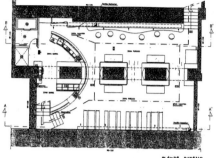

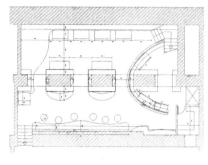

PLANTA SOTANO

The locale has a marvellous terrace and two floors noted for their happy Mexican color.

Le local dispose de deux étages aux couleurs gaies propres au Mexique et une merveilleuse terrasse.

Das Lokal hat zwei Geschosse, die wegen ihrer mexikanischen Farbenpracht hervortreten, und eine herrliche Terrasse.

The ground floor of the Rita Blue is watched over by the image of the Verge de la Mercè (patron of the city).

L'étage inférieur où préside la statue de la Vierge de la Merci.

Das Erdgeschoß des Rita Blue wird von der Figur der Gottesmutter der Barmherzigkeit beherrscht.

The tough and comfortable furniture belongs to the collection of Muebles Amat. Lighting is by Santa & Cole. The stools are designed by Agatha Ruiz de la Prada.

Le mobilier, résistant et confortable appartient à la collection de Muebles Amat. L'éclairage est de Santa & Cole. Les tabourets sont dessinés par Agatha Ruiz de la Prada.

Die stabilen und bequemen Möbel stammen aus der Kollektion von Muebles Amat. Die Beleuchtung ist von Santa & Cole. Die Hocker wurden von Agatha Ruiz de la Prada entworfen.

Shed 54

London, United Kingdom
2000
Photography | Photo | Fotografie: Chas Wilshere.

The Wapping Project is the result of a complete remodeling of the Wapping Hydraulic Power Station, a Victorian building dating from the 1890s, which was originally one of the five power stations along the Thames that provided electricity to London. In charge of the restoration was Josha Wright, who sought to bring out the contrast between the old and new elements, by maintaining the industrial and technical history of the power station. At present, the Wapping Project has an outstanding restaurant and seeks to anticipate the art production of the XXIst century. As such, Wapping has been baptized with a new Tate Gallery, as its choice customers come to this post-modern cathedral of old industrial machinery to discover that the Wapping is not just a restaurant, but also a magical enclave where anything can happen.

Le Wapping Project est le résultat de la rénovation du Wapping Hydraulic Power Station, un édifice victorien de la dernière décade du XIXe siècle qui était une des cinq stations qui, tout au long de la Tamise, fournissaient en électricité la ville de Londres. La réhabilitation de cet espace est de Wright qui a essayé de mettre en évidence le contraste entre les éléments anciens et les nouveaux, tout en gardant le passé industriel et technologique de la station. Actuellement, le Wapping Projet n'est pas seulement un restaurant mais il est connu par sa volonté de devancer la production artistique du XXIe siècle. Le Wapping a été surnommé la nouvelle Tate Gallery car ses clients se déplacent jusqu'à cette cathédrale post-moderne de vieilles machines industrielles pour y découvrir un endroit magique où tout peut arriver.

Das Wapping Project ist das Ergebnis der Renovierung der Wapping Hydraulic Power Station, eines viktorianischen Gebäudes aus dem letzten Jahrzehnt des 19. Jh. Ursprünglich war es eines der fünf an der Themse gelegenen Kraftwerke, welche die Stadt London mit Strom versorgten. Für die Restaurierung verantwortlich war Josha Wright, der die Gegensätze zwischen den alten und den neuen Elementen herauszustellen versuchte, wobei er die industrielle und technologische Vergangenheit des Werkes bestehenließ. Heute gilt das Wapping Project nicht nur als ausgezeichnetes Restaurant, sondern auch als Vorreiter der Kunst des 21. Jahrhunderts. Deshalb wurde das Wapping als "neue Tate Gallery" bezeichnet, denn seine vornehmen Gäste pilgern zu diesem postmodernen Tempel alter Industriemaschinen und stellen fest, daß das Wapping eher ein magischer Ort ist, wo alles Mögliche passieren kann, als bloß ein Restaurant.

Wapping Project

As well as its excellent wine list, the Wapping is a pioneer of design. Its European and American furniture can be bought in the establishment itself.

Le Wapping, un bar pionnier du design, offre en plus de son excellent choix de vins, la possibilité d'acheter sur place les meubles contemporains européens et américains.

Das Wapping hat nicht nur eine ausgezeichnete Weinkarte, sondern ist auch im Bereich des Designs bahnbrechend. Die präsentierten zeitgenössischen Möbel aus Europa und Amerika können hier auch gekauft werden.

Café Royale

Modest Baquedano

Barcelona, España
2000
Photography | Photo | Fotografie: Martí Llorens.

The idea of creating a night spot where the classicism of cocktail bars was turned upside down arose from the out-of-use concept of the 1950s and '60s clubs. A dose of modernity with cosmopolitan pretensions was injected, that would meet a desire to play with the visible and the barely seen. Seen and not seen was the proposal: a play of floor-bar, wall-ceiling, wall-wall. The first example occurs in the entrance where a water-cement floor is resolved with a patchwork pattern. Then starts the corridor with full cat-walk glamour, flanked on its left by a luminous glassy panel that projects an accompanying light that yet half-conceals. Perhaps because of these magical ambiguities, this was the place chosen for Almodóvar's party to celebrate the Goya 2000 prize for his highly distinguished film All about my mother. A few steps further on, the glassy radiance is repeated in the lobby of the authentic dance area.

Sous une conception désuète de club des années 50 et 60, l'idée de créer un établissement nocturne où le classicisme des cocktailleries bousculerait son format. L'injection d'une dose de modernité bien comprise avec des prétentions cosmopolites, jointes au désir de jouer avec le visible et l'imperceptible. Vu et non vu, c'est l'intention: créer un jeu entre le sol-comptoir et le mur-plafond, mur-mur. Le premier exemple se trouve à l'entrée où un stock hydraulique résout cette introduction avec un patchwork. Ensuite, le couloir commence avec le meilleur glamour des passerelles, flanqué à sa gauche d'un panneau vitré éclairé qui projette une lumière familière tout en permettant de se cacher un peu. Ce sont peut-être ces équivoques magiques qui ont fait que cet établissement ait été choisi pour la fête de Almodóvar pour célébrer son prix Goya 2000 pour son film "Todo sobre mi madre". Après quelques pas, la splendeur vitrée se reproduit dans l'antichambre de ce qui est la véritable piste de danse.

Die Idee, ein Nachtlokal zu schaffen, wo das Altherkömmliche der Cocktailbars ein völlig neues Gesicht erhält, beruht auf dem veralteten Konzept der Clubs der 50er und 60er Jahre. Dazu war eine beträchtliche Dosis Modernität mit kosmospolitischen Ansprüchen notwendig, die den Wunsch beinhaltet, mit dem Sichtbaren und dem kaum Wahrzunehmenden zu spielen. Gesehen und nicht gesehen werden, das ist hier die Absicht: ein Spiel mit Fußboden-Theke, Wand-Decke, Wand-Wand schaffen. Das erste Beispiel dafür ist das Patchwork am Eingang. Auf ganz glamouröser Weise geht es weiter in das Innere des Lokals mit einer beleuchteten Glaswand auf der linken Seite, die den Raum erhellt, aber gleichzeitig auch eine intime Stimmung schafft. Vielleicht wählte Almodóvar das Lokal wegen dieses magischen Spiels zum Feiern seines Goya 2000-Preises für den berühmten Film Alles über meine Mutter. Die Glaspracht wiederholt sich im Vorraum der Tanzfläche.

Glass is the key element that
confers on the Café Royale the
class it takes such pride in: the
panels, superposed on wood,
isolate, reflect and project the light
in an almost yellowish manner,
playing with ambivalence. Guests
sink into the comfortable arm-chairs
upholstered in orange velvet.

*Le verre est l'élément roi qui attribue
la classe octroyée au Café Royale:
les panneaux superposés sur le bois
isolent, renvoient et projettent la
lumière presque jaunâtre, en jouant
avec les équivoques. De confortables
fauteuils tapissés en velours orange
accueillent les invités.*

Das Glas verleiht dem Café Royale
den Glanz, für den es bekannt ist:
die auf Holz aufgebrachten
Glasplatten dämpfen, reflektieren
und werfen ein fast gelbliches Licht
und treiben dabei ein verwirrendes
Spiel. Bequeme, mit orangenem
Samt bezogene Sessel laden den
Gast zum Ausruhen ein.

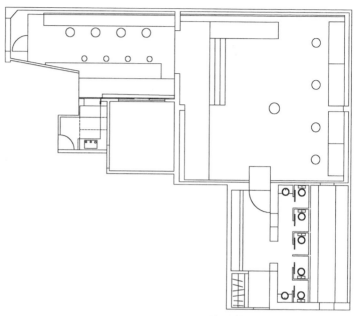

Three different spaces and three colors, green, orange and blue, marry the structure and the wooden floor. The rest rooms were designed to look something like a toy room.

Trois espaces différents et trois couleurs, vert, orange et bleu se marient avec la structure et le parquet en bois. Les cabinets de toilette ont été placés presque comme dans un jeu.

Drei verschiedene Räume und drei Farben –grün, orange und blau– passen zur Struktur und dem Fußboden aus Holz. Die Waschräume ähneln denjenigen eines Puppenhauses

Café Royale

Andrée Putman

Paris, France
2001
Photography | Photo | Fotografie: Mihail Moldoveanu.

Escaping from Baroque images or from extreme lyricism seems to be the genius that Andrée Putman has distilled in the Pershing Hall hotel, example of sobriety and already catapulted to fame as emblem of Parisian ultramodernity. Starting in the bar-lounge, meeting point of the city's most exclusive people, the decoration is absent, even cold if you look at the gray wooden floor, the bar of polished aluminium and the mirrors with a sanded finish. The bar contributes the main lighting: when you climb the few steps you reach a long narrow space, where dark tones of smoke, aubergine and beige coexist, conveying a combination of shine and silence on the surroundings, ideal for photographic exhibitions. Low tables of golden wood, sofas, arm-chairs and poufs (Andrée Putman design for Techno) are spread around there and the atmosphere becomes more intimate, almost monastic. The restaurant awaits on the ground floor, where pearl curtains ensure the privacy of the diners.

Fuir du baroque ou du lyrisme trop marqué semble avoir l'idée du génie de Andrée Putman dans l'hôtel Pershing Hall, exemple de sobriété qui a été catapulté comme emblème du style le plus ultra parisien. En commençant par le bar-lounge, point de réunion de la gens la plus exclusive de la ville, le décor est absent, plutôt froid comme le sol en bois gris, le comptoir en aluminium poli et les glaces à finition sablée. Le comptoir apporte l'éclairage principal: en montant les marches du court escalier on accède à un espace long et étroit où cohabitent les nuances sombres, la couleur fumée, les couleurs aubergine et les beiges, là où l'atmosphère forme un duo de brillance-silence, idéal pour accueillir des expositions de photos. La sont disposées des tables basses en bois doré, des divans fauteuils et poufs (design d'Andrée Putman pour Techno) et le cercle devient plus intime, presque monacal. Pour ceux qui désirent dîner, le restaurant attend à l'étage en-dessous où les rideaux en perles accueille la privacité des commensaux.

Mit dem Vermeiden eines barocken und übertrieben lyrischen Stils gelang es Andrée Putman, dem Hotel Pershing Hall, das jetzt schon Sinnbild des Plus Ultra Parisien ist, einen ausgesprochen nüchternen Stil zu verleihen. Die Dekoration der Bar-Lounge, Treffpunkt des Jet-Sets der Stadt, kann in Anbetracht des grauen Holzfußbodens, der Theke aus Aluminium und den Spiegeln als karg oder sogar kalt bezeichnet werden. Das Licht der Theke stellt die Hauptbeleuchtung dar: nach wenigen Treppenabsätzen erreicht man einen langen, schmalen Raum, wo dunkle, rauchfarbene, auberginenfarbene und beige Farbtöne vorherrschen, vielleicht um die Stimmung eines Duetts aus Glanz und Stille zu schaffen, was für fotografische Ausstellungen sehr geeignet ist. Hier stehen niedrige Tische aus goldfarbenem Holz, Sofas, Puffs (von Andrée Putman für Techno entworfen), die dem Raum eine intime, fast klösterliche Atmosphäre geben. Für das Abendessen bietet sich das Restaurant im Erdgeschoß an, wo Vorhänge aus Perlen die Gäste vor neugierigen Blicken schützen.

The bar-lounge of the Pershing Hall radiates light in an overall context where dark tones, smoke, aubergine and beige practice the art of sobriety. Restaurant, Lounge and the 24 rooms of the hotel respond to what has been called the art of the anti-chic, the absence of decorative motifs achieved with a neutral palette and almost priestly will-power.

Le bar-lounge du Pershing Hall irradie sa lumière dans un ensemble où les nuances sombres, couleur fumée, aubergine et les beiges pratiquent l'art de la sobriété. Restaurant, Lounge et les 24 chambres de l'hôtel répondent à ce qui est connu comme art de l'antichic, l'absence de motifs décoratifs obtenue à partir d'une palette de neutres et d'une idée presque monacale.

Die Bar-Lounge des Pershing Hall ist die Lichtquelle des nüchternen, in dunklen, rauchfarbenen, auberginefarbenen und beigen Tönen gehaltenen Raumes. Das Restaurant, die Lounge und die 24 Zimmer des Hotels verkörpern die sogenannte Anti-Chic-Kunst, die vom Fehlen an Dekorationsmotiven unter Verwendung einer neutralen Farbpalette, und einer fast klösterlichen Atmosphäre geprägt wird.

Pershing Hall

Paradigm of elegance made discipline and then denied are these curtains of glass pearls used as dividing screens in the Pershing Hall restaurant, built on what was the residence of General John Pershing. Another unmistakable sign of the concept of combined exclusivity and silence is the vertical garden that rises in the courtyard, idea of Patrick Blanc that unifies the hotel and which is visible both from the rooms and from the Lounge and restaurant.

Paradigme de l'élégance faite discipline et reniée ensuite voici ce que sont ces rideaux de perles de cristal qui s'intègrent comme séparateurs dans le restaurant du Pershing Hall, construit sur ce qui avait été la résidence du général John Pershing. Une autre preuve indéniable de la combinaison conceptuelle entre l'exclusivité et le silence est le jardin vertical qui monte au patio, conçu par Patrick Blanc unifiant l'hôtel et qui est visible des chambres, du Lounge et du restaurant.

Musterbeispiel der Eleganz sind die aus Kristallperlen gefertigten Vorhänge, die als Trennwände im Restaurant des Pershing Hall dienen. Das Hotel wurde auf dem Grundstück des ehemaligen Wohnsitzes des Generals John Pershing errichtet. Ein weiteres eindeutiges Zeichen für die konzeptliche Verbindung zwischen Exklusivität und Stille ist der vertikal angelegte Garten im Hof, der von Patrick Blanc entworfen wurde und dem Hotel ein einheitliches Bild verleiht. Sowohl von den Zimmern wie auch von der Lounge und dem Restaurant hat man einen Ausblick auf den Garten.

Kurvenstar

Stefan Schilgen

**Berlin, Deutschland
1997
Photography | Photo | Fotografie: Pablo Castagnola.**

Hip-hop and electronic music flow through this universe of light and across this stage inspired by the most famous psychodelic clubs of the 1970s. Berlin's Kurvenstar has become a cult destination and reference for lovers of disco "Neo-Baroque". Lavishly decorated, each element is reinforced by its proximity to the others. The walls of the entire club are covered with paper painted in geometric motifs and colorful patterns, while circular shapes run into a spiral of curves picked up too by the tips of the choice furniture. An eclectic combination picked out carefully to avoid unnecessary clashes. Lighting is a fundamental part of this same aesthetic. The built-in spots and lamps hanging from the ceiling give the background illumination, intensified by beams of light at strategic points.

Le hip-hop et la musique électronique règnent dans cet univers de lumières qui a été inspiré dans les clubs les plus psychédéliques des années soixante. Le Kurvenstar berlinois est devenu un local de culte, une référence pour les amateurs du "néo-baroque" de discothèque. Profusion dans la décoration où chacun des éléments en place renforce son protagonisme associé à l'ensemble. Les murs du local sont revêtues de papiers peints aux motifs géométriques et dessins de couleurs alors que les formes circulaires font pénétrer dans une spirale aux courbes reprises dans les coins des meubles choisis. Une éclectique combinaison réalisée avec mesure évite les stridences superflues. L'éclairage est, d'autre part, un élément fondamental qui aide à l'esthétique. Les luminaires encastrés et les lampes suspendues au plafond sont la source d'éclairage de base qui est nuancée par les faisceaux de lumière aux points stratégiques.

Hip-Hop und elektronische Musik durchströmen dieses Lichteruniversum und den von den bedeutendsten psychedelischen Clubs der 70er Jahre inspirierten Raum. Der Berliner Kurvenstar ist zu einem Kultlokal und einem Begriff für die Fans des "Disco-Neubarocks" geworden. Jedes Element der prunkvollen Dekoration tritt in Verbindung mit den anderen hervor. Die Wände des Lokals wurden mit farbenfrohen und mit geometrischen Motiven bedruckten Tapeten tapeziert; wogegen die kreisförmigen Muster den Gast in eine Spirale von Kurven hineinziehen, die sich auch an den Ecken und Kanten der Möbel wiederholt. Eine eklektische Kombination, die mit Maß durchgeführt wurde, damit die Innenausstattung nicht zu überladen wirkt. Die Beleuchtung ist ein weiteres wichtiges Element, das die Ästhetik hervorhebt. Die Strahler und die an der Decke hängenden Lampen stellen die hauptsächliche Lichtquelle dar, die durch strategisch angeordnete Strahlen abgestuft wird.

The walls of the entire club are covered with paper painted in striking colors and characteristic 1970s motifs.

Les murs du local ont été revêtus de papier peint aux couleurs attrayantes et aux motifs caractéristiques des années soixante-dix.

Die Wände des Lokals wurden mit farbenfrohen und mit Motiven der 70er Jahre bedruckten Tapeten tapeziert.

Kurvenstar

The circular shapes are repeated on the mirrors, the items of decoration and the openings in the building's structure.

Les formes circulaires sont reprises sur les glaces, dans les éléments décoratifs et dans les ouvertures structurelles pratiquées dans le local.

Die runden Formen wiederholen sich bei den Spiegeln, den Dekorationselementen und den strukturellen Öffnungen des Lokals.

Medusa

Barcelona, España
1998
Photography | Photo | Fotografie: Pep Escoda.

Medusa has become a reference point of Barcelona night life for those looking for a contemporary space of versatile colors and tones. Its walls are decorated with pastel colors on a uniform and completely white cement background. Metal and silver are features of other items, such as the bar-columns or the row of stools at the bar. The furnishing consists mainly of recycled pieces and has been reupholstered in brightly-colored PVC that breathes life into this 300 square-meter room. Arm-chairs and low tables are the most common pieces, placed in small groups in different corners of the locale. Numerous hanging balloons are the main source of light, complemented and nuanced by some low lamps, and interrupted by the brightness given off by the slides projected onto the walls. Color, material and light meet in this fashionable spot.

Le Medusa est devenu un référent des sorties nocturnes de Barcelone pour tous ceux qui désirent profiter de son espace au décor contemporain et aux nuances variées. Sur un fond uniforme en ciment, avant tout à fait blanc, des couleurs pastel ont été appliquées sur les murs. En d'autres éléments le métal et l'argent ont été travaillés, comme les colonnes du comptoir et les tabourets alignés devant. Le mobilier choisi, la plupart des pièces ont été récupérées, a été tapissé de skay aux couleurs très vives qui apportent une nuance vivace à cette salle de 300 mètres carrés environ. Les fauteuils et les tables basses sont les pièces les plus récurrentes, distribuées en petits ensembles dans différents coins de l'établissement. Les nombreux ballons suspendus constituent la principale source de lumière, complétée et nuancée par quelques lampes basses, nuance cassée par l'éclair de la projection de diapositives sur les murs. Couleur, matière et lumière se donnent rendez-vous dans cet établissement.

Im Barceloner Nachtleben ist Medusa zu einem Begriff für diejenigen geworden, die sich an einem zeitgenössischen und mehrfarbigen Raum erfreuen wollen. Die ehemals ganz weißen Zementwände wurden in Pastellfarben gestrichen. Bei anderen Elementen, wie die Säulen der Theke und die davorstehenden Hocker, wurden Metall und Silber verwandt. Das ausgewählte Mobiliar, größtenteils recycelte Stücke, wurde mit farbenfrohem Kunststoffleder neu gepolstert, was dem 300 m2 großen Saal ein lebhaftes Aussehen verleiht. Zahlreiche Sessel und niedrige Tische stehen in kleine Gruppen angeordnet in verschiedenen Ecken des Lokals. Viele hängende Kugelleuchten sind die wichtigste Lichtquelle, welche von einigen niedrigen Lampen ergänzt und vom Schein der auf die Wände projizierten Dias unterbrochen wird. Farbe, Materie und Licht treffen in diesem Trendlokal zusammen.

The variation of tones contributed by the walls, lights and upholstery make Medusa an entire universe of color relationships.

La variation de nuances apportée par les murs, les lumières et les tapisseries du mobilier font que Medusa soit tout un univers de relations chromatiques.

Die verschiedenen Farbtöne der Wände, die Lichter und der Polsterstoff der Möbel machen aus Medusa ein Universum der Farbverbindungen.

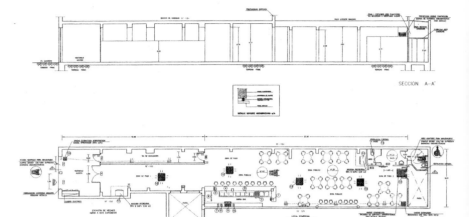

SECCION A-A'

PLANTA

The pieces of furniture chosen to give atmosphere to the locale are recycled, although they have been restored and reupholstered to give them a much more up-to-date look.

Les pièces de mobilier choisi pour donner de l'ambiance au local sont récupérées et tapissées de neuf pour leur donner un air plus actuel.

Für das Lokal wurden recycelte Möbelstücke ausgewählt, die allerdings restauriert und neu gepolstert worden sind, um ihnen einen aktuelleren Look zu geben.

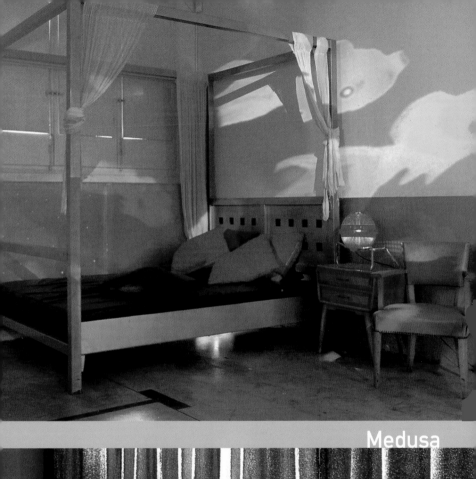

Medusa

The lighting is also one of its decor keys. In addition to the sources of overall light, numerous lamps and neon are placed to create suggestive games of intensity.

L'éclairage est également une des clés dans la décoration. En plus des sources de lumière générale, on a disposé de nombreuses lampes et néons qui forment de suggestifs jeux d'intensité.

Die Beleuchtung ist einer der Stützpunkte der Dekoration. Neben den Hauptlichtquellen wurden zahlreiche Lampen und Neonlichter installiert, die auf suggestiver Weise mit der Intensität des Lichtes spielen.

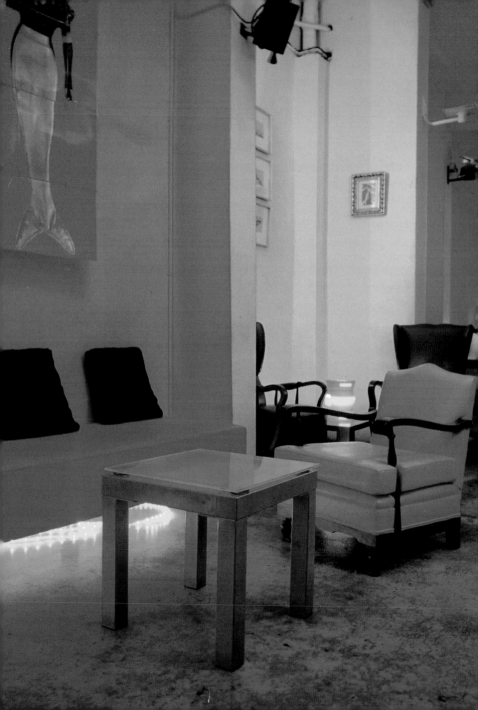

Sidecar

Alex Giménez Imirizaldu

Preliminary Plan | Avant-Projet | Vorentwurf: Beth Galí y Jaume Benavent
Barcelona, España
Reform | Réforme | Erneuerung: 2001
Photography | Photo | Fotografie: Martí Llorens.

Located in Barcelona's Plaza Real, Sidecar is a survivor from the 1980s rock scene. Originally a 'hole in the wall' with a side-door and a small terrace, 2001 saw its authentic opening to the street with the demolition and then glazing of the previously bricked-in windows and a new access from the square. But Sidecar wanted to conserve its mouthy and rebellious spirit by taking as the basis of its new project the powerful graphic image of Boixader and Sallés - an anarcho-glam leaflet - and by introducing new elements onto its main floor: a hanging bar of steel enamelled with car paint, light outlets made with glasses built into the wall, 'pop-sordid' furnishing, etc.. However, its cellar maintains the same structure and surroundings and still puts on one of the best live programmes in the city. You see, old rockers never die.

En pleine plaça Reial barcelonaise, Sidecar est un des survivants de la scène rock des années 80. Posé comme un local maudit, avec une petite porte latérale d'accès et une petite terrasse, c'est en 2001 que sa véritable ouverture sur la rue par la démolition du mur bouchant les fenêtres et la pose de vitres et la création d'un nouvel accès depuis la place. Mais Sidecar a voulu garder son esprit contestataire et rebelle en prenant comme origine du projet la puissante image graphique de Boixader & Sallés, un pamphlet anarcho-glam- et en ajoutant d'autres éléments à son étage principal: un comptoir suspendu en acier émaillé avec de la peinture pour carrosserie de voitures, des points de lumière avec des verres encastrés, le mobilier, mauvais goût-pop, etc. Par ailleurs, son sous-sol garde sa structure et son décor initial pour continuer à accueillir une des meilleurs programmations scéniques de la ville. Les vieux du rock ne meurent jamais!

Am Barceloner Plaza Real gelegen, ist Sidecar ist eines der überlebenden Lokale aus der Rokker-Szene der 80er Jahre. Als "Gaunerlokal" gedacht, mit einer kleinen seitlichen Eingangstür und einer kleinen Terrasse, wurde es 2001 erst richtig zur Straße hin geöffnet, indem die zugemauerten Fenster aufgebrochen und verglast wurden. Außerdem wurde ein neuer Eingang direkt vom Platz aus geschaffen. Sidecar wollte jedoch seinen nonkonformistischen und rebellischen Geist nicht aufgeben, deshalb wurde das Projekt auf die starke Graphik von Boixader & Sallés –eine Anarcho-Glam-Pamphlet– aufgebaut. Dabei wurden im Hauptgeschoß neue Elemente hinzugefügt: eine abgehängte Theke aus mit Autolack gespritztem Stahl, eingesetzte Trinkgläser als Lichtpunkte, Möbel im "schlichten Pop-Stil", usw. Hingegen wurde die ursprüngliche Struktur sowie auch die Ambientierung des Kellergeschosses beibehalten, so daß hier weiterhin die besten Musikgruppen auftreten können. Denn die alten Rocker sind unsterblich.

The hanging bar and rest-rooms are some of the innovations. However, the cellar retains the same structure as when it opened in 1982.

Le comptoir suspendu et les toilettes sont quelques uns des nouveaux éléments. Par contre, le sous-sol de l'établissement maintient sa structure d'origine, celle de son inauguration en 1982.

Die abgehängte Theke und die Waschräume sind einige der neuen Elemente. Dagegen stammt die Struktur des Kellergeschosses noch von 1982, als das Lokal eröffnet wurde.

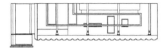

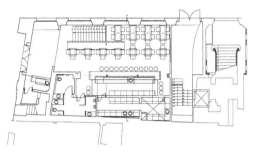

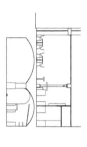

Access to the cellar from the rehabilitated and opened-out main floor has been made very much easier by the reforms.

Depuis l'étage principal qui a été rénové et ouvert actuellement, l'accès au sous-sol du local est bien plus aisé.

Der Zugang von der renovierten und jetzt offenen oberen Etage her zum Kellergeschoß wurde umgebaut und dadurch beträchtlich erleichtert.

Sidecar

Jubinal

Achim Keyser y Serder Wetzmann

Berlin, Deutschland
1998
Photography | Photo | Fotografie: Pablo Castagnola.

Warm feelings by candle-light. Located in one of the select areas of Berlin's night-time leisure scene, Jubinal is a place where all its meaning comes from the combination of aesthetic styles. A small entrance-hall welcomes customers with the impact of warm-toned neon lighting. These same lighting effects are repeated inside, where a large C-shaped bar stands before a line of futuristic stools. An area of small leather sofas accompanied by tables and stools with metallic structures and dark upholstery has been positioned in front of the big windows. Beside the entrance, and as a contrast, some square arm-chairs upholstered in white leather create a much more intimate area for relaxing. Current lines combine with 1960s and '70s lines under a certain outer space feel suggested by the neon lighting.

De chaudes sensations à la lumière d'une bougie. Situé dans une zone choisie des loisirs nocturnes de Berlin, Jubinal est un local où le mariage des esthétiques acquiert toute sa signification. Un vestibule réduit accueille les clients sous le choc des néons aux tons chauds. Ces effets de lumières se reproduisent à l'intérieur, présidé par un grand comptoir en forme de C face auquel s'alignent les tabourets d'inspiration futuriste. Face aux verrières une zone avec de petits canapés en cuir autour de tables et des tabourets à la structure métallique et tapissés couleur sombre. Près de l'entrée, et faisant contraste, quelques fauteuils carrés tapissés en cuir blanc créent une zone de séjour beaucoup plus intime. Des lignes actuelles ou des années 60 et 70 se marient sous un certaine aspect galactique renforcé par les néons.

Angenehme Stimmung bei Kerzenschein. In einer der beliebtesten Gegenden des Berliner Nachtlebens gelegen, ist Jubinal ein Lokal, in dem mehrere Ästhetiken im wahrsten Sinne des Wortes miteinander verbunden sind. In einem kleinen Vorraum mit wärmeausstrahlenden Neonlichtern werden die Gäste empfangen. Diese Lichteffekte wiederholen sich im Inneren, das von einer großen Theke in Form eines offenen C beherrscht wird, vor der die futuristisch anmutende Hocker stehen. Vor den großen Fenstern wurde ein Sitzbereich geschaffen, bestehend aus kleinen Ledersofas, Tischen und metallischen, dunkel gepolsterten Hockern. Im Kontrast dazu stehen am Eingang einige viereckige Sessel aus weißem Leder, die eine viel intimere Atmosphäre schaffen. Aktuelle und aus den 60er und 70er Jahren stammende Linien vermischen sich hier, wobei die Neonlicher einen leichten Anflug von galaktischer Stimmung geben.

The tables and chairs with metallic legs and a round base are contrasted with the square white-leather armchairs situated next to the entrance.

Les tables et les chaises à la base circulaire en métal contrastent avec les fauteuils aux formes carrées tapissés en cuir blanc, placés à l'entrée.

Die runden Tisch- und Stuhlbeine aus Metall kontrastieren mit den viereckigen Sesseln aus weißem Leder, die am Eingang stehen.

Jubinal

The numerous neon lights in various tones, along with the lighted candles on all the tables, help create a warm atmosphere.

Les nombreux néons aux différentes nuances contribuent à créer une atmosphère chaude renforcée par la présence des bougies qui allumées sur les tables.

Die zahlreichen Neonlichter in verschiedenen Farbtönen schaffen eine warme Atmosphäre, was noch von den auf allen Tischen brennenden Kerzen betont wird.

Alphabet

Jenny Jones y Spike Marchant

London, United Kingdom
1997
Photography | Photo | Fotografie: Chas Wilshere.

Located in Oxford Circus, Alphabet harbors welcome surprises. The wide ground floor is in a fairly conventional style of wooden floors weathered by the passage of time, a bar with rotating-top stools and groups of tables and chairs. However, to step downstairs is to enter a new completely distinct world. A striking city plan of London's Soho painted on the floor traces impossible routes from one to the other side of the room. The furniture consists of curious sofas and recycled arm-chairs, with small wheels fitted, tables improvised from tyres and various low stools also recovered from junk. All these pieces are like vehicles able to travel from one point to another on the street map that gives them their raison d'être.

Situé à Oxford Circus, Alphabet renferme d'agréables surprises dans son intérieur. Le rez-de-chaussée, grand, possède une esthétique assez conventionnelle avec son sol en bois vieilli par les années, un comptoir entouré de tabourets tournants et un ensemble de chaises autour des tables. Mais, descendre les marches conduisant à l'étage inférieur c'est entrer dans un nouveau monde qui a peu ou rien à voir avec ce qui est à l'étage supérieur. Un plan urbain du Soho de Londres a été peint sur le sol en traçant des parcours impossibles d'un côté et de l'autre de la salle. Le mobilier se compose de curieux canapés et des fauteuils récupérés auxquels on a mis des petites roues, des tables improvisées avec des pneus et quelques petits tabourets bas, çà et là. Tous ces éléments ressemblent à des véhicules pouvant se déplacer d'un point à l'autre sur le plan des rues qui leur sert de base.

Am Oxford Circus gelegen, bereitet Alphabet seinen Gästen angenehme Überraschungen. Der ausgetretene Holzfußboden, die Theke, die davorstehenden Drehhocker und die aus Tisch und Stühlen bestehenden Sitzgruppen verleihen dem geräumigen Erdgeschoß ein herkömmliches Aussehen. Über eine Treppe gelangt man in das untere Stockwerk, das mit dem oberen kaum etwas gemeinsam hat. Auf einem auffallenden, auf den Fußboden aufgemalten Stadtplan des Londoner Soho werden unmögliche Strecken von einer Seite des Saales auf die andere gezeichnet. Das Mobiliar dieses Geschosses besteht aus eigenartigen, recycelten Sofas und Sesseln, an die kleine Räder angebracht wurden, aus mit Reifen hergestellten Tischen und aus einigen ebenfalls restaurierten Hockern. Diese Möbelstücke stellen Fahrzeuge dar, die von einer Straße des Stadtplans zur anderen fahren können.

Recycled arm-chairs have been upholstered in leather and had small wheels fitted for moving about the room.

Les fauteuils récupérés ont été tapissés de cuir, et les petites roues permettent de les déplacer dans la salle.

Die recycelten Sessel wurden mit Leder überzogen und mit kleinen Rädern versehen, wodurch diese innerhalb des Saales herumgefahren werden können.

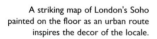

A striking map of London's Soho painted on the floor as an urban route inspires the decor of the locale.

Un plan du Soho londonien est peint sur le sol comme itinéraire urbain inspirant la décoration de l'établissement.

Die Dekoration des Lokals wird von dem auf den Fußboden aufgemalten Stadtplan des Londoner Soho inspiriert.

Alphabet

The upper street-level floor is in a
much more conventional style:
wooden floors, a bar with stools,
and groups of chairs and tables.

*Le niveau supérieur possède une
esthétique plus conventionnelle: des sols
en bois, un comptoir avec des tabourets
et des ensembles des tables et de chaises.*

Das obere Stockwerk weist ein
herkömmliches Aussehen auf:
Holzfußböden, eine Theke mit Hockern
und aus Tischen und Stühlen
bestehende Sitzgruppen.

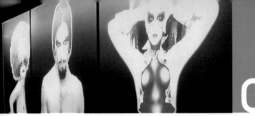

Cool

Tomás Alía
Madrid, España
2001
Photography | Photo | Fotografie: Uxío da Vila.

In a journey to 1970s geometry, like a mirage of electric blue fluoride and hanging silver balls, Cool is introduced to Madrid's night-life. From the entrance to the dance floor, still shots of decor ideas are reproduced from a few decades ago, when the sensationalism of glitter and light was found everywhere. Two private rooms for chilling out look over the dance floor from glass balconies on the mezzanine. Here the exciting realm of colors, glitter, psychodelic shapes of chairs and hand-painted paper is completed by the neon lighting pouring into every corner. The black back-drop to the ground floor is interrupted by the large photographic panels in stainless-steel boxes that give the touch of light. On the dance floor the night assumes the identity of "neon, mirrors, rustless effect, glitter and more glitter". A stage raised above the dance floor and three steel panels behind give it the look of a room in space.

Comme un voyage dans la géométrie des années 70, comme un mirage de fluor bleu électrique et des ballons argentés en suspension, c'est ainsi que se présente le Cool, un des choix de la nuit madrilène. De l'entrée à la salle de danse, des instantanées de schémas décoratifs se reproduisent, rappelant le décor vieux de quelques décennies, lorsque s'imposait partout l'effet des brillances et de la lumière. Deux privés avec chill-out et balustrades se penchent, de l'étage intermédiaire, sur la piste de danse qui se trouve en bas. Ici est évoqué le royaume amusant des couleurs, des brillances, des formes psychédéliques des chaises et papier peint à la main allié au néon présent dans tous les coins. Le fond noir de l'étage inférieur est cassé par les grands panneaux photographiques sous encadrements en acier inox qui ajoutent une touche de lumière. Arrivés sur la piste de danse, la nuit prend le nom de "néon, glaces, effet inox, brillances et encore plus d'éclats". Une scène élevée au-dessus de la piste et au fond trois panneaux en acier rendent le cadre presque galactique.

Bei einer Reise zum Geometrismus der 70er Jahre, wie eine Illusion aus bläulichem Fluor und schwebenden silbernen Kugeln, gelangt man zum Cool des Madrider Nachtlebens. Vom Eingang bis zur Tanzfläche hin werden auf Fotos Dekorationsstile, die vor einigen Jahrzehnten üblich waren, als überall ein übertriebenes Spiel mit Glanz und Licht getrieben wurde, gezeigt. In der Zwischenetage befinden sich zwei Privaträume mit Chill-Out, von deren verglasten Balkons man auf die im unteren Stockwerk liegende Tanzfläche herabblicken kann. Hier wird das lustige Reich der Farben, des Glanzes und der psychedelischen Formen der Stühle und handgemalten Tapeten evoziert, hinzu kommen noch die allgegenwärtigen Neonlichter. Unterbrochen wird der schwarze Hintergrund von großen Abbildungen, die auf Kästen aus Inox-Stahl, die etwas Helligkeit abgeben, haften. An der Tanzfläche wird die Nacht von "Neonlichtern, Spiegeln, Metalleffekten, Glitzern und Glänzen" bestimmt. Eine über der Tanzfläche liegende Bühne und drei Stahlplatten im Hintergrund verleihen diesem Saal eine fast galaktische Atmosphäre.

From the famous Bombo chairs, designed by Stefano Giovannoni, on the mezzanine floor, you can watch the dancers' rhythmic movements. Hand-painted geometric patterns, finished with glossy protector varnish, cover the walls with revival shapes. The steel-perforated sound-proof panels on descending the entrance stair (see next page) reflect the overall blue light.

Réunion des fameuses chaises Bombo, design de Stefano Giovannoni, à l'étage intermédiaire, d'où on peut observer les mouvements rythmés du personnel. Les imprimés géométriques dessinés à la main et finis au vernis satiné revêtent les murs aux formes revival. Les panneaux d'insonorisation en acier perforé sont placés sur l'escalier de l'entrée (page suivante) reflétant la lumière bleue de l'ensemble.

Für das Zwischengeschoß, von wo aus die rhythmischen Bewegungen der Tanzenden beobachtet werden können, wählte man die berühmten Bombo-Stühle, welche von Stefano Giovannoni entworfen wurden. Die geometrischen Revival-Muster der Wände sind handgemalt und wurden mit Satinlack überstrichen. Die Lärmschutzplatten aus Stahl an der Eingangstreppe (nächste Seite) werfen das blaue Licht zurück.

Cool

The dance floor and stage are in stained wengé
wood, on which hard-wearing glossy varnish has been
painted. The floor is divided by a set of squares
throwing up light. The pillars, perforated by shiny
polished Inox and coated in opal methacrylate, reach
the upper floor. On them, mirror neons play at color
changes. Three great balls of mirrors round off the
1970s image.

*La piste de danse et la scène sont en bois wengué teint
avec une application de vernis satiné haute résistance
et délimitée par un quadrillé de lumière. Les colonnes
remontent au niveau supérieur, elles sont en inox poli et
recouvertes en méthacrylate opale; à l'intérieur des néons
et des glaces jouent à changer les couleurs. Trois grands
ballons en verre complètent l'ambiance des années
soixante dix.*

Bis auf eine viereckige beleuchtete Fläche sind
Tanzfläche und Bühne aus gefärbtem, mit
hochbeständigem Satinlack geschütztem Wengé-Holz.
Die bis zur oberen Etage hin reichenden Säulen
wurden aus gelöchertem, hochglanzpoliertem
Inox-Stahl gefertigt und mit opalem Methacrylat
verkleidet; darin wechseln Neonlichter ständig ihre
Farben. Drei große glitzernde Kugeln runden die
Stimmung der 70er Jahre ab.

Roberto Musco

**Barcelona, España
1998
Photography | Photo | Fotografie: Martí Llorens.**

Fifty years a furniture shop, it is now a place that must be seen. The Café titled "Muebles Navarro" (Navarro Furniture) takes its inspiration from the former shop despite its change of use. Even the shop sign has been adopted as a leitmotif. Since it opened in 1998, the Café has become a reference point in Barcelona's reformed Raval area and has a varied and faithful clientèle. The result fulfils the aim of its creator Robert Musco, which was to achieve a relaxing and welcoming atmosphere. He took advantage of the difficult initial lay-out, with three separate corridors, and planned a space with groups of sofas, easy-chairs, centre-tables and lamps. The bar is also a fundamental piece, outstanding for its simplified Art Nouveau shapes. Serenity and good taste in a locale that also exhibits works by city artists.

Pendant cinquante ans ce fût un magasin de meubles et actuellement un point de rencontre obligée. Le Café qui se nomme "Muebles Navarro" est inspiré de l'ancien établissement qui est maintenant tout à fait adapté à ses nouvelles fonctions. Même l'enseigne du magasin qui reste encore est le leitmotiv. Depuis son inauguration en 1998, le Café est devenu un point de référence dans le quartier rénové du Raval et il compte avec une clientèle variée et fidèle. Le résultat est bien celui que son créateur, Roberto Musco, avait projeté: créer un climat accueillant et reposant. Pour cela, la distribution compliquée d'origine, avec ses trois couloirs séparés, a été transformée et un espace accueillant un ensemble de canapés, de fauteuils et de tables basses et de lampes. Le comptoir est également un des éléments fondamentaux avec ses formes modernistes simplifiées. Placidité et bon goût dans un établissement qui accueille des expositions d'oeuvres d'artistes urbains.

Fünfzig Jahre lang ein Möbelgeschäft und heute ein Muß. Die Aufschrift am Eingang des Cafés, ''Muebles Navarro'', erinnert an die ehemalige Tätigkeit des Lokals, obwohl diese heute nicht mehr ausgeführt wird. Das noch erhaltene Schild des Geschäfts diente als Leitmotiv bei der Namensgebung des Lokals. Seit seiner Eröffnung im Jahre 1998 ist das Café im sanierten Barceloner Viertel Raval zu einem Begriff geworden und erfreut sich einer treuen und verschiedenartigen Kundschaft. Das Ergebnis entspricht dem Ziel seines Schöpfers, Roberto Musco, der dem Lokal eine entspannende und gemütliche Atmosphäre geben wollte. Dafür wurde die komplizierte ursprüngliche Aufteilung mit drei getrennten Fluren übernommen und ein Raum mit aus Sofas, Sesseln, Couchtischen und Lampen bestehenden Sitzbereichen gestaltet. Die Theke stellt ein weiteres Grundelement dar und besticht wegen ihrer vereinfachten modernistischen Formen. Ruhe und Geschmack in einem Lokal, in dem außerdem Werke von Künstlern der Stadt ausgestellt werden.

The furniture recalls the cafés of yesteryear. Wrought iron, wood and marble are the main materials.

Le mobilier récupéré rappelle celui des vieux cafés. Fer forgé, bois et marbre dont les principaux matériaux utilisés.

Die restaurierten Möbel erinnern an diejenigen der alten Cafés. Schmiedeeisen, Holz und Marmor sind die meistverwandten Materialien.

The Café's walls welcome exhibitions of new local and international talents.

Les murs du Café accueillent, un temps, des expositions des talents locaux et internationaux.

Im Café finden Wechselausstellungen von neuen Talenten der Stadt und aus dem Ausland statt.

The bar of simplified Art Nouveau shapes is one of the
elements defining the character of the café.

*Le comptoir aux formes modernistes simplifiées est un des
éléments de base qui contribue au caractère particulier de
l'établissement.*

Die Theke mit vereinfachten modernistischen Formen ist
eines der Grundelemente und prägt den Charakter des
Lokals.

El Café que pone Muebles Navarro

so_da

Marc Escursell y Macarena Obrador

Barcelona, España
2000
Photography | Photo | Fotografie: Pep Escoda.

Look around you, find out what art and design inspires in other houses, and search among past tastes, mostly recovered from flea markets such as Barcelona's Encants or in Perpignan. This is the inspiration of Marc and Macarena to make their shop-bar, bar-shop, a meeting point of recent trends in the city of Barcelona. Among fuchsia, red and orange, versatile furniture switches between day and night use. Furniture with wheels functions as night equipment. The dressing-rooms change their face with the moon and are used as lights. Shelving, chests of drawers and basket chairs make up a shop-window that is easily integrated into the night's atmosphere. Part of this peculiar furnishing with a certain retro touch and, even more, futuristic, is designed by Christian Bilkler. The 170 square meters are spread over two areas, one larger in which stands the bar of wood and stainless steel from which the colorful coming and going of people who are, above all, modern can be contemplated.

Observer le panorama, voir ce que l'art et le design produit dans d'autres lieux et parmi les goûts d'antan, rechercher des éléments récupérés chez les brocanteurs comme les Encants à Barcelone ou d'autres à Perpignan. C'est ce que Marc et Macarena ont fait pour leur magasin-bar, bar-magasin, point de rencontre des dernières tendances de la ville de Barcelone. Entre fuchsias, rouges et orangés se trouve un mobilier versatile à utilisation diurne/nocturne. Les meubles à roues sont des équipement de nuit. Les vestiaires changent avec la lune et sont utiles pour éclairer. Les étagères, les commodes et les chaises araignée composent une devanture qui s'intègre sans confusion dans le décor nocturne. Une part de ce mobilier spécial a une touche rétro, l'autre étant beaucoup plus futuriste, appartiennent au design de Christian Bilkler. Les 170 mètre carrés sont distribués en deux zones, la plus grande accueille le comptoir en bois et acier inoxydable d'où on peut observer l'alternance des gens avant tout très à la page.

Kunst- und Designtendenzen anderer Orte erkunden und nach Objekten vergangener Zeiten suchen, hauptsächlich auf Flohmärkten wie die Barceloner Encants und andere in Perpignan. Dies ist der Grundsatz, nach dem Marc und Macarena vorgingen, um in ihrer Laden-Bar, oder Bar-Laden, ein Zusammentreffen der neuesten Trends der Stadt Barcelona zu ermöglichen. Im von rosa, roten und orangenen Farbtönen beherrschten Lokal stehen Möbel, die sowohl bei Tag als auch bei Nacht ihren Zweck erfüllen. Die Möbel mit Rädern werden nachts verwandt. Die Umkleidekabinen werden bei Einbruch der Dunkelheit zu Lampen. Die Regale, Kommoden und netzförmigen Stühle bilden ein Ensemble, das sich ohne weiteres in die Nachtdekoration einfügt. Ein Teil dieses eigenartigen Mobiliars, mit einem gewissen Retro-Look und einem weitaus futuristischeren Aussehen, wurde von Christian Bilkler entworfen. Die Gesamtfläche von 170 m2 ist in zwei Bereiche aufgeteilt. Im größeren steht die Theke aus Holz und rostfreiem Stahl, von wo aus das gemischte, vor allem moderne Publikum beobachtet werden kann.

The bar is the meeting-place of the most modern people of the city. The furniture meets their pretensions: padded leather arm-chairs, various kinds of basket chairs and strategic lights within a setting of explosive color.

La pièce accueillant le comptoir réunit les gens les plus à la page de la ville. Le mobilier répond aux prétentions: des fauteuils recouverts de cuir, les chaises araignée, aux formes les plus disparates et les projecteurs stratégiquement situés s'entrecroisent dans un cadre aux couleurs explosives.

Im Thekenraum trifft man das modernste Publikum der Stadt an. Das Mobiliar entspricht den Anforderungen: Ledersessel, verschiedenartige netzförmige Stühle und strategisch angeordnete Leuchten passen gut zu den knalligen Farben des Raumes.

so_da

Barbugatti

Luigi Caccia Dominioni

Milano, Italia
2000
Photography | Photo | Fotografie: Paola D´Amico.

The Barbugatti is the outcome of the reconstruction of the former Barattini factory to improve the use of space without modifying its original characteristics. The harmonious adaptation of the existing volumes improved the site's beauty by endowing it with a fascination and luminosity that is not at all common in this kind of industrial building. This extraordinary space houses, as well as a restaurant, the University of Image and the Industrial Gymnasium, revealing clearly its relationship with its owners Fabrizio and Alessandra Ferri: for he is photographer and stylist while she is a leading dancer at La Scala. The decor by Barbugatti expresses this relationship with the worlds of images and the body: a minimalist chic style, with a healthy menu of biological products and drinks such as apple, carrot and fresh kiwi, in an environment of relaxed rhythms and classical music.

Le Barbugatti est le résultat du travail de reconstruction de l'ancienne fabrique Barattini qui a permis de fonctionnaliser l'espace sans en modifier le caractère d'origine. Les volumes existants ont été adaptés au perfectionnement du local en lui conférant une fascination et une luminosité assez rares dans des structures industrielles de ce genre. Cet espace extraordinaire héberge, en plus du restaurant, l'Université de l'Image et le Gimnase Industria, en relation avec les propriétaires, Fabrizzio et Alessandra Ferri: lui étant photographe et styliste et elle danseuse célèbre de la Scala.
Le décor du Barbugatti est l'expression de sa relation avec le monde de l'image et du corps. Un style minimaliste-chic où un menu sain à base de produits biologiques et de boissons à base de jus de pomme, de carottes et de kiwi frais sont servis dans un environnement au rythme reposant de musique classique.

Barbugatti ist das Ergebnis des Umbaus der ehemaligen Fabrik Barattini, womit die Funktionalität des Raumes verbessert werden sollte, ohne jedoch ihre ursprünglichen Merkmale zu verändern. Die harmonische Umgestaltung der vorhandenen Räume verbesserte das Aussehen des Lokals und gab ihm eine Attraktivität und Helligkeit, die bei Fabriken dieser Art ziemlich seltsam anmutet. Dieser außergewöhnliche Raum beherbergt, vom Restaurant abgesehen, die Schule für Fotokunst, und das Fitness-Center Industria, wobei die Beziehung zu den Eigentümern Fabrizio y Alessandra Ferri herausgestellt wird. Er ist Fotograf und Maskenbildner, und sie, eine bekannte Tänzerin der Scala. Ausdruck ihrer Beziehung zur Welt von Bild und Körper ist die im Minimal-Chic-Stil gehaltene Dekoration des Barbugatti, wo ein gesundes Menü aus Bio-Produkten, sowie auch Apfel-, Möhren- und Kiwisäfte angeboten werden, alles bei entspannenden Rhythmen und klassischer Musik.

The stainless-steel bar contrasts with the splashes of color on the luminous walls to offer a minimalist chic adaptation of the old Barattini factory.

Le comptoir du bar en acier inoxydable contraste avec les taches de couleur sur les murs éclairés donne une esthétique minimaliste-chic à ce qui fût autrefois la fabrique Barattini.

Die Theke aus Inox-Stahl kontrastiert mit den Farbflecken an den leuchtenden Wänden und verleiht der ehemaligen Fabrik Barattini eine Minimal-Chic-Ästhetik.

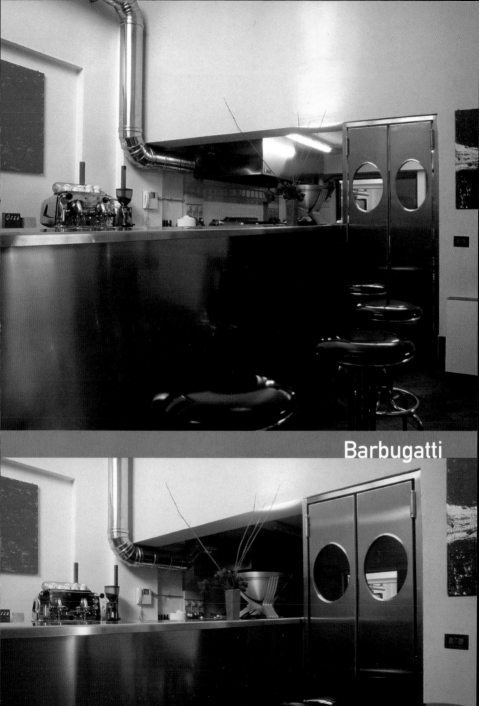

Barbugatti

· West Street

Wells Mackere 71

London, United Kingdom
2001
Photography | Photo | Fotografie: Chas Wilshere.

The West Street is housed in a fine two-storey building that uses the concept of the vertical to play with material, color and structure. From top to bottom, the locale undergoes a gradual change. At the top, the high ceilings frame a setting defined by its ethereal and fickle character. The nakedness of its lighted spaces is interrupted only by a flying sculpture like steam, whose silhouette rises towards infinity. Back down to hard reality, the ground floor brings dark colors and solidity. The leather sofas and furniture in noble woods exemplify a lower floor characterized by its body mass. And so the West Street customer cannot help glancing with longing, up from the solid world of things, towards the upper storey, towards the world of lightness, where objects have lost their ballast.

Le West Street est un prestigieux établissement à deux étages qui, à partir de sa verticalité, joue avec la matière, les couleurs et la projection structurelle. De haut en bas, le local présente une gradualité progressive. La partie supérieure aux plafonds hauts renferme une ambiance définie et éthérée et légère. La nudité des espaces lumineux est uniquement interrompue par la présence d'une sculpture légère, vaporeuse, dessinant une silhouette qui s'élève vers l'infini. De retour à l'inaltérable réalité, le rez-de-chaussée revient aux couleurs sombres et à la matière. Les canapés en cuir et le mobilier en bois nobles confèrent au plan inférieur la caractéristique corporelle des volumes. C'est que les clients du West Street, à partir de la contingence du monde des objets ne peuvent pas éviter d'adresser un regard de désir vers la partie supérieure, vers le monde de la légèreté où les objets ont perdu leur poids.

West Street ist in einem privilegierten zweistöckigen Lokal untergebracht, in dem anhand des Vertikalitätskonzeptes mit Materie, Farbe und Strukturprojektion gespielt wird. Das Lokal ist von oben nach unten hin abgestuft. Im Obergeschoß grenzen die hohen Decken eine ätherische und leichte Atmosphäre ab. Die Kargheit der hellen Räume wird lediglich von der Gegenwart einer federleichten Skulptur unterbrochen, die sich wie eine ins Endlose steigende Silhouette abhebt. Wieder zurück in der unveränderlichen Wirklichkeit wird das Erdgeschoß von dunklen Farben und Materialität geprägt. Die Ledersofas und die Möbel aus Edelholz sind ein Beispiel für die Körperlichkeit der Räume des unteren Geschosses. Von der Welt der Objekte her kann der Gast des West Street nicht vermeiden, sehnsüchtig nach oben zu blicken, zur Welt des Ätherischen, wo die Gegenstände in der Luft schweben.

The West Street is housed in a
fine two-storey building that
uses the concept of the vertical
to play with material, color and
structure.

*Le West Street est un
établissement prestigieux à deux
étages jouant à partir du concept
de la verticalité avec la matière,
les couleurs et la projection
structurelle.*

West Street befindet sich in
einem privilegierten
zweistöckigen Lokal, in dem
anhand des Vertikalitätkonzeptes
mit Materie, Farbe und
Strukturprojektion gespielt wird.

West Street

The leather sofas and furniture in noble woods occupy
a lower floor characterized by its body mass.

*Les canapés en cuir et le mobilier en bois nobles se trouvent
au rez-de-chaussée caractérisé par la corporéité des volumes.*

Die Ledersofas und die Möbel aus Edelholz sind ein Beispiel für das
Körperliche der Räume des Erdgeschosses.

Patrick Monoghan

London, United Kingdom
1997
Photography | Photo | Fotografie: Peter Cook (VIEW).

Despite its name, this London club has little to do with a typical English tavern or pub. Located next to a big park, its interior design breaks with this natural dynamic to become a frankly welcoming design refuge. The white surfaces of its general structure contrast with the round yellow columns repeated throughout the building. White, combined now with fuchsia, is repeated in the upholstery of arm-chairs and stools. A simple but striking color range that links seamlessly to the clear wood of its tables and the aluminium of the furniture's structures. A panel of illuminated white glass at the bar is a general source of light, along with the spots built into the ceiling and the panels of bluish light from the bottle rack.

Malgré son nom, cet établissement londonien n'a rien de commun avec les tavernes typiques ou les pubs anglais. Situé près d'un grand parc, son intérieur rompt la dynamique naturelle pour devenir un refuge au design franchement accueillant. Les surfaces blanches de ses structures générales sont en contraste avec les colonnes jaunes qui se trouvent dans tout l'établissement. Cette couleur est reprise sur les tapisseries et les fauteuils, les tabourets, en combinaison avec la couleur fuchsia. Une simple, mais éclatante gamme chromatique se marie sans stridences avec le bois clair de ses tables et avec l'aluminium des structures de base du mobilier. Un panneau en verre blanc éclairé est disposé sur le comptoir et constitue une source de lumière générale associée aux luminaires encastrés dans les plafonds et aux panneaux de lumière bleutée de la vitrine aux bouteilles.

Dieses Londoner Lokal hat trotz seines Namens kaum etwas mit einer typischen englischen Taverne oder Pub zu tun. An einem großen Park gelegen, bricht seine Innendekoration mit der äußeren Naturwelt und wird zu einem gemütlichen Ort. Die weiße Oberfläche der Grundstrukturen kontrastiert mit den gelben runden Säulen, die überall im Lokal zu sehen sind. Ebenfalls gelb, aber mit rosa kombiniert, sind die Polsterbezüge der Sessel und Hocker. Eine einfache, aber auffallende Farbpalette, die gut zum Holz der Tische und zum Aluminium der Grundstrukturen der Möbel paßt. An der Theke wurde außerdem eine beleuchtete weiße Glasplatte aufgestellt, die zusammen mit den Deckenstrahlern und dem mit bläulichem Licht beleuchteten Flaschenregal eine Lichtquelle darstellt.

The club is lit by a combination of spots built into the ceiling and glass panels on surfaces such as the bar or bottle rack.

L'éclairage de l'établissement a été projeté comme une combinaison de luminaires encastrés dans les plafonds et les panneaux en verre sur des surfaces notables, comme le comptoir ou la vitrine aux bouteilles.

Das Beleuchtungssystem des Lokals besteht aus Deckenstrahlern und Glasplatten an wichtigen Stellen, wie die Theke und das Flaschenregal.

Tavern on the Green

The round yellow columns are a
structural element that creates a
unifying dynamic for all the various
zones of the club.

*Les colonnes cylindriques couleur jaune
sont un élément structurel créant une
dynamique qui contribue à l'unité de
toutes les ambiances de la salle.*

Die gelben, runden Säulen sind ein
Strukturelement, das alle Ambienten
des Saales vereinheitlicht.

Clip's

Giorgio Zerbi

Milano, Italia
1997
Photography | Photo | Fotografie: Paola D'Amico.

Three elements combine to create a homogenous whole. Water, stone and iron are the material and aesthetic basis of Clip's, a suggestive Milan nightspot whose forms and textures produce a strange feeling of melancholic beauty. The apparent coldness of the materials used is perfectly countered by the placing of elements and resources whose curving lines provide the warmth needed. The circular tables with white marble tops, alongside chairs made of iron, but with red leather seats, are a perfect example of this. The irregular ceilings break the linearity governing the other structures. In addition, the decor to coat the columns and the bar's front wall appear to imitate the incessant movement of water, as if a sea was taking on life on top of the lifeless base. Water is again present in the images projected onto the side walls.

Trois combinés pour créer un tout homogène. Eau, pierre et fer sont les bases matérielles et esthétiques du Clip's, un établissement milanais suggestif où les formes et les textures produisent une étrange sensation de beauté mélancolique. L'apparente froideur des matériaux utilisés est parfaitement contrecarrée par la disposition des éléments et des ressources dans lesquels les lignes courbes apportent la chaleur désirée. Les tables circulaires à dessus en marbre blanc entourées de fauteuils à la structure en fer, mais aux sièges en cuir rouge sont un bon exemple. Les plafonds irréguliers sont en rupture avec les lignes régnantes dans les structures générales. De plus, la décoration pratiquée pour revêtir les colonnes et le mur d'exposition du comptoir semble imiter le mouvement continuel de l'eau, comme si une mer se réveillait sur la base inerte. L'eau à nouveau est présente sous forme de projection sur les murs latéraux.

Drei Elemente, die zur Gestaltung eines einheitlichen Ganzen verbunden wurden. Wasser, Stein und Eisen sind die materiellen und ästhetischen Grundlagen des Clip's, eines suggestives Mailänder Lokals, in dem Formen und Texturen ein eigenartiges Gefühl von melancholischer Schönheit hervorrufen. Die scheinbare Kälte der verwandten Materialien wird von der Anordnung der Elemente, deren geschwungenen Linien dem Raum die nötige Wärme verleihen, ausgeglichen. Die runden Tische mit weißen Marmorplatten und die dazugehörigen Sessel mit Eisenstruktur und roten Lederpolstern sind ein gutes Beispiel dafür. Die abgestuften Decken brechen mit der Linearität der anderen Strukturen. Außerdem scheint die Verkleidung der Säulen und der Rückwand des Flaschenregals die endlosen Hin- und Herbewegungen des Wassers nachzuahmen, als ob ein Meer auf der leblosen Grundfläche ins Leben gerufen würde. Auch auf den Seitenwänden ist das Wasser als projiziertes Bild vorhanden.

The irregular ceilings, the bar decor and the light projected on the walls are warming lines that help break the coldness of the basic materials used.

Les plafonds irréguliers, la décoration du comptoir et la projection de lumière sur les murs sont des éléments aux lignes chaudes qui contribuent à rompre avec la froideur des matériaux utilisés.

Die warmen Linien der abgestuften Decken, der Thekendekoration und der auf die Wände geworfenen Lichtbilder gleichen die Kälte der verwandten Materialien aus.

Clip's

The grouped metal chairs
and tables, with white marble
tops and red leather seats,
are grouped together on the
stone floors.

*Sur les sols en pierre sont
disposées, avec leurs structures
métalliques, les tables à dessus
en marbre blanc et les chaises
à siège en cuir rouge.*

Auf den Steinfußböden
gruppieren sich Tische mit
weißen Marmorplatten und
Stühle mit roten Ledersitzen,
ihre Struktur ist aus Metall.

Lab

Paul Daily

London, United Kingdom
2000
Photography | Photo | Fotografie: Chas Wilshere.

In the heart of London's Soho, Lab is an authentic journey back to television series such as Charlie's Angels. 1970s styling is present in almost the elements of this club. The brick walls painted in an almost fluorescent green combine with others in orange and copper tones that hark back to the shine of Farrah Fawcett's long hair. Rounded edges almost in capsule form are also repeated as a motif on the bar, the shelving and even on the mirrors of the entire club, with varnished wood and steel the main materials. Stools of different heights, but with identical circular lines, flood the bar and the surrounds of the tables, so that as many customers as possible can sit down. The colored spots also help create the club's characteristic retro look.

Situé en plein Soho londonien, le Lab est comme un véritable voyage de retour aux scénarios des feuilletons de télévision comme les Anges de Charlie. L'esthétique des années soixante dix se retrouve pratiquement dans tous les éléments du local. Les murs en brique ont été peints en vert presque fluorescent en alliance avec les autres nuances orangées et cuivres qui rappellent la lumière de la longue chevelure de Farrah Fawcett. Coins arrondis et formes presque capsulaires se retrouvent comme un motif dans le comptoir, sur les étagères et même sur les glaces du local où prédominent le bois laqué et l'acier. Des tabourets à hauteurs différentes mais aux lignes circulaires identiques se situent près du comptoir et autour des tables pour que le plus grand nombre de clients puisse s'asseoir aisément. Les Projecteurs de couleur contribuent à créer cette atmosphère rétro caractérisant cet établissement.

Mitten im Londoner Soho gelegen, stellt Lab eine Rückkehr zu den Schauplätzen von Fernsehserien wie Drei Engel für Charlie dar. Die Ästhetik der 70er Jahre ist im Lokal fast allgegenwärtig. Die Backsteinwände wurden in einem leuchtenden Grün gestrichen, während andere wieder in orangen und kupferfarbenen Tönen, die an das glänzende lange Haar von Farrah Fawcett erinnern, gehalten sind. Abgerundete Ecken und kapselähnliche Formen wiederholen sich auch als Motiv an der Theke, an den Regalen und sogar an den Spiegeln des Lokals, wobei lackiertes Holz und Stahl die meistverwandten Materialien sind. Zahlreiche runde Hocker verschiedener Höhen stehen bei der Theke und an den Tischen, damit so viele Gäste wie möglich Platz nehmen können. Das farbige Licht der Strahler trägt zur Gestaltung der für das Lokal so typischen Retro-Atmosphäre bei.

The circular base of the stools
and the regular shape of the tables
create a dynamic of curves that is
repeated even on the edges of the
shelves and mirrors.

*La base circulaire des tabourets
et la forme régulière des tables
créent une dynamique de courbes
qui se retrouvent sur les contours
des étagères et des glaces.*

Die runde Grundfläche der Hocker
und die gleichförmigen Tische
schaffen eine Kurvendynamik, die
auch bei den Regalen und den
Spiegeln wiederzufinden ist.

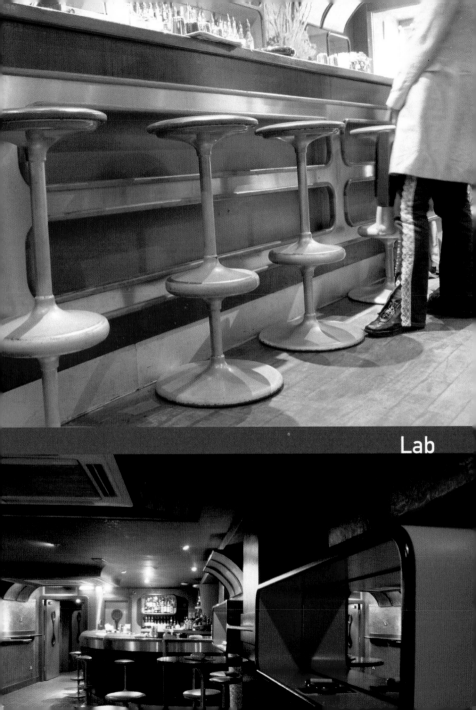

Lab

The golden coloring of some of the walls could well serve as homage to the long blonde mane of Farrah Fawcett.

Les nuances dorées appliquées sur certains murs pourraient être un hommage à la blonde chevelure de Farrah Fawcett.

Vielleicht wurden die goldfarbenen Wände zu Ehren des blonden Haars von Farrah Fawcett so gestrichen.

The Pop Bar

Francisca Rovira y Susana Navalón

Barcelona, España
2001
Photography | Photo | Fotografie: Pep Escoda.

An extremely kitsch entrance welcomes you into a small bar - 94 square meters - that re-creates exactly the aesthetic style of the 1960s. The idea arose from a trip by the owner to London and was translated on her return to Barcelona into this commitment to a totally pop decor. The most valuable feature is the painting work in the reproduction of the famous wall-paper of that era: geometrical borders in orange, brown and white, painted with acrylic enamels. The illuminated pillars follow the same design. Half-moon leather sofas in orange and red are placed on both sides, synthesising with the coloring of the bar. Very disco-y silver lamps. The more peaceful back of the bar recovers the 1960s vertical lines of the entrance; and the corner is spattered with blue, white and orange, perhaps to draw a more intimate zone. The rest-room gives the counter-point, with its cold drawn shapes and colors.

Une entrée très kitsch s'ouvre sur un petit bar de 94 mètres carrés qui recrée presque en la calquant l'esthétique des années 60. La propriétaire en conçut l'idée à partir d'un voyage qu'elle fît à Londres et à son retour à Barcelone elle misa sur une décoration tout à fait pop. Le travail de peinture qui reproduit le fameux papier peint qui couvrait les murs de cette période est remarquable: des bordures géométriques à la peinture acrylique aux couleurs orange, marron et blanc. Des colonnes éclairées suivent le même design. Des canapés en demi lune en cuir orange et rouge se trouvent sur les côtés, en harmonie avec les couleurs de l'établissement. Des lampes argentées font très discothèque. La zone du fond a un caractère plus paisible, reprenant les rayures verticales très année soixante de l'entrée qui parsèment le coin de bleu, blanc et orange dessinant une sphère peut-être plus intime. Les toilettes apportent un contrepoint à partir d'une palette froide dans les formes, les dessins et les couleurs.

Ein Eingang im Kitsch-Look empfängt die Gäste der kleinen, nur 94 m2 großen Bar, in der sich die Ästhetik der 60er Jahre widerspiegelt. Die Idee entstand bei einer London-Reise der Inhaberin des Barceloner Lokals und wurde nach ihrer Rückkehr in die Tat umgesetzt; sie setzte dabei auf eine ausgesprochene Pop-Dekoration. Am erwähnenswertesten ist die Nachbildung der für jene Epoche typischen Tapete: mit orangenem, braunem und weißem Acryllack gemalte Randstreifen mit geometrischen Mustern. Die beleuchteten Säulen entsprechen dem gleichen Design. Halbmondförmige Sofas aus orangenem und rotem Leder sind auf beiden Seiten aufgestellt und stehen im Einklang mit dem Farbenspiel des Lokals. Silberne Lampen im reinsten Disco-Look. Im hinteren Bereich der Bar herrscht eine gedämpftere Stimmung, hier wiederholen sich die ebenfalls für die 60er Jahre typischen Längsstreifen des Eingangs, und die blauen, weißen und orangenen Farbtöne schaffen eine intimere Atmosphäre. Die Waschräume bilden den Kontrast dazu durch ihre kalten Formen und Farben.

A kitsch impact on entering The Pop Bar. Once inside, garish red curtains on one side and a wall of painted vertical lines on the other are the aperitif to the crazy patterns of the ground floor.

Impression kitsch lorsqu'on découvre l'entrée de The Pop Bar. En passant la porte des rideaux rouge foncé d'un côté et un mur aux rayures verticales constituent l'apéritif du schéma fou recréé à l'étage inférieur.

Der Eingang von The Pop Bar ist im Kitsch-Look gehalten. Hinter der Tür hängt auf einer Seite ein weinroter Vorhang, auf der anderen Seite befindet sich eine mit Längsstreifen versehene Wand, ein Vorgeschmack auf die verrückte Innendekoration des Erdgeschosses.

The world of the 1960s is interpreted through valuable painting work that reproduces the geometrical borders of the famous wall-paper of that era. Acrylic enamels in orange, brown and white flow across the walls and both the bottom and top of the bar.

Le monde des années 60 est interprété à nouveau à partir d'un remarquable travail de peinture reproduisant les bordures géométriques du papier peint si caractéristique qui couvrait les murs à cette époque. On a employé des émaux acryliques orange, marron et blanc pour les reproduire sur les murs et sur les parties inférieure et supérieure du comptoir.

Die Welt der 60er Jahre wird durch die gelungene Nachbildung der für jene Zeit typischen, mit geometrischen Randstreifen versehenen Tapete, wiedergegeben. Dafür wurden die Wände, sowie der obere und untere Rand der Theke mit orangenem, braunem und weißem Acryllack bemalt.

The Pop Bar

The sofas and poufs are red and orange, integrated into the bar's color pattern. High temperatures! At the back, the rest rooms stir the color palette again, opting for drawn motifs on a white background.

Les canapés et les poufs sont rouges et oranges et s'intègrent bien dans la gamme chromatique de l'établissement. Haute température! Au fond, les toilettes changent la palette de couleurs et misent sur les motifs dessinés sur fond blanc.

Die rot und orangenen Sofas und Puffs passen gut zu den Farben des Lokals. Heiß! Die hinten gelegene Waschräume sind in kälteren Farben gehalten, hier erscheinen die Motive auf weißem Grund.

Salero

Pilar Líbano
Barcelona, España
1997
Photography | Photo | Fotografie: Pep Escoda.

A luminous refuge in the heart of the great city. El Salero (The Salt Store), so called because it stands on the site of an old salted cod warehouse, is known for its immaculate look and its beautiful selection of items that go to create this look. Situated in one of Barcelona's oldest quarters. Pilar Líbano, in charge of the project, has opted for sophisticated recycling: the new materials used to recover structures and create new elements combine perfectly with familiar pieces and furniture. As such, there is nothing odd in seeing a bar lined with rotating 1950s-style stools alongside white tubular chairs with plastic bottoms, followed by an area of tables and chairs from distinct styles and periods. The relaxed atmosphere that governs the locale is, to a great extent, due to its warm lighting.

Un refuge lumineux au milieu de la grande ville. Le Salero -nom qui provient d'un ancien dépôt de morue- est situé dans un des plus vieux quartiers de Barcelone: il est remarquable par son blanche silhouette et les pièces choisies avec soin pour créer son ambiance. Les matériaux nouveaux pour récupérer de vieilles structures et pour créer de nouveaux éléments s'allient à la perfection aux choses et aux meubles de toujours. C'est pourquoi on n'est pas surpris de voir un comptoir avec une file de tabourets tournants inspirés des années 50 ainsi que des tables et des chaises à structure tubulaire et bases en plastique blanc; ensuite une zone de tables et de chaises récupérées au style et époques différents. L'atmosphère détendue que l'on trouve dans cet établissement est dû en grande partie à l'éclairage accueillant.

Ein heller Zufluchtsort mitten in der Großstadt. Salero, so benannt, weil es in einem ehemaligen Stockfisch-Lager in einem der ältesten Stadtviertel Barcelonas untergebracht ist, besticht wegen seines makellosen Aussehens und der exquisiten Auswahl der Dekorationselemente. Pilar Líbano, die für das Projekt Verantwortliche, setzte auf ein sinnvoll durchgeführtes Recycling: die zur Restaurierung von Strukturen und zur Schaffung neuer Elemente verwandten neuen Materialien passen gut zu den altherkömmlichen Möbelstücken. Deshalb wirkt der Anblick der Theke, vor der Drehhocker im Stil der 50er Jahre stehen, sowie der Tische und Stühle mit Rohrstruktur und Grundflächen aus weißem Kunststoff, zusammen mit dem dahinterliegenden Bereich, in dem restaurierte Tische und Stühle verschiedener Stile und Epochen zusammengewürfelt sind, nicht befremdend. Die entspannende Atmosphäre des Lokals ist hauptsächlich auch auf die warme Beleuchtung zurückzuführen.

The general lighting with a series of hanging bulbs is complemented by
numerous candles and Chinese lanterns.

*L'éclairage général par une série d'ampoules suspendues au plafond
s'allie aux nombreuses bougies et des lampions.*

Die aus von der Decke herabhängenden Glühbirnen bestehende Hauptbeleuchtung
wurde durch zahlreiche brennende Kerzen und Lampions ergänzt.

Salero

The great many mirrors on the walls give lots of varying views into all the corners of the bar.

Les nombreuses glaces disposées sur les murs permettent d'avoir de perspectives variées de tous les coins du local.

Die vielen Wandspiegel bieten verschiedene Perspektiven aller Ecken und Winkel des Lokals.

Ragoo

Leonardo Davighi, Edmondo Campus
Milano, Italia
2000
Photography | Photo | Fotografie: Paola D'Amico.

The Ragoo is located on the small Martesana canal in Milan. This cocktail-bar has opted for an aesthetic following the boldest trends, reason for the establishment becoming famous among artists and cosmopolitans. The Ragoo, a bar with atmosphere tasting of 1970s high-tech, and with yellow and ochre walls, houses the daring furniture and weird lamps thought up by Davighi and Campus, who define their output as "incorrect design", in the sense that it is easy to reproduce their decor items, because of the materials used and the way they have been made. This makes the Ragoo a kind of geometrical hallucination formalized in the boldest way. During the summer, this bar of the "sauce of your dreams", in reference to the famous Italian sauce, spreads out along the bank of the Martesana to serve its highly original cocktails.

Le Ragoo est situé dans le petit canal de la Martesana de Milan. Le cocktail bar reprend une esthétique prenant parti pour les tendances les plus osées, motif pour lequel cet établissement est devenu le plus connu chez les artistes et les cosmopolites de tout genre. Le Ragoo, un local à ambiance au goût des années 70 high-tech, aux murs jaunes et ocres, accueille les meubles osés et les lampes aux formes étranges conçus par Davighi et Campus, qui définissent leur oeuvre comme un "design incorrect", en ce que les objets décoratifs sont faciles à copier, à cause des matériaux et leur réalisation. Ainsi, le Ragoo est une sorte d'hallucination géométrique formalisée le plus intrépidement possible. De plus, le local de la "sauce of your dreams", faisant référence à la fameuse sauce italienne, s'étend pendant la saison estivale tout au long des berges de la Martesana pour servir les cocktails les plus originaux.

Ragoo befindet sich am kleinen Martesana-Kanal in Mailand. Die Ästhetik der Cocktail-Bar liegt voll in den gewagtesten Trends, weshalb das Lokal zu einem Treffpunkt von Künstlern und Kosmopoliten geworden ist. Im Ragoo, einem Ambient-Lokal mit High-Tech-Stimmung der 70er Jahre und gelben und ockerfarbenen Wänden, stehen die gewagten Möbel und die seltsam geformten Lampen von Davighi und Campus, die ihre Werke als "inkorrektes Design" bezeichnen, da die Dekorationsgegenstände aufgrund der verwandten Materialien und Herstellungsmethoden leicht nachzubilden sind. Deswegen ist Ragoo eine Art geometrischer Halluzination, die auf die kühnste Art und Weise verwirklicht wurde. Während der Sommermonate breitet sich das Lokal der "sauce of your dreams", einer berühmten italienischen Sauce, am Ufer des Martesana-Kanals aus und bietet hier die originellsten Cocktails an.

Davighi and Campus are two young designers and artists who claim to practise "incorrect design", as the objects of decoration in the Ragoo can be easily reproduced.

Davighi et Campus sont deux jeunes artistes dessinateurs qui affirment qu'ils pratiquent un "design incorrect" car les objets de décoration proposés dans le Ragoo peuvent être facilement copiés.

Davighi und Campus sind zwei junge Designer und Künstler, welche behaupten, ein "unkorrektes Design" zu entwerfen, denn die Dekorationsobjekte des Ragoo sind leicht nachzubilden.

Ragoo

The general idea the designers
wanted to put across was a 1960s
American bar. As well as the
own-creation lamps on this page,
its highly original luminous table
made out of recycled materials
can be seen on the following page.

*L'idée générale que les dessinateurs
ont voulu transmettre est celle d'un
local américain des années 60.
En plus des lampes originales, sur
cette page, il faut observer sur la
page suivante la très originale table
lumineuse réalisée à partir de
matériaux recyclés.*

Absicht der Designer war, der Bar
die Stimmung eines amerikanischen
Lokals der 60er Jahre zu geben.
Interessant sind nicht nur die
originellen, auf dieser Seite
abgebildeten Lampen, sondern auch
der eigenartige, beleuchtete Tisch,
der aus Recycling-Materialien
gefertigt wurde.

Gold Bar Café

Hudson Featherstone
London, United Kindom
1997
Photography | Photo | Fotografie: Chas Wilshere.

A retro style countered by design items and pieces. The main feature of the Gold Bar Café, in the West of London's Soho, is two light boxes with images by the photographer Tim Brotherton, treated by the artist and graphic designer Christian Soukias, which are a pop art reference in the entrance and at the back. The inside of a refrigerator, unrecognisable in the middle of the country, can be seen in them. As the café is lengthy almost to a fault, the front has been opened to the outside to nuance the spatial depth. The walls are painted in yellows and greens that contrast with the reds, browns and blues of the furnishing. The vinyl stools along the walnut bar are designed by Robin Day, and the hanging lamps by Verner Panton. Other design features distancing the café from retro are the mirrors with circular lamps and the glass-covered holes in the floor.

Une esthétique rétro compensée par des éléments et des pièces de design. Le Gold Bar Café, situé dans la zone ouest du Soho londonien, compte deux panneaux lumineux protagoniste présentant des vues du photographe Tim Brotherton, traitées par l'artiste et dessinateur graphique Christian Soukias, une référence pop art à l'entrée et au fond du local. On peut y discerner l'intérieur d'un frigo, méconnaissable sur fond de prairie. La façade presque trop longue a été ouverte sur l'extérieur pour en harmoniser la profondeur spatiale. Les murs sont peints en jaunes et verts en contraste avec les tons rouges, marrons et bleus du mobilier. Les tabourets en vinyle rangés face au comptoir ont été dessinés par Robin Day et les lampes suspendues sont de Verner Panton. Les autres éléments de design s'éloignant du rétro sont les glaces aux appliques circulaires et les perforations en verre pratiquées sur le sol.

Retro-Look, durch Designer-Elemente und -Möbelstücke ausgeglichen. Das Gold Bar Café liegt im Westen des Londoner Soho. Besonders auffallend sind die beiden jeweils am Eingang und hinten im Lokal befindlichen beleuchteten Pop-Art-Kästen mit Bildern des Fotografen Tim Brotherton, welche vom Künstler und Graphikdesigner Christian Soukias bearbeitet wurden. Auf den Bildern ist das Innere eines Kühlschrankes zu sehen, unerkennbar mitten im Feld stehend. Wegen der fast übermäßigen Länge des Lokals wurde die Fassade nach außen hin optisch erweitert, um die räumliche Tiefe zu reduzieren. Das Gelb und Grün der Wände kontrastiert mit den roten, braunen und blauen Farbtönen des Mobiliars. Die vor der Theke aus Nußbaumholz stehenden Hocker aus Vinyl wurden von Robin Day entworfen, die Hängelampen stammen von Verner Panton. Weitere vom Retro-Stil abweichende Designer-Elemente sind die Spiegel mit kreisförmigen Verzierungen und die in den Fußboden gebohrten und mit Glas bedeckten Löcher.

The mirrors with circular wall-lamps and the Verner Panton bar lights are some of the design features that distance the style of the bar from being just retro.

Les glaces avec appliques circulaires et les lampes de Verner Panton qui éclairent le comptoir sont les éléments de design qui éloignent l'esthétique du local de ce qui est purement rétro.

Die Spiegel mit kreisförmigen Verzierungen und die von Verner Panton stammenden Lampen, welche die Theke beleuchten, sind einige der Designer-Elemente, die die Ästhetik des Lokals vom reinsten Retro-Look distanzieren.

Gold Bar café

The yellow and green on the walls contrast with the stronger colors of the furniture.

Les couleurs jaunes et verts appliquées sur les murs contrastent avec les tons plus foncés du mobilier.

Die gelben und grünen Farbtöne der Wände kontrastieren mit den dunkleren Farben der Möbel.

Red vinyl stools designed by Robin Day line up in front of the walnut bar.

Face au comptoir revêtu de bois de noyer s'alignent les tabourets en vinyle rouge design de Robin Day.

Vor der mit Nußbaumholz verkleideten Theke stehen Hocker aus rotem Vinyl, die von Robin Day entworfen wurden.

Milk

Milk S.L.

Barcelona, España
2001
Photography | Photo | Fotografie: Pep Escoda.

New York imitation, the Milk is noted as a small apartment-club with highly sensationalist effects. Lounge, club, stair-case and drinking area, each part exploits to the maximum a concept which, if it can be expressed in just one word, would be "colorist". Like one box inserted inside another, and always maintaining its feel of narrowness, first comes the lobby, then the bar, which receives its night customers on pretty and well-designed flame-red stools; then a stair-case that leads to intimate corners and other parentheses, behind a multi-colored curtain; then, a total-red sitting-room whose sofa is more than an invitation to spend the night and from which stairs to nowhere descend; and finally, the area of mingling. A very mixed club. A destination which does not lower the level of color clashes, for here white is crossed by beams of bright blue light and projections that round off an atmosphere of explosive starry cocktail bar.

Avec un style prétendument new-yorkais, le Milk s'érige en petit appartement-club où les pièces qui le composent sont traitées de façon très spectaculaire. Lounge, club, escalier et zone de bar, chacun exploite au maximum un concept unique que pourrait être qualifié de "coloriste". Comme une boîte encastrée dans l'autre, gardant toujours son sens longitudinal partout, se succèdent l'annexe proche au comptoir, qui reçoit le client nocturne sur des hauts tabourets dernier cri, d'un rouge éclatant, un escalier conduisant vers des coins intimes et vers d'autres parenthèses, en passant un rideau aux perles multicolores, un salon rouge absolu où le canapé est plus qu'une invitation au repos, de là on peut aller vers nulle part par un petit escalier; et finalement, l'aire de rencontre, un club très mixte. Une fin de route qui ne rabaisse pas le niveau de tension chromatique: ici le blanc est nuancé par des faisceaux de lumière bleue ciel et des projections donnent une finition à cette ambiance de mélange explosif et stellaire.

Typisch für New York. Milk weicht als kleiner Appartement-Club mit effektvoll gestalteten Bereichen von den übrigen Lokalen ab. Wenn die voneinander unabhängigen Konzepte von Lounge, Club, Treppe und Ausschankbereich vereinheitlicht werden könnten, wäre das Ergebnis nichts anderes als "kunterbunt". Wie bei einer Matruschka, wo eine Puppe in einer anderen steckt, immer längs verlaufend, folgen aufeinander: der Raum vor der Theke, in dem aparte, feuerrote Hocker im brandaktuellen Design die Nachtschwärmer empfangen; eine Treppe, die zu intimen Winkeln und anderen mit bunten Perlschnurvorhängen abgeschlossenen Eckchen führt; ein Aufenthaltsraum rouge absolu, in dem das Sofa zum Hinsetzen einlädt und von wo aus eine Treppe ins Nirgendwo hinunterführt; und schließlich, der Raum für geselliges Zusammensein von Gästen aus allen Kreisen. Am Ende der Route ist das Gefecht der Farben untereinander nicht weniger hart: hier wird das Weiß durch die himmelblauen Lichtstrahlen nuanciert, was eine explosive galaktische Stimmung schafft.

A clear New York idea emerges
in both the furniture and
the lay-out, as if it was part of
an apartment at night.

*Une évidente conception
new-yorkaise émerge tant de la
distribution que du choix du mobilier
qui semble distribué comme dans
un appartement à vie nocturne.*

Eine offensichtlich New Yorker
Konzeption prägt sowohl die
Aufteilung des Raumes als auch die
ausgewählten Möbelstücke, die zu
einem Appartement, in dem sich
das Leben nachts abspielt, gehören
scheinen.

Each color gives meaning to each
of the areas of this long narrow
club. The sitting-room or lounge
is the totally red heart, a corner
of intimacy or communication,
depending on the intention.
A stair-case leads from here
down to nowhere.

*Chaque couleur donne un sens à
chacune des zones de ce club étroit
et tout en profondeur. Le salon en
est le coeur rouge absolu, un recoin
d'intimité ou de communication,
selon les intentions. De là, un
escalier descend vers nulle part.*

Jede Farbe gibt jedem einzelnen
Raum dieses langgestreckten Clubs
einen anderen Sinn. Der Aufenthaltsbereich oder Lounge ist das Herz
rouge absolu, ein je nach Absicht intimes oder zur Geselligkeit einladen-
des Eckchen. Von hier aus führt eine
Treppe ins Nirgendwo hinunter.

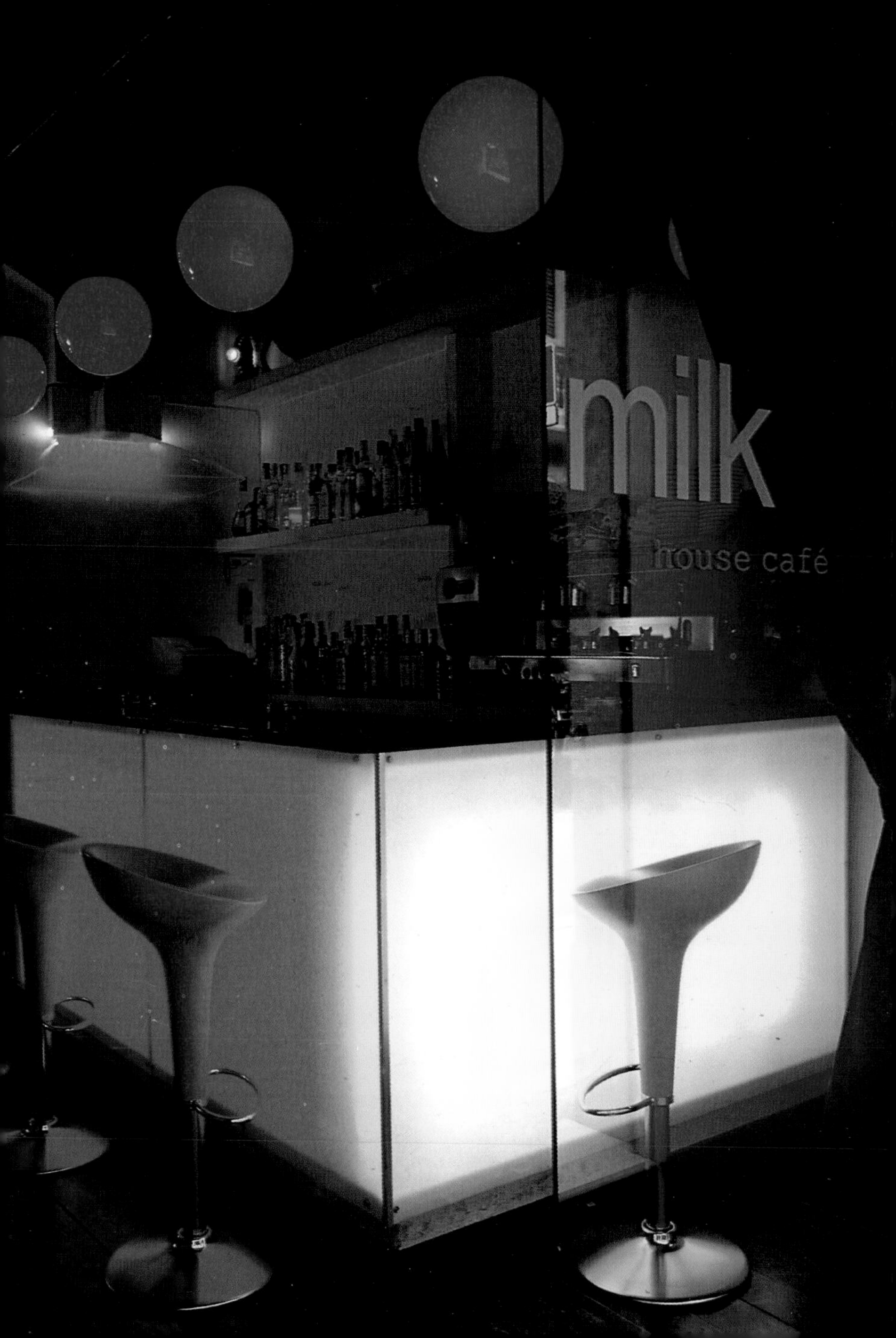
milk
house café

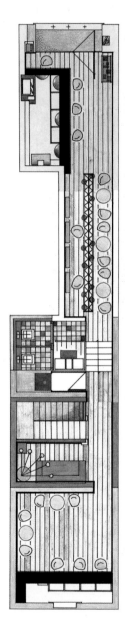

The depth of the club has been used to put together its different areas like pieces on a thread, with a play of different levels.

L'utilisation de la profondeur du local a permis de traiter les pièces aux différents usages, les encastrant les unes dans les autres, jouant avec les différents niveaux.

Durch die Ausnutzung der Tiefe des Lokals gelang es, verschiedenartige Räume unterzubringen, wobei mit mehreren Ebenen gespielt wurde.

Structured like a box or various boxes, each one uncovered within a bigger one. The ceilings have had to be lowered.

Structuré comme une boîte, ou plusieurs, qui se laissent découvrir à l'intérieur d'une plus grande. Les plafonds ont dû être rabaissés par rapport au local précédent.

Wie eine oder mehrere Kisten strukturiert, die ineinanderstecken. Die Decken mußten beim Umbau des Lokals herabgesetzt werden.

Milk

In the last room, at the back of Milk, the most fluorescent light is concentrated, the sky-blue that contradicts the back-ground white. The bar is a source of beams of colors, ideal for attracting its mixed public. Blue stools, for less fiery tastes than the red ones at the entrance.

Au fond du Milk, la lumière qui se concentre dans la dernière salle est plus fluorescente, l'esthétique bleue nuance la blancheur du fond. Le comptoir est une source de faisceaux de couleurs, idéale pour attirer la mixture de clients. Des tabourets bleus pour des goûts moins "allumés" que les rouges de l'entrée.

Der letzte Raum des Milk wird von gleißendem Licht überflutet, der weiße Hintergrund wird von himmelblauen Strahlen nuanciert. Die Theke strahlt farbige Lichtstrahlen aus, was das verschiedenartige Publikum des Lokals anzieht. Blaue Hocker für diejenigen, denen das Rot des Eingangs nicht so gut gefällt.

Schwarzenraben

Kruse & Roers

Berlin, Deutschland
1997
Photography | Photo | Fotografie: Pablo Castagnola.

A perfect soft combination of coloring: chocolate, pistachio and coconut mixed in equal parts as in one of the many delicious dishes served up in Schwarzenraben. Posed as a bar-restaurant, this Berlin locale is known for its simple, modern lines. The superfluous or unnecessary elements have been avoided so as to prioritize basic structures and the comfort of the customers. Its large windows let natural light flood the entire space: this only has to be complemented by a few hanging lights. The leather sofas adjoin the side walls, as a seat for those who want to savor any of the dishes served on functional square tables, accompanied by traditional wooden chairs. These pieces make up the basic and almost the only furniture, which is repeated throughout the locale, whose walls are practically bare, except one, which is dominated by a large black and white photograph.

Une parfaite et douce combinaison de nuances, chocolat, pistache et noix de coco mélangées à parts égales comme une des délicieuses recettes servies au Schwarzenraben. Conçu comme bar-restaurant, cet établissement berlinois est caractérisé par ses lignes simples et modernes. Les éléments superflus ont été évités pour donner la priorité aux structures de base et au confort des clients. Ses grande baies vitrées permettent à la lumière naturelle d'envahir tout l'espace et seules quelques lampes suspendues au plafond la complètent. Les bancs tapissés en cuir sont adossés aux murs latéraux attendant les gourmets qui désirent savourer les plats servis sur des tables fonctionnelles carrées, entourées de chaises en bois aux lignes classiques. Ces éléments constituent le mobilier essentiel dispersé dans tout le local dont les murs sont pratiquement vides, sauf celui où est accrochée une grande photo blanc et noir.

Eine perfekte und sanfte Kombination von Farbtönen: Schokolade, Pistazien und Kokos gemischt zu gleichen Teilen wie bei einem der vielen köstlichen Rezepte des Schwarzenraben. Als Bar-Restaurant konzipiert, charakterisiert sich dieses Berliner Lokal durch seine schlichten, modernen Linien. Man hat auf überflüssige und unnötige Elemente verzichtet und den Grundstrukturen und dem Komfort der Gäste Vorrang gegeben. Dank der großen Fenster wird der ganze Raum von Licht überflutet, so daß nur einige wenige Hängelampen nötig sind. An den Seitenwänden stehen Ledersofas, in denen die Gäste Platz nehmen können, um das Essen, welches auf den funktionalen viereckigen Tischen serviert wird, zu genießen. Auf der anderen Seite der Tische stehen herkömmliche Stühle aus Holz. Diese Stücke stellen das Grundmobiliar dar, das überall im Lokal wiederanzutreffen ist. Die Wände sind fast völlig schmucklos, bis auf eine, die mit einer großen Schwarzweißfotografie dekoriert ist.

The basic furniture consists of sofas in stony colors, conventional wooden chairs and ordinary square tables.

Le mobilier essentiel du local est composé de canapés couleur pierre, de chaises en bois classiques et de tables carrées aux lignes régulières.

Das Grundmobiliar besteht aus steinfarbenen Sofas, herkömmlichen Stühlen aus Holz und viereckigen, geradlinigen Tischen.

Schwarzenraben

The abundant natural light from the large windows is only supported by some hanging lamps that give out very faint light.

Les flots de lumière naturelle venant des grandes baies vitrées ne sont renforcés qu'avec quelques lampes suspendues au plafond donnant des faisceaux de lumière douce.

Da ausreichend Tageslicht durch die großen Fenster strömt, sind nur einige Hängelampen, die schwaches Licht abgeben, notwendig.

Café Schilling

Sandra Tarruella Esteva e Isabel López Vilalta

Barcelona, España
1997
Photography | Photo | Fotografie: Martí Llorens.

The former Schilling gun shop has given way to a traditional sort of café. This initial idea of the owner Adrián Mateu converted the project more into a restoration than reform job, since on the inside shelves, for example, bottles replaced arms. In addition, varnished supports were installed and a rack for glasses in previously aged stainless steel was placed on the bar. Several mirrors and shelving were deployed to give the impression of greater depth. Traditional Catalan white marble paving was fitted and the ceilings with mouldings round the edges were splashed with gold paint and covered with an ochre sheen to recall the stains deposited by long years of tobacco smoke. Finally, large sumptuous especially designed lamps in brass and fabric were put in. No-one would say that Schilling did not look and feel like a hundred year-old café.

L'ancienne armurerie Schilling a laissé la place à un café comme ceux d'autrefois. À partir de cette idée initiale du propriétaire Adrián Mateu, le projet est devenu plus une oeuvre restauration que de réforme. Dans les vitrines intérieures, par exemple, les bouteilles ont remplacé les armes. D'autre part, les accoudoirs DM ont été vernis, et un porte-verres en acier inox vieilli a été placé au dessus du comptoir. Les glaces et les étagères donnent plus de profondeur à l'espace. Le pavement, en marbre blanc du pays, a été mis à la manière traditionnelle, et les plafonds avec des moulures sur tout leur périmètre ont été parsemés de peinture dorée et recouverts d'une patine couleur ocre imitant la trace que la fumée du tabac laisse avec le temps. Finalement, de somptueuses lampes spécialement conçues en tissu et laiton ont été installées. Qui dirait que le Schilling, par son aspect et son ambiance, n'est pas un café centenaire ?

Die ehemalige Waffenhandlung Schilling beherbergt heute ein altherkömmliches Café. Wie vom Inhaber Adrián Mateu beabsichtigt, kann das Projekt nicht als Umbau, sondern eher als Restaurierung bezeichnet werden, da zum Beispiel in den Regalen die Flaschen den Platz der Waffen einnahmen. Ferner wurden die Kehlleisten aus lackiertem DM verwandt; über der Theke wurde eine Gläserhaltevorrichtung aus gealtertem rostfreiem Stahl angebracht. Zur optischen Vergrößerung des Raumes wurden mehrere Spiegel und Regale angebracht. Der Fußboden aus weißem Marmor wurde auf herkömmliche Art verlegt und die Decken mit umlaufenden Zierleisten wurden mit Goldfarbe besprenkelt und mit einer ockerfarbenen Patina versehen, was an die Spuren, die der Tabakrauch mit der Zeit hinterläßt, erinnern sollte. Schließlich wurden große, prachtvolle, eigens dafür entworfene Lampen aus Stoff und Messing installiert. Wegen seiner Ästhetik und Stimmung würde kaum jemand glauben, daß Schilling kein altes ehrwürdiges Café ist.

The choice of furniture and
the design of the bar area
responded to the desire to
imitate to the full the style of
traditional old cafés.

*Le choix du mobilier
et la conception du comptoir
répondent au désir d'imiter
en tout le style des cafés
les plus classiques.*

Die Auswahl der Möbel und
die Gestaltung der Theke
entsprechen dem Wunsch,
den Stil der altherkömmlichen
Cafés nachzuahmen.

The shelves that now hold
a spectacular array of bottles
displayed in their day the goods
of the former gun-shop.

*Les étagères, où s'aligne maintenant
une magnifique collection
de bouteilles, accueillaient autrefois
les pièces d'armurerie.*

Auf den Regalen, auf denen
heute eine umfangreiche
Flaschensammlung zu sehen ist,
waren früher die Waren der
ehemaligen Waffenhandlung
ausgestellt.

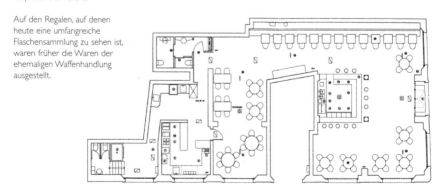

Café Schilling

Manaus

Carles Riu Pou

**Mataró (Barcelona), España
2000
Photography | Photo | Fotografie: Martí Llorens.**

Losing yourself in room after room in a large house, as in the film *Eyes wide shut* would appear to be the intention of Carles Riu in opening Manaus. At least this is the feeling that this rehabilitation of a hundred-year old house gives. All its old splendor is restored in its conversion into a sophisticated night spot in which the constant changes in level create confusion. Between walls of genuine brick and behind ancient doors, spaces decorated with lamps and furniture recovered from various periods and styles are hidden. A stair-case finished in black and white marble leads to the upper floor of the house, where the rest room, cloak-room and a bar can be found. On the ground floor there are two dance floors with their respective bars. Yellow is the dominant color of the walls and the iron girders supporting the roof, to which a delicate sky blue tone has been added.

Se perdre de pièce en pièce dans la grande maison comme dans le film Eyes wide shut *semble avoir été l'intention de Carles Riu lorsqu'il a conçu Manaus. C'est au moins la sensation que l'on a après la rénovation de cette maison centenaire qui lui a rendu toute sa splendeur, et l'a convertie en un local de nuit sophistiqué où les changements de niveaux constants portent à confusion.*

Parmi les murs en brique authentique et derrière les vieilles portes se cachent des espaces décorés avec des lampes et des meubles récupérés, de différentes époques et styles. Un escalier en marbre noir et blanc conduit au niveau supérieur où se trouve un comptoir, les toilettes et les vestiaires. A l'étage du bas se trouvent deux pistes de danse et leurs comptoirs respectifs. Le jaune domine sur les murs et sur les poutres en fer du plafond, parsemées de bleu ciel.

In einem großen Haus von einem Zimmer zum anderen irren, wie im Film Eyes wide shut, war scheinbar die Absicht von Carles Riu als er Manaus entwarf. Dies ist jedenfalls das Gefühl, das man nach dem Umbau eines über hundert Jahre alten Hauses hat, dem damit sein ehemaliger Glanz zurückgegeben werden sollte. Gleichzeitig sollte es als vornehmes Nachtlokal, in dem die vielen verschiedenen Ebenen verwirrend wirken, hergerichtet werden. Zwischen Backsteinwänden und hinter alten Türen verbergen sich Räume, die mit restaurierten Lampen und Möbel verschiedener Epochen und Stile ausgestattet wurden. Eine Treppe aus schwarzem und weißem Marmor führt zum oberen Geschoß des Hauses, wo die Theke, die Waschräume und die Garderobe liegen. Im Erdgeschoß sind zwei Tanzflächen mit den dazugehörigen Theken untergebracht. Bei den Wänden ist Gelb die vorherrschende Farbe, wie auch bei den Eisenträgern der Decke, auf denen auch noch ein feiner himmelblauer Ton aufgetragen wurde.

Practically all the pieces of furniture used in the different spaces are antique.

Pratiquement toutes les pièces du mobilier décorant les différents espaces ont été restaurées.

Fast alle Möbelstücke, die in den verschiedenen Räumen zu sehen sind, wurden sorgfältig restauriert.

The lights that run across the front of the house can be seen from a distance, and welcome visitors.

Les lumières qui suivent les lignes principales de la façade sont une réclame qui accueille au loin tous les visiteurs.

Die den Hauptlinien der Fassade folgenden Lichter locken die Gäste schon von weitem an und heißen sie willkommen im Haus.

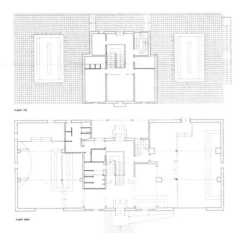

PLANTA PIS

PLANTA BAIXA

The ground floor bars are laid with a mahogany-stained compound surface.

Les comptoirs de l'étage inférieur ont été revêtus d'une surface en DM teint en couleur acajou.

Die Theken des unteren Geschosses wurden mit mahagonifarbenem DM verkleidet.

Manaus

A majestic new stair-case
finished in black and white
marble leads to the upper floor.

Un escalier majestueux,
tout neuf, revêtu de marbre blanc
et noir, conduit au niveau supérieur
de la maison.

Eine stilvolle neu gebaute Treppe
aus weißem und schwarzem
Marmor führt zur oberen Etage
des Hauses.

Adidas Sport Café

Ron Arad Associates
Toulon, France
1997
Photography | Photo | Fotografie: Ron Arad Associates.

Its name says everything, or nearly everything. The Adidas Sport Café of Toulon is a joint project between the well-known brand of sports clothes and Kronenbourg with the aim of creating a new concept of theme café specializing in sports. Restaurant, bar, book-shop and shop, the enormous room is equipped with interactive technology that allows sporting broadcasts and simulations to be enjoyed from individual tables. The customers can occupy their seats on the benches placed throughout the café as if they were in a stadium ready to admire the spectacle offered by the high screens. In addition, the transparent restored front of the building means that all the sporting images are an attraction to the potential customers who can watch them from the street. And from transparency, the café moves on to a scale of grays and blacks that form the main color range, only distorted by the red of the numerous chairs.

Son nom dit tout ou presque tout. L'Adidas Sport Café de Toulon est un projet conjoint réalisé par la célèbre marque de vêtements de sport et Kronenbourg, afin de créer un nouveau concept de local thématique spécialisé dans les sports. Restaurant, bar, librairie et magasin, cette salle aux grandes dimensions est équipée d'une technologie interactive permettant de jouir de retransmissions et de simulations sportives depuis les tables individuelles. Les clients peuvent s'asseoir sur des bancs situés au long du local comme s'ils se trouvaient sur un stade pour admirer le spectacle qui s'offre à leurs yeux sur les grands écrans. De plus, la façade transparente, préparée pour que toutes ces images sportives soient une réclame pour les clients potentiels qui les voient de l'extérieur. De la transparence on passe à une palette de gris et noirs, principale gamme chromatique, rompue par le rouge des nombreuses chaises.

Sein Name sagt praktisch alles oder fast alles. Das Adidas Sport Café in Toulon ist ein von der bekannten Sportartikelmarke Adidas und Kronenbourg gemeinsam durchgeführtes Projekt mit dem Ziel, ein neues Konzept eines auf Sport spezialisierten thematischen Lokals zu schaffen. Der großflächige Raum, bestehend aus Restaurant, Bar, Buchhandlung und Geschäft, ist mit interaktiver Technologie ausgestattet, die es ermöglicht, von individuellen Tischen aus Sportübertragungen und -simulationen zu verfolgen. Die Gäste können auf den Bänken, die im ganzen Lokal aufgereiht stehen, Platz nehmen und das Spektakel, das ihnen auf den großen Bildschirmen dargeboten wird, genießen als wären sie Zuschauer in einem Stadion. Aber dies ist noch nicht alles, dank der durchsichtigen Fassade läßt sich das Schauspiel auch von der Straße her betrachten, so daß dadurch mögliche Gäste angelockt werden können. Die Durchsichtigkeit geht über zu einer Palette von grauen und schwarzen Farbtönen, die nur vom Rot der zahlreichen Stühle unterbrochen wird.

The predominating range of blacks
and grays contrasts with the lively
reds and blacks of the chairs.

*La gamme prédominante des noirs
et des gris est rompue par le rouge
et autres couleurs vives choisies
pour les chaises.*

Die vorherrschenden schwarzen
und grauen Töne kontrastieren mit
dem Rot und den anderen
lebhaften Farben, die für die Stühle
ausgewählt wurden.

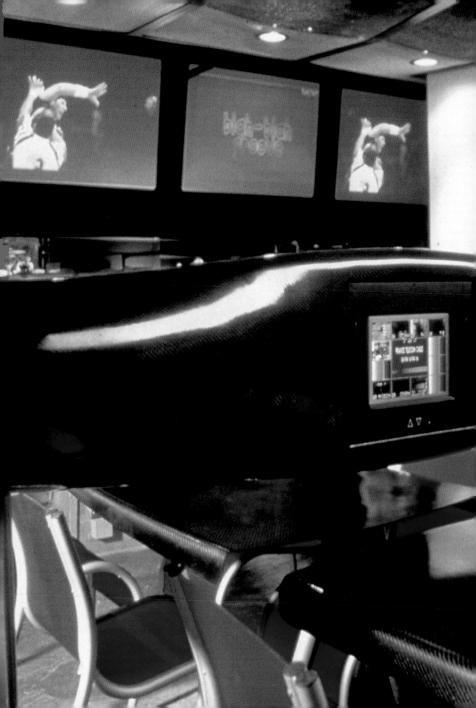

The project used the very latest
generation of techniques and
materials such as carbon fiber,
resins and steel.

*Le projet a été réalisé en utilisant
des techniques et des matériaux
de dernière génération comme la fibre
de carbone, quelques résines et l'acier.*

Bei der Ausführung des Projekts
wurden hochmoderne Techniken
und Materialien, wie Kohlefaser,
einige Harze und Stahl, verwandt.

ALL: SAINT GERMAIN 2 - MARSEILLES 0 BASKETBALL: CHICAGO BULLS

Adidas Sport Café

Cuore

Leonardo Davighi y Edmondo Campus

Milano, Italia
1998
Photography | Photo | Fotografie: Paola D'Amico.

Davighi and Campus proposed a remodeling of this cocktail bar in order to create an atmosphere which would tempt the customer to poke about and discover surprises. This half-magical, half-romantic intention led to the division of the space into endless shelves full of lamps and diverse decorative items. In addition, the weak lighting attempts to accentuate - and achieves it - the difficulty in perceiving space, making the discovery of the different objects still more interesting. This is a leisure proposal full of surprises, an experiment in materials, colors and lights. Avant-garde sallies, winks at a certain retro evocation, incursions into the world of dreams. All are requisites making this establishment an original and architecturally unique bar, where, whilst feeling yourself part of an alternative cosmos, you can sip the most bizarre cocktails in the company of the most eccentric characters of Milan's night life.

Davighi et Campus ont proposé une rénovation du local pour recréer une ambiance où le client serait tenté par la curiosité à rechercher de surprises. Cette intention, magique et romantique, a fait que l'espace soit divisé en une infinité de salles remplies de lampes et d'objets de décoration disparates. L'éclairage faible prétend accentuer (et il y parvient) la difficulté à percevoir l'espace et rendre encore plus intéressante la découverte des différents objets. Il s'agit d'une proposition ludique pleine de surprises; une expérimentation des matériaux, des couleurs et des lumières. Des éclairs d'avant-garde, des clins d'oeil à une certaine évocation rétro, de légères intrusions dans le monde onirique. Ce sont des qualités qui font de cet établissement un local original et à l'architecture unique, où en plus de se sentir part d'un cosmos alternatif on peut déguster les cocktails les plus spéciaux en compagnie des personnages les plus excentriques du Milan nocturne.

Zur Schaffung eines Ambiente, das die Neugier des Gastes erweckt, wurde von Davighi und Campus der Umbau des Lokals vorgeschlagen. Zur Ausführung dieser halb magischen, halb romantischen Idee wurde die Bar in viele, mit Lampen und verschiedenen Dekorationsgegenständen angefüllte Räume unterteilt. Außerdem wird mit der schwachen Beleuchtung versucht, das Wahrnehmen der Gegenstände im Raum schwieriger zu machen, so daß das Entdecken dieser Objekte nur noch interessanter wird. Es ist ein Spiel voller Überraschungen, ein Experimentieren mit Materialien, Farben und Lichtern. Avantgardistische Tupfer, eine gewisse Retro-Evozierung, kleine Streifzüge in die Welt der Träume. All diese Merkmale machen die Bar zu einem originellen, architektonisch einzigartigen Lokal, wo der Gast sich nicht nur Teil eines alternativen Kosmos fühlt, sondern auch noch die ungewöhnlichsten Cocktails in Gesellschaft der exzentrischsten Menschen des Mailänder Nachtlebens trinken kann.

The Cuore is a cocktail bar
with just one setting, whose
furniture and lighting are all
made of innovative materials.

*Le Cuore se montre comme un
cocktail bar à l'ambiance unique
où meubles et lampes sont créés
à partir de matériaux innovateurs.*

Cuore ist eine Cocktail-Bar
mit einem einmaligen Ambiente,
in der Möbel und Lampen
aus innovativen Materialien
gefertigt sind.

Cuore

The formal experiments of the designers Davighi and Campus are present in each of the decor elements, some different from others. The wooden pillars were recoated with soft silvery-colored materials.

L'expérimentation formelle des dessinateurs Davighi et Campus est présente dans chacun des éléments de décoration, différents les uns des autres. Les piliers en bois ont été recouverts de matériaux souples aux couleurs argentées.

Bei jedem einzelnen der voneinander abweichenden Dekorationselemente kommt zum Ausdruck, daß die Designer Davighi und Campus mit den Formen experimentiert haben. Die Säulen aus Holz wurden mit weichen Materialien in silbernen Farbtönen verkleidet.

Philippe Starck

London, United Kingdom
2000
Photography | Photo | Fotografie: Mihail Moldoveanu.

A particular and mysterious aesthetic and cultural sensibility is found in the alliance between the famous hotelier Ian Schrager and the renowned designer Philippe Starck. Located inside the Hotel Sanderson, in the heart of London's Soho, the Long Bar once more puts into practice the idea of mixing baroque with modern creations that overflow with daring and imaginative originality. Formal limits disappear and so it becomes annex of the adjoining Spoon restaurant as an place to taste *tapas*, caviar, oysters or an extraordinary sushi almost informally, as well as to have a drink. The diners sit on lofty stools in purest Starck style: silvery structure and upholstered back-supports with a woman's eye on the back. A total work of art, the bar is planned as an extensive rectangle of onyx illuminated in green. The protruding ends of the table top are in stainless steel. We cannot avoid affirming that we are looking at a new architecture of hotel design.

Une sensibilité esthétique et culturelle particulière et mystérieuse s'allie dans la collaboration entre l'emblématique hôtelier Ian Schrager et l'archi connu Philippe Starck. Situé dans l'Hôtel Sanderson, au coeur du Soho londonien, le Long Bar est encore une fois un mélange de baroque et de créations modernes débordant d'originalité osée et imaginative. Les limites formelles disparaissent : le Long Bar devient le voisin du restaurant Spoon, tel un annexe pour déguster des tapas, du caviar, des huîtres ou un unique sushi de façon presque informelle, et prendre un verre. Les clients s'installent sur de hauts tabourets au plus pur style Stark : structure argentée et dossiers tapissés avec le dessin d'un oeil féminin sur la partie arrière. Le comptoir, tout à fait artistique, est conçu comme un immense rectangle d'onyx vert lumineux. Les accoudoirs qui débordent de la surface du plan du comptoir sont en acier inox. On peut affirmer qu'une nouvelle architecture se consolide en ce qui concerne le design des hôtels.

Das Lokal ist ein gemeinsames Werk des angesehenen Hoteliers Ian Schrager und des schon sehr bekannten Designers Philippe Starck, das von einer besonderen, mysteriösen Sensibilität geprägt wird. Im Hotel Sanderson gelegen, mitten im Londoner Soho, ist Long Bar eine Mischung aus Barock und modernen Kreationen, die eine gewagte und phantasievolle Originalität ausströmen. Die Grenze zum nebenanliegenden Restaurant Spoon ist nicht festumrissen und so wird die Bar zu einem Nebenraum, in dem man Appetithappen, Kaviar, Austern oder einen einmaligen Sushi ungezwungen essen und auch einen Drink nehmen kann. Die Gäste sitzen auf eleganten Hockern von Starck: silberne Struktur und gepolsterte Lehnen, auf deren Rückseite das Auge einer Frau eingraviert wurde. Die künstlerisch gestaltete Theke ist ein großes, grün beleuchtetes Rechteck aus Onyx. Die Vorsprünge der Theke sind aus rostfreiem Stahl gefertigt. Abschließend muß unbedingt erwähnt werden, daß wir vor dem Durchbruch einer neuen Innenarchitektur für Hotels stehen.

The fluid communication between the Long Bar and the Spoon restaurant is achieved by removing walls, just as so many other formal boundaries are eliminated from the hotel's public rooms. The dishes of the well-known chef Alain Ducasse can be tasted in all these spaces.

Le passage aisé entre le Long Bar et le restaurant Spoon a obligé à renoncer aux murs, et à deux les autres limites formelles annulées dans les autres locaux communs de l'hôtel. Dans les deux endroits on sert les fameux plats d'Alain Ducasse.

Das direkte Ineinanderübergehen von Long Bar und Restaurant Spoon wurde durch den Verzicht auf die Wände erreicht; in den übrigen öffentlichen Räumen des Hotels wurde Ähnliches vorgenommen. Die Gerichte des renommierten Küchenchefs Alain Ducasse werden sowohl in der Bar als auch im Restaurant angeboten.

Long Bar

The idea of the Urban Spa underlies the concept of the Sanderson Hotel, with added artistic value in the furnishings: from the foyer with its romantic sofa shaped like lips to the stools by Starck on whose back a woman's eye is engraved, photographed by Ramak Fazel.

L'idée de l'Urban Spa plane sur la conception de l'hôtel Sanderson, car le mobilier est une valeur artistique ajoutée : du vestibule, où se trouve un canapé romantique en forme de lèvres, jusqu'aux tabourets made by Starck avec leur dossier imprimé d'un oeil féminin, pris d'une photo de Ramak Fazel.

Das Konzept des Hotel Sanderson wird von der Idee des Urban Spa beeinflußt, was dem Mobiliar einen künstlerischen Wert verleiht: vom Vestibül her, wo ein romantisches lippenförmiges Sofa steht, bis zu den von Starck entworfenen Hockern hin, auf deren Rückenlehne das von Ramak Fazel fotografierte Auge einer Frau eingraviert wurde.

Purple Bar

Philippe Starck
London, United Kingdom
2000
Photography | Photo | Fotografie: Chas Wilshere.

The Purple Bar is an authentic symphony of violets, purples and lavender blues. The result is an intimate chic lounge, perfect for a drink and quiet chat. Burlesque expression of the always different Starck, the atmosphere created has a high ingredient of witch-craft and magic. Typical of this are the tables in Venetian glass that go with the stools imported from Africa, which have stainless steel backs, and the violet Queen Anne-style chairs, which are disproportionately small, creating an effect both tender and bizarre at the same time, characteristic of a doll's house. An unpolished Nero Apsoluto slab of stone becomes material for the bar, recreating organic shapes that look like a meteorite fallen from the sky. The flooring uses the same black granite, and the walls and ceiling lined with violet silk curtains create an effect characteristic of theatre sets.

Le Purple Bar est une véritable symphonie de violets, mauves et bleus lavande. Le résultat est un lounge intime à l'ambiance chic, parfait pour prendre un verre et avoir des conversations tranquilles. Expression burlesque de l'inénarrable Starck, l'atmosphère créée a une forte dose d'envoûtement et de magie.
Les tables en verre vénitien sont caractéristiques et s'allient avec les tabourets importés d'Afrique, aux dossiers en acier inox. Les chaises violettes style Queen Anne, trop petites, produisent un effet de tendresse et bizarrerie, celui d'une maison de poupées. Une pierre non polie Nero Apsoluto devient le matériau du comptoir, en reprenant les formes organiques rappellant un météorite tombé du ciel. Le pavement est fait de la même pierre de granit noir et les murs et le plafond sont recouverts de voiles violets rappelant la scène d'un théâtre.

Purple Bar ist eine echte Symphonie von violetten, malvenfarbenen und lavendelblauen Tönen. Das Ergebnis ist eine intime Lounge mit Chic-Ambientierung, ein idealer Ort für einen Drink und eine angenehme Unterhaltung. Die hier geschaffene Atmosphäre, eine burleske Äußerung des stets innovierenden Starcks, ist äußerst bezaubernd und magisch.
Typisch für das Lokal sind die Tische aus venezianischem Glas, welche zu den aus Afrika importierten Hokkern mit Inox-Rücklehnen passen, und die verhältnismäßig kleinen, im Queen-Anne-Stil gehaltenen violetten Stühle, die einen sowohl rührenden als auch extravaganten Eindruck machen und wie Stühlchen eines Puppenhauses anmuten. Die Theke ist aus unpoliertem Nero-Apsoluto-Stein, der mit seinen organischen Formen einem vom Himmel gefallenen Meteoriten ähnelt. Für den Fußboden wurde der gleiche schwarze Granitstein verwandt; die mit violetten Seidenvorhängen bespannten Wände und Decke erinnern an die Bühne eines Theaters.

The Purple Bar is an authentic symphony of violets, purples and lavender blues, that create a chic and intimate lounge.

Le Purple Bar est une véritable symphonie de mauves, violets et lavande qui créent un lounge à l'atmosphère chic et intimiste.

Purple Bar ist eine echte Symphonie von violetten, malvenfarbenen und lavendelblauen Tönen, die die Lounge chic und intim erscheinen lassen.

Purple Bar

Tables of Venetian glass, African
stools and disproportionately tiny
chairs. A bar hewn from rough
stone and curtains of violet silk
create a bizarre atmosphere, similar
to a theatrical *mise-en-scène*.

Tables en verre vénitien, tabourets
africains et chaises trop petites.
Un comptoir en pierre naturelle
et des tentures en soie violacée
recréent l'ambiance bizarre
des scène de théâtre.

Tische aus venezianischem Glas,
afrikanische Hocker und winzig kleine
Stühle. Eine Theke aus unpoliertem
Stein und Vorhänge aus violetter
Seide schaffen eine seltsame
Stimmung, die an das Bühnenbild
eines Theaters erinnert.

Dot

Ellen Rapelius, Xavier Franquesa (Studio-X)

Barcelona, España
1997
Photography | Photo | Fotografie: Martí Llorens.

Dot is right in the middle of Barcelona's Gothic Quarter, on Nou de Sant Francesc street, a refuge for lovers of avant-garde clubs. Crossing its door-step takes you onto an authentic stage-set. Seventy square meters, divided into two areas, and a "beam me up" circular platform with a beam of light, that tele-transports customers from one area to another. The first area is dominated by red and orange tones. 1950s-style stools in deep blue PVC line the bar. An atmosphere of discreet glamour contrasting with the space universe at the back of the club. A futuristic dance floor in mainly blues and greens, pierced by the rapid-blinking pulses of light from the continuous projection of movies. Cold and heat. Ice and fire. An impressive duality defining this particular urban cave.

En plein quartier gothique barcelonais émerge le Dot, dans la rue Nou de Sant Francesc, comme un refuge pour les amateurs des établissements d'avant-garde. Passer la porte c'est pénétrer dans une ambiance particulière. Soixante-dix mètres carrés, divisés en deux ambiances et un "beam me up" (une plateforme circulaire comme source de lumière) permet à ceux qui s'approchent de ce local de se télé-transporter d'une zone à une autre. La première est dominée par les nuances rouges et orangées. Face au comptoir sont alignés les tabourets style années 50 en skay rouge. Une atmosphère très discrète d'un certain glamour contraste avec l'univers galactique créé au fond du local. C'est là que se trouve une piste de danse au décor futuriste où prédominent les bleus et les verts nuancés par les faisceaux de lumière clignotante partant de la projection continue de light movies. Froid et chaud, glace et feu. Une dualité choquante qui définit bien cette exclusive grotte urbaine.

Dot liegt im gotischen Viertel von Barcelona, in der Calle Nou de Sant Francesc, und ist ein Zufluchtsort für Anhänger der avantgardistischen Lokale. Hinter der Eingangstür herrscht eine unverfälschte Stimmung. Die Fläche von 70 m2 ist in zwei Ambienten und ein "beam me up" (runde Plattform, die als Lichtquelle dient), das die Gäste von einem Bereich in den anderen transportiert, aufgeteilt. Der erste wird von roten und orangenen Farbtönen beherrscht. Vor der Theke stehen Hocker aus Kunststoffleder im Stil der 50er Jahre. Eine leicht glamouröse Atmosphäre, die mit dem galaktischen Universum des hinteren Teils des Lokals kontrastiert. Dort befindet sich eine futuristisch anmutende Tanzfläche, in der blaue und grüne Töne vorherrschen. Diese Farben werden von den ausgehenden Lichtstrahlen der ständig vorgeführten Light-Movies nuanciert. Kälte und Wärme. Eis und Feuer. Eine eindrucksvolle Dualität, die diese eigenartige Stadthöhle charakterisiert.

A futuristic "beam me up"
defines the boundary between
the club's two zones.

*Un "beam me up" futuriste
permet d'établir les limites entre
les deux zones du local.*

Ein futuristisches "beam me up"
macht es möglich, die beiden
Bereiche abzugrenzen.

Lights and materials in reddish and orangey tones
mark the basic color range in the warm hemisphere of

*Lumières et matériaux aux tons rougeâtres et orangés,
gamme chromatique de base dans l'hémisphère chaud du Dot.*

Die rötlichen und orangenen Töne der Lichter und Materialien
stellen die Farbenpalette der "heißen Hemisphäre" des Dot dar.

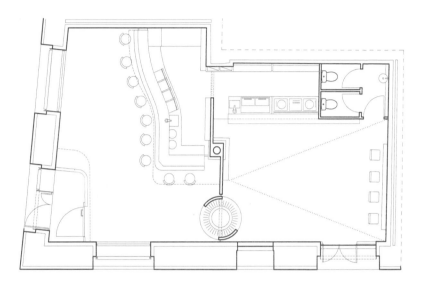

The contrast of tones on its own
defines the two areas clearly.

*Les deux ambiances sont parfaitement
définies par le simple contraste
des tonalités.*

Der Farbenkontrast ist hier ganz
offensichtlich, da jedes der beiden
Ambienten von einer Farbe
definiert wird.

Dot

Maurice Renoma

Paris, France
2001
Photography | Photo | Fotografie: Mihail Moldoveanu.

Maurice Renoma, renowned artist and photographer, pays homage to the art of the photograph, to contemporary design and to architecture, in his new idea of restaurant for his Renoma Café Gallery. In this establishment Maurice Renoma projects a space that exalts the social ritual of the café. Thanks to the rehabilitation of a loft, in the purest New York style, the Renoma Café Gallery has become a fusion space, a photograph and design exhibition gallery, that extends into a library-smoking room and a trend-setting bar-restaurant. Legendary figure of the 1970s generation of *prêt-à-porter* photographers, Maurice Renoma proposes a gallery-café devoted to his own works of art. However, when night falls on the Renoma, the customer perceives how the focus of the establishment's decor shifts towards a semi-circular bar giving off a pale blue light.

Maurice Renoma, artiste et photographe consacré, rend hommage à l'art de la photographie, au design contemporain et à l'architecture en présentant un concept nouveau de la restauration pour son Renoma Café Gallery. Avec cet établissement Maurice Renoma projette un espace qui se transforme en une exaltation du rituel social du café. Ainsi, grâce à la rénovation d'un loft, du plus pur style new-yorkais, le Renoma Café Gallery devient un espace de fusion apte à devenir une exposition de photographie et design se prolongeant en bibliothèque fumoir et en un bar restaurant dernier cri. Figure emblématique du prêt-à-porter de la génération des photographes des années soixante dix, Maurice Renoma propose une galerie café où consacrer ses oeuvres d'art. Cependant lorsque la nuit tombe sur le Renoma, le client perçoit que le poids compositif de la décoration de l'établissement se déplace vers un comptoir en demi-cercle qui émet une pâle lumière bleutée..

Maurice Renoma, ein angesehener Künstler und Fotograf, huldigt der Kunst der Fotografie, dem zeitgenössischen Design und der Architektur mit seinem neuen Konzept der Gastronomie für seine Renoma Cafe Gallery. Maurice Renoma wollte bei diesem Projekt ein Ort schaffen, in dem das gesellschaftliche Ritual der Cafés verherrlicht werden soll. Durch den Umbau eines Lofts nach New Yorker Art wurde die Renoma Café Gallery zu einem Mehrzwecklokal, das sich als Saal für Fotografie- und Designausstellungen eignet und gleichzeitig einen Raucher- und Leseraum, sowie ein voll im Trend liegendes Bar-Restaurant beherbergt. Maurice Renoma, Symbol der Fotografengeneration der 70er Jahre, präsentiert ein Galerie-Café, in dem seine eigenen Kunstwerke ausgestellt werden sollen. Bei Nacht hat der Gast jedoch das Gefühl, daß sich der Schwerpunkt der Dekoration des Renoma zu der schwaches, bläuliches Licht ausstrahlenden halbrunden Theke hin verschiebt.

The Renoma Café Gallery has taken a New York-style loft and converted it into a space of fusion, as photograph and design exhibition gallery, that extends into a library-smoking room and a trend-setting bar-restaurant. Must be visited: the luminous bar is the star of the Renoma night.

Le Renoma Café Gallery reprend un loft style new-yorkais et devient un espace de fusion apte à se transformer en galerie exposition de photo et design qui se prolonge en une bibliothèque fumoir et en un bar restaurant dernier cri. Visite obligée : le comptoir lumineux, le grand protagoniste de la nuit.

Die in einem nach New Yorker Stil umgebauten Loft untergebrachte Renoma Cafe Gallery ist zu einem Mehrzwecklokal geworden, das sich als Saal für Fotografie- und Designausstellungen eignet und gleichzeitig einen Raucher- und Leseraum, sowie ein modisches Bar-Restaurant beherbergt. Ein Muß: die beleuchtete Theke, Mittelpunkt des Lokals bei Nacht.

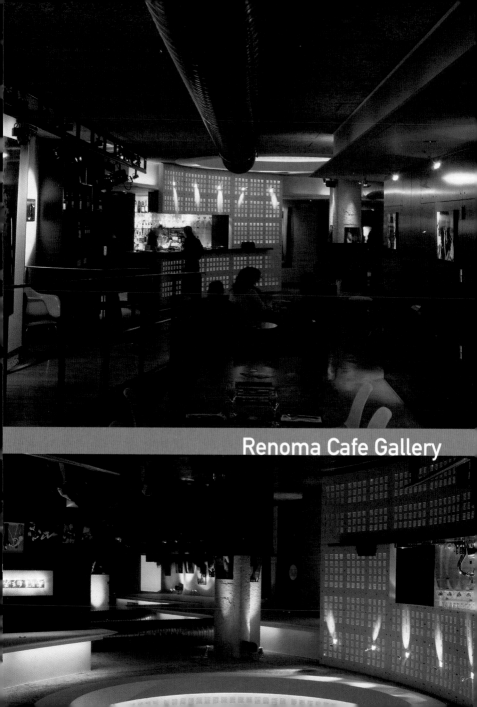

Renoma Cafe Gallery

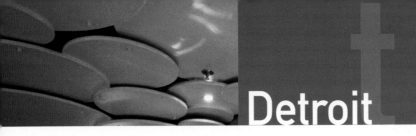

Detroit

Quentin Reymolds
London, United Kingdom
1995
Photography | Photo | Fotografie: Chas Wilshere.

A bar that seems to have been dug under Covent Garden, but whose sandy textures belong more to mythical exotic deserts rather than to central London. The walls of the Detroit are, in fact, covered with a mix of resin and sand brought from the Adriatic sea. Designed originally as a restaurant, the site had sufficient contrasts and potential to acquire a new function. The strange angles of the ceiling and the non-linearity of its surfaces were mitigated by the introduction of curved shapes. Now, the different areas are like natural caverns to which the changing floors and high ceilings help add a certain air of mystery. Movies like *Star Wars* or *Mad Max* seem to have inspired the lighting, based on spots in port-holes giving out phantasmagoric beams of light. The tubular chairs and red and blue bench-seats are the only note at all discordant with style details such as the purple staircase that leads up to nowhere.

Un bar qui semble avoir été creusé sous le Covent Garden mais dont les textures sableuses semblent plutôt appartenir à des mythiques déserts. Et en fait, les murs du Detroit sont recouverts d'un mélange de résine et de sable provenant de l'Adriatique. Conçu à l'origine comme restaurant, l'établissement comptait avec des contrastes et potentialités suffisantes pour acquérir une nouvelle fonction. Les angles étranges du plafond et la non linéarité de ses surfaces ont été mitigées avec l'introduction de lignes courbes. Actuellement, les différentes zones sont comme des cavernes naturelles où les sols changeants et les hauts plafonds contribuent à créer un certain mystère. Des films comme Star Wars ou Mad Max semblent avoir inspiré également l'éclairage, fait de plafonniers perforés émettant des faisceaux de lumière fantasmagorique. Les chaises tubulaires et les banquettes rouges et bleues sont les seules notes discordantes face aux éléments de style comme l'escalier pourpre, ne menant nulle part.

Eine Bar, die wie ein unter Covent Garden ausgeschachteter Grubenbau anmutet, deren sandige Texturen aber nicht zum Stadtzentrum von London zu gehören scheinen, sondern eher zu mythischen und exotischen Wüsten. Die Wände des Detroit sind mit einer Mischung aus Harz und extra vom Adriatischen Meer herbeigeschafftem Sand behaftet. Das ursprünglich als Restaurant konzipierte Lokal verfügte über ausreichende Kontraste und Möglichkeiten, um umfunktioniert werden zu können. Die seltsamen Winkel der Decke und die nicht linearen Oberflächen wurden abgerundet. Jetzt wirken die einzelnen Bereiche wie von der Natur geschaffenen Höhlen, in denen die unterschiedlichen Fußböden und die hohen Decken dem Raum eine mysteriöse Stimmung verleihen. Allen Anschein nach haben Filme wie Star Wars oder Mad Max die Gestaltung der Beleuchtung mit gespenstisches Licht abgebenden Lochstrahlern entscheidend beeinflußt. Die röhrenförmigen Stühle und die roten und blauen Sitzbänke stellen den einzigen Kontrast zu stilvollen Elementen, wie die purpurfarbene, ins Nirgendwo führende Treppe, dar.

The circle is a motif on the
ceilings and on the zinc doors
that separate the different zones
of the bar.

*Le cercle est le motif des plafonds
et des portes de zinc séparant
les différentes zones du local.*

Der Kreis ist das bestimmende
Motiv an Decken und an den
Zinktüren, die die Bereiche des
Lokals voneinender trennen.

Detroit

The lighting, based on spots in
port-holes giving out diffuse beams of
light, helps create a futuristic atmosphere.

*L'éclairage au moyen de plafonniers perforés
qui émettent des faisceaux de lumière diffuse
permet de créer une atmosphère futuriste.*

Das von den Lochstrahlern abgegebene
diffuse Licht schafft eine futuristische
Atmosphäre.

Il Volo

Andrea Raddrizani
Milano, Italia
1998
Photography | Photo | Fotografie: Paola D'Amico.

Il Volo is a unique place leading the Milanese revolution in favor of aperitifs. Conceived according to the centuries-old technique of the Feng Shui, this cocktail-bar takes the five essential elements of the Chinese tradition, earth, metal, fire, wood and water, in order to create areas that, through their proper spatial orientation, manage to transmit harmonious energy that favors personal relationships. Located in a beautiful court-yard, Il Volo offers an idyllic setting for a romantic *tête-à-tête*. The elegant black canopies, a dark marble bar, the little fountain in the middle, and trickling streams symbolize the continuous flow of energy. With a highly sophisticated pace, Il Volo is a classic establishment frequented by a clientèle that dresses naturally in Armani, improvising a casual style with shirts outside trousers. This garden inhabited by ancient plants is a perfect stage for enjoying the *Dolce Vita* whilst sipping a Martini rosso.

Il Volo est un exemplaire unique en tête de la révolution milanaise en faveur de l'apéritif. Conçu selon la technique millénaire du Feng Shui, ce cocktail-bar reprend les cinq éléments fondamentaux de la tradition chinoise, terre, métal, feu, bois et eau, afin de créer des ambiances qui, selon son orientation adéquate dans l'espace, transmettent une énergie harmonieuse facilitant les relations entre les personnes. Situé dans un beau patio, Il Volo offre une ambiance idyllique pour un romantic cheek to cheek. Des stores noirs très élégants, un comptoir bar en marbre sombre, une petite fontaine au centre et des petites rigoles qui symbolisent le flux continu de l'énergie. Il Volo, au rythme de l'ambiance la plus sophistiquée, est un classique établissement fréquenté par une clientèle habillée très simplement par Armani, qui improvise le style décontracté chemise hors du pantalon. De là que ce jardin habité par des plantes millénaires soit un cadre parfait pour jouir de la Dolce Vita en dégustant un Martini rosso.

Il Volo ist anführend bei der Mailänder Revolution zugunsten des Aperitifs. In der nach der tausendjährigen Feng-Shui-Technik konzipierten Cocktail-Bar wird auf die fünf Grundelemente der chinesischen Tradition - Erde, Metall, Feuer, Holz und Wasser- zurückgegriffen, um Ambienten zu schaffen, die bei richtiger Lage im Raum eine harmonische, die zwischenmenschlichen Beziehungen fördernde Energie ausstrahlen. In einem schönen Innenhof gelegen, ist Il Volo aufgrund seiner idyllischen Ambientierung für ein romantic cheek to cheek ideal. Elegante schwarze Markisen, die Theke aus dunklem Marmor, der in der Mitte liegende kleine Brunnen und die Bächlein, die das ständige Fließen der Energie symbolisieren. Il Volo ist ein klassisches Lokal, das von Gästen aufgesucht wird, die bei auserwählter Ambient-Musik mit Nonchalance Armani-Kleidung tragen und einen ungezwungenen Stil, mit dem Hemd lässig aus der Hose heraushängend, improvisieren. Deswegen ist dieser Garten mit über tausend Jahre alten Pflanzen ein idealer Ort, um bei einem Martini Rosso das Dolce Vita zu genießen.

Il Volo boasts of being the first locale in Italy that was planned on the basis of a reading of space in the Feng Shui. Converted into a classic of the Milan cocktail hour, this special spot takes its name from an enormous canopy covering the main bar in the garden and which recalls a parapenting wing preparing to take flight.

Il Volo se veut le premier local en Italie projeté à partir d'une lecture de l'espace du Feng Shui. Devenu un classique à l'heure de l'apéritif milanais, cet enclave privilégié prend son nom d'une énorme toile couvrant le comptoir du jardin et qui rappelle une aile de parapente prête à prendre son élan.

Il Volo rühmt sich, das erste Lokal Italiens zu sein, das nach der Feng-Shui-Philosophie räumlich gestaltet wurde. Diese idyllisch gelegene Cocktail-Bar, mittlerweile ein Begriff für die Mailänder Aperitiv-Fans, wird nach dem riesigen Tuch, das die große Theke im Garten überspannt und an einen großen abflugbereiten Delta-Flügel erinnert, benannt.

Il Volo

It is surprising to see how Il Volo fits into the old walls of the Viale Caldara. Its warm interior decor, designed for a Prince's palace, is noted for the delicate streams that flow among the customers' tables.

Il est surprenant de voir comment Il Volo s'insinue dans les vieilles murailles du Viale Caldara. Sa chaude décoration intérieure projetée comme un palais de princes est remarquable par les délicieux ruisseaux qui coulent entre les tables des commensaux.

Es kann mit Erstaunen festgestellt werden, daß Il Volo die alten Mauern des Viale Caldara andeutet. Bei seiner warmen Innendekoration, die wie ein Fürstenpalast anmutet, sind die zwischen den Tischreihen der Gäste durchlaufenden kleinen Bäche hervorzuheben.

GiovanniMaria Torno

Milano, Italia
1999
Photography | Photo | Fotografie: Paola D'Amico.

Italian tradition mixed with the rhythmic beat of rock and roll. That's Amore is an update of the classic New York cafés and bars of the 1950s. Taking as reference and inspiration the scenes of some of the pictures set in this period, such as American Graffiti, this club of little more than 200 square meters has a suggestive curving bar in perforated steel, fronted by chrome stools with seats of different colors. The neon lights create, however, a more artificial atmosphere, countered by the wengé wood floors, which in turn contrast with the silvery table tops and the lightly acid colors of the walls. The seats round the tables are upholstered in lively colors with white borders. Some of them are heart-shaped.

Tradition italienne mêlée aux accords rythmés du rock and roll. That's Amore est une révision actuelle des cafés classiques et des locaux new-yorkais des années 50. Les scènes de certains films de l'époque ont été référence et inspiration, par exemple, American Graffiti, de ce local de 200 mètres carrés au moins, avec un comptoir suggestif sinueux réalisé en acier perforé où s'accumulent les tabourets à la structure chromée et aux sièges tapissés de différentes couleurs. Les lumières néon créent, cependant, une atmosphère plus artificielle, contrastée par les parquets en bois de wengué qui à leur tour choquent avec les dessus de table argentés et les couleurs légèrement acides des murs. Les chaises autour des tables sont tapissées de vives couleurs avec lisière blanche, quelques fois leurs dossiers ont une forme de coeur.

Italienische Tradition vermischt mit rhythmischen Rock-and-Roll-Klängen. That's Amore ist eine aktualisierte Version der klassischen New Yorker Cafés und Lokale der 50er Jahre. Bei der Raumgestaltung dienten die Schauplätze einiger in dieser Zeit spielenden Filme, wie zum Beispiel American Graffiti, als Vorbild. Das etwas mehr als 200 m2 große Lokal verfügt über eine suggestive, geschwungene Theke aus gelöchertem Stahl, vor der Hocker mit verchromter Struktur und verschiedenfarbenen Polstersitzen stehen. Die Neonlichter schaffen jedoch eine kältere Atmosphäre, die von den Fußböden aus Wengé-Holz ausgeglichen wird, der wiederum mit den silberfarbenen Tischplatten und den leicht zitrusfarbenen Wänden kontrastiert. Die um den Tischen herumstehenden Stühle sind in lebhaften Farben gepolstert und weiß verbrämt, einige davon haben herzförmige Rücklehnen.

The coldness of some materials and elements, such as the structural parts of the chairs and tables, contrasts with the warm colors chosen for the seats' upholstery.

La froideur de certains matériaux et éléments, comme les structures des tables et des chaises contraste avec les tons chauds choisis pour les tapisseries des sièges.

Die Kälte mancher Materialien und Elemente, wie die Struktur von Tischen und Stühlen, kontrastiert mit der Wärme der für die Polster aller Sitze ausgewählten Farben.

That's amore

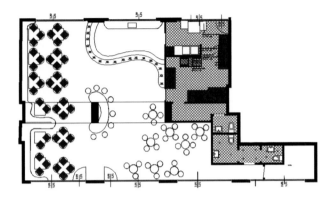

The curving bar is made of perforated steel. The lighting in this area is much more warm and intimate.

Le comptoir aux formes sinueuses a été fabriqué en acier perforé. L'éclairage choisi pour cette zone a un nuance plus chaude et intimiste.

Die geschwungene Theke wurde aus gelöchertem Stahl gefertigt. Die Beleuchtung wirkt in diesem Bereich viel wärmer und intimer.

Café Salambó

Francisco García Lasaosa, Emili Taltavull Gimeno

Barcelona, España
1992
Photography | Photo | Fotografie: David Manchón.

The Café Salambó has become one of the main meeting points of Barcelona's Gràcia quarter. Its style of a 1920s café where groups of people would regularly meet was achieved after a complete overhaul of the factory formerly on the site. All the furniture on the main floor is in iroko wood, the floor is inlaid with sucupira and the walls are finished by Venetian fire-plated stucco. A wrought-iron stair-case leads to the upper floor, which is L-shaped. These 120 square meters, with floors of solid oak, hold two billiard tables, a bar and furnishing similar to that on the ground floor. The café is lit by a border strip round the walls, cylindrical table-lamps with parchment shades, alabaster masses and the light which the glass shelving within the bar gives out. Those who frequent the Salambó consider it, despite the passing of time, a lasting part of their own personal history and an enigmatic enclave with a cinematic tinge.

Café Salambó est devenu un des points de rencontre préféré du quartier barcelonais de Gràcia. Son esthétique de café-salon des années 20 a été réalisée après une rénovation totale de l'ancienne nef qu'il occupe. Tout le mobilier de l'étage principal est en bois de iroco, le sol est en parquet de sukupira et les murs sont finis au stuc vénitien repassé au feu. On accède par un escalier en fer, on accède à l'étage du haut qui a une forme en L de 120 mètres carrés au sol en chêne massif, occupé par des tables de billard, un comptoir et un mobilier semblable à celui de l'étage du bas. L'éclairage est résolu par une bordure sur tout le périmètre, des lampes en parchemin cylindriques pendues sur les tables, des volumes en albâtre et la lumière qui sort des étagères en verre, du côté du comptoir. Ceux qui fréquentent le Salambó le considèrent, malgré le temps, comme une trace durable de leur propre histoire et un énigmatique enclave aux teintes cinématographiques.

Café Salambó ist zu einem der beliebtesten Treffpunkte des Barceloner Stadtviertels Gràcia geworden. Durch Umbau der alten Halle, in der das Lokal untergebracht ist, bekam es das Aussehen eines Kaffeehauses der 20er Jahre. Im Hauptgeschoß sind alle Möbel aus Iroko-Holz gefertigt, der Parkettfußboden ist aus Sucupira-Holz und die Wände sind mit venezianischem Stuck verziert. Über eine schmiedeeiserne Treppe wird das obere, L-förmige Geschoß erreicht. Dieser 120 m2 große, mit Eichenholzparkett ausgestattete Raum beherbergt zwei Billardtische, eine Theke und dem Mobiliar der unteren Etage ähnliche Möbelstücke. Das Lokal wird von einem umlaufenden Lichtrandstreifen, von über den Tischen hängenden zylindrischen Pergamentpapierlampen, von Alabasterkästen und von dem von den Glasregalen der Theke ausgestrahlten Licht beleuchtet. Der Stammgast des Salambó empfindet, daß das Café ein unvergänglicher Teil seines eigenen Lebens darstellt und ein geheimnisvoller Ort mit der Stimmung eines Filmes ist.

The upper floor contains
two billiard tables, a bar
and furnishing similar to
that on the ground floor.

*L'étage supérieur accueille
deux tables de billard , un
comptoir et un mobilier
semblable à celui de l'étage
du bas.*

Im oberen Geschoß
wurden zwei Billardtische,
eine Theke, sowie dem
Mobiliar der unteren Etage
ähnelnde Möbelstücke
aufgestellt.

Café Salambó

Le Biciclette

Luca Bernasconi

Milano, Italia
1988
Photography | Photo | Fotografie: Paola D'Amico.

The Biciclette was opened in 1988. Though its architectural structure has remained unchanged since then, its decor has been periodically updated. It is famous for having become a key promoter of the work of new generations of artists. Its modern, minimalist atmosphere, welcoming and exquisite, was chosen for the always good purpose of becoming an ideal place to exhibit any kind of art. As an "Art Café", it hosts exhibitions of artists who are still at the very start of their creative lives. The iron furniture with very chic lines contrasts with the transparent floor that exhibits a surprising collection of bicycles, from the most rickety to the most futuristic. The row of red stools gives way to an annex of clean lines, only interrupted by the colors of the photographs and pictures on exhibit.

Le Biciclette a été inauguré en 1988 et, bien que sa structure architecturale a toujours été la même, sa décoration a été périodiquement rénovée. Il a une bonne renommée et est devenu un établissement clé car il soutient le travail des nouvelles générations d'artistes. Son ambiance, moderne et minimaliste, accueillante et exquise, a été conçue avec la toujours bonne intention de devenir l'endroit idéal pour l'exposition de n'importe quel type d'art. Comme dans un Art Café, il accueille des expositions d'artistes à la genèse de leur projection créative. Le mobilier en acier, aux lignes très chic, contraste avec le sol transparent exposant une surprenante collection de bicyclettes, de la bécane à la plus futuriste. Le défilé de tabourets rouges précède un annexe aux lignes pures, interrompue uniquement par les couleurs des photographies et des tableaux exposés.

Le Biciclette wurde 1988 eröffnet und seitdem ist seine Dekoration von Zeit zu Zeit erneuert worden, die architektonische Struktur hingegen hat keine Veränderung erfahren. Die Philosophie des Lokals beruht auf der Förderung von Nachwuchskünstlern, was ihm allgemeine Anerkennung eingebracht hat. Die hier geschaffene Ambientierung, modern und minimalistisch, gemütlich und exquisit, soll das Lokal zu einem idealen Ausstellungsort aller Kunstrichtungen machen. Nach der Art eines "Art Cafés" werden Wechselausstellungen von Künstlern, die erst am Anfang ihrer Laufbahn stehen, beherbergt. Die aus Stahl gefertigten Möbelstücke im Chic-Stil kontrastieren mit dem durchsichtigen Fußboden, unter dem eine erstaunliche Sammlung von Fahrrädern, von den klapprigsten hin bis zu den futuristischsten Designermodellen, zu sehen ist. Nach der langen Reihe von roten Hockern gelangt man zu einem Nebenraum mit kahlen Wänden, an denen lediglich die Farben der ausgestellten Fotografien und Gemälde auffallen.

The atmosphere of Le Biciclette is a modern and minimalist solution which provides an ideal art exhibition space. Its decor is complemented by non-stop sounds with the latest lounge numbers.

L'ambiance de Le Biciclette est une solution moderne et minimaliste qui tente d'offrir un espace idéal pour l'exposition d'oeuvres d'art. Sa décoration est parachevée par la musique toujours présente, avec les mélodies lounge les plus actuelles.

Die Ambientierung des Le Biciclette ist eine moderne und minimalistische Lösung, mit der ein für Ausstellungen von Kunstwerken idealer Raum geschaffen werden soll. Ergänzt wird die Dekoration durch die ständige Ausstrahlung der aktuellsten Lounge-Musik.

The techno chic motifs in steel and glass make it an original space, inspired by the world on two wheels.

Les motifs techno chic en acier et en verre transforment le local en un espace original, inspiré dans le monde des deux roues.

Die Techno-Chic-Motive aus Stahl und Glas machen das Lokal zu einem originellen, von der Fahrradwelt inspirierten Raum.

Le Biciclette

Plaza

Roberto Ercill, Miguel Ángel Campo

Vitoria, España
2000
Photography | Photo | Fotografie: César San Millán.

This bar is located next to the Plaza de España, on a pedestrian-only street of the Basque capital. Its activity takes place on two floors, with the cellar as a service area. At street level, the Plaza has a bar and an area of chairs and tables, which are clearly differentiated. Upstairs, however, is a lounge area with a magnificent view over the street. The main difficulty of the project was the joining of two separate buildings. This formal lack of definition arising from the union of the two places was confronted by a simple strategy of materials and shapes. The white ceilings and structures, the hard-wearing wood floors and the stainless steel in the most exposed places complete the small range of finishes. A huge pane of glass like a screen on the South wall highlights its image as a café. Comfort above all: the double layer of glass regulates the heat of the bar.

Dans une rue piétonne de la capitale basque, proche de la Plaza de España, se trouve ce local dont l'activité se déroule sur deux étages, plus le sous-sol réservé au services. Au rez-de-chaussée, le Bar Plaza dispose d'un comptoir et d'une zone de tables et chaises nettement différenciée. L'étage supérieur, par contre, a été conçu comme une zone salon où on peut jouir d'une magnifique vue sur la rue. La principale difficulté du projet a été de grouper deux édifices différents. Cette indéfinition formelle dérivée de l'union des deux locaux a été réussie au moyen d'une simple stratégie de matériaux et de formes. Les plafonds et les structures peintes en blanc; les sols en bois très résistant et l'acier inox dans les zones les plus fréquentées complètent la palette réduite des finitions. Une grande baie vitrée comme écran sur la façade sud souligne la silhouette du café. Avant tout, le bien-être : la double peau en verre règle la température du local.

Dieses Lokal liegt in einer Fußgängerstraße der baskischen Hauptstadt, in der Nähe vom Plaza de España. Es ist in zwei Stockwerke gegliedert, wobei der Kellerraum dem Dienstbereich vorbehalten ist. Im Erdgeschoß befindet sich die Theke und ein deutlich abgezeichneter Bereich mit Tischen und Stühlen. Das obere Geschoß hingegen ist als Aufenthaltsbereich konzipiert worden, von dem man einen wunderbaren Ausblick auf die Straße hat. Das Schwierigste an dem Projekt war, zwei verschiedene Gebäude miteinander zu verbinden. Die hier nicht vorhandene formale Einheit wurde durch den strategischen Einsatz von Materialien und Formen erreicht: weiß gestrichene Decken und Strukturen; Fußböden aus strapazierfähigem Holz, sowie rostfreier Stahl an abnutzungsgefährdeten Stellen. Das Innere des Cafés wird von einer Glaswand und der Südfassade hervorgehoben. Komfort ist hier das Wichtigste: dank der Doppelglasscheibe ist die Temperatur im Lokal immer angenehm.

One of the project's main difficulties was the integration of the two separate buildings that make up the current space of the bar.

Une des principales difficultés a été l'intégration de deux édifices différents composant l'espace actuel du local.

Eine der Schwierigkeiten des Projekts war, die zwei verschiedenen Gebäude, die den heutigen Raum des Lokals darstellen, miteinander zu verbinden.

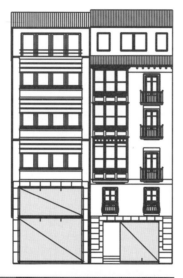

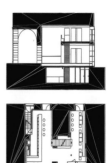

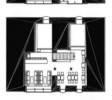

White ceilings and structures contrast with the hard-wearing wood floors and with the stainless steel in its most exposed places.

Plafonds et structures blanches en contraste avec les sols en bois très résistants et avec l'acier inoxydable des zones les plus exposées.

Die weiß gestrichenen Decken und Strukturen kontrastieren mit den Fußböden aus strapazierfähigem Holz und dem rostfreien Stahl der abnutzungsgefährdeten Stellen.

Plaza

The preceding page shows how the stairs connecting the two floors of the bar start in the dividing wall between the two buildings. The old shop-window has been conserved and is used for temporary art exhibitions.

Sur la page précédente, on apprécie l'escalier qui relie les deux étages du local qui naît du mur mitoyen. De l'autre côté, l'ancienne devanture qui est conservée pour des expositions d'art temporaires.

Auf der vorhergehenden Seite ist ersichtlich, wie die die beiden Etagen miteinanderverbindende Treppe von der die beiden Lokale trennende Wand ausgeht. Im ehemaligen Schaufenster sind heute wechselnde Kunstausstellungen zu sehen.

Dani Freixes, Victor Argentí, Vicente Miranda
Barcelona, España
1992
Photography | Photo | Fotografie: David Manchón.

To recover the tradition of taking tapas and aperitifs was the main aim of this locale, whose reform and rehabilitation won the Grand FAD Prize for Interior Design in 1992. Located on Barcelona's Rosellón street, Seltz has a store area in the semi-basement, a comfortable and huge bar with tables against the wall and some tables grouped together next to the practical kitchen. The glass, wood and the finish painted with slate, which lets the day's tapas be written up on the walls, are the basic materials used. There is also an interesting finish with sliding glass panels lit by the fluorescent lights on the wall in front of the bar and on the stairs leading to the upper floor. This giant graphic collage, consisting of various logos of vermouth brands is undoubtedly the main visual attraction of the locale and an excellent invitation to sample its gastronomic dishes.

Récupérer la tradition des tapas et l'apéritif est l'objectif principal de ce local qui a reçu le Grand Prix FAD d'Intériorisme en 1992. Situé dans rue barcelonaise de Rosellón, Seltz compte une zone de magasin au sous-sol, un grand comptoir confortable avec des tables adossées et un espace de tables groupées près de la cuisine, très pratique. Le verre, le bois et la finition de peinture ardoise qui permet d'inscrire sur les murs l'offre de tapas de la journée, sont les matériaux de base utilisés. D'autre part, on remarque la finition avec des panneaux coulissants en verre, illuminés grâce aux fluorescents du mur en face du comptoir et des escaliers d'accès au niveau supérieur. Ce gigantesque collage graphique, composé par différents logotypes de marques de vermouth, constitue, sans doute, le principal attrait visuel du local et une invitation en toute règle à la dégustation de son offre gastronomique.

Hauptziel dieses Lokals, für dessen Umbau im Jahre 1992 der Große FAD-Preis für Innenarchitektur verliehen wurde, war die Rückkehr zur Tradition der "Tapas" und der Aperitifs. Das in der Barceloner Calle Rosellón gelegene Seltz verfügt über einen Lagerbereich im Souterrain, eine geräumige Theke mit angebauten Tischen, sowie einen neben der praktischen Küche liegenden Bereich mit einzelnen Tischen. Die hauptsächlich verwandten Materialien sind Glas, Holz und Schieferfarbe, die es ermöglicht, die "Tapas" des Tages an die Wand zu schreiben. Hervorgehoben werden muß außerdem die durchlaufende, von Leuchtröhren beleuchtete Glaswand, die sich gegenüber der Theke und der zum oberen Geschoß führenden Treppe befindet. Diese riesige Collage aus verschiedenen Logos von Wermutweinmarken, zweifellos das attraktivste Element des Lokals, lädt zum Genießen des gastronomischen Angebots ein.

The graphic collage with logos of various vermouths on the illuminated glass panels is the most impressive element of decoration in the locale.

Le collage graphique de logotypes de marques d'apéritifs sur les murs de verre illuminés est l'élément le plus surprenant de la décoration de ce bar.

Die graphische Collage aus Logos von verschiedenen Wermutweinmarken auf der beleuchteten Glaswand stellt das auffälligste Dekorationselement des Lokals dar.

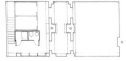

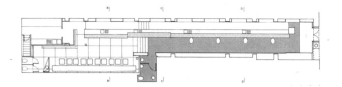

Seltz

Zapping

Studio Simonetti
Riccione, Italia
1997
Photography | Photo | Fotografie: Alberto Ferrero.

Zapping is an authentic metropolis of the future. Soft organic forms follow each other on an ordered stage where audiovisual and multimedia devices are indispensable. This video-pub seeks to communicate the speed of today's multimedia web: an expansion of time and space, characteristic of global communication. The decor has an artificial look: it is based on carefully laid-out geometry to which color adds particular importance. A theatrical and evocative atmosphere which breathes a certain fascination with the night and where each element becomes transformed. The shafts of light from the central pillars and the bar inside are points of vitality, whereas on the roof voluptuous thick clouds accompany a huge map on which all the continents are sketched. The furniture is laid out in circles with the bar at the circles' centre, so muting the vertical and horizontal lines of flooring, walls and ceilings.

Zapping est une authentique métropole du futur. Les formes organiques et douces se succèdent en un scénario ordonné où la présence d'éléments et d'appareils audiovisuels et multimédia se fait indispensable. Ce vidéo-pub veut communiquer la vitesse du réseau multimédia actuel: une dilatation du temps et de l'espace, propre à la communication globale. La décoration semble artificielle; elle repose sur une géométrie étudiée où la couleur apporte une valeur particulière. Une atmosphère théâtrale et évocatrice où palpite une certaine fascination de la nuit et où chaque élément semble se transformer. Les faisceaux de lumière des colonnes centrales et le comptoir placé dans l'aire interne sont des points de vitalité alors que sur les plafonds des nuages voluptueux et denses accompagnent une carte gigantesque où se profilent tous les continents. D'autre part, le mobilier s'articule en sens circulaire ayant comme centre le comptoir, nuançant la verticalité et l'horizontalité des pavements, des murs et des plafonds.

Zapping ist eine echte Metropole der Zukunft. In einem ordentlich eingerichteten Schauplatz, in dem die Audiovisual- und Multimedia-Elemente und -Geräte unerläßlich sind, wechseln sich organische und sanfte Formen ab. In diesem Video-Pub soll die Geschwindigkeit des heutigen Multimedianetz zum Ausdruck kommen: eine für die globale Kommunikation typische Ausdehnung der Zeit und des Raumes. Die futuristisch aussehende Dekoration stützt sich auf eine durchdachte Geometrie, in der die Farbe eine besondere Rolle spielt. Eine theatralische und evozierende Atmosphäre, in der eine gewisse Faszinierung von der Nacht zu spüren ist und jedes Element sich zu verwandeln scheint. Die Lichtstrahlen der in der Mitte stehenden Säulen und die in ihrer Nähe befindliche Theke beleben den Raum, während an der Decke üppige Wolken eine riesengroße Landkarte, auf der alle Erdteile dargestellt sind, umgeben. Zur Abschwächung der Vertikalität und Horizontalität der Fußböden, Wände und Decken sind die Möbel kreisförmig um die Theke angeordnet.

The bar and illuminated central pillars are the key
points of this futuristic stage-set, under an
artificial night sky, full of thick voluptuous clouds.
The idea is of curving surfaces, as a free
interpretation of constructing an architecture
beyond the literal sense of the term.

*Le comptoir et les colonnes centrales éclairées
constituent les points vitaux de ce scénario futuriste
placé sous un ciel nocturne artificiel, rempli de nuages
voluptueux et denses. L'idée projette une surface de
lignes courbes qui est comme une interprétation libre
pour construire une architecture dépassant le sens
littéral du terme.*

Die Theke und die beleuchteten, in der Mitte
stehenden Säulen sind wesentliche Elemente dieses
futuristischen Schauplatzes, über dem ein
künstlicher, mit schweren Wolken besäter
Nachthimmel schwebt. Der Entwurf
kurvenförmiger Oberflächen stellt eine freie
Interpretierung einer über die wörtliche Bedeutung
des Begriffes hinausgehenden Architektur dar.

Zapping

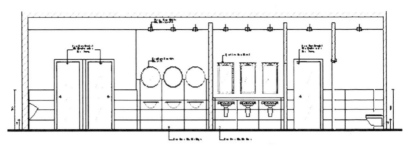

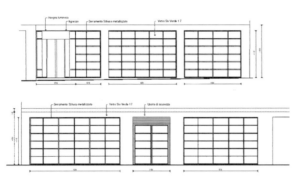

Lamps made out of numerous slides that act as light reflectors, creating curious and continuous effects, are set into the banister running round the bar.

Incorporées à la balustrade qui entoure le comptoir on remarque des lampes faites d'innombrables diapositives qui diffusent la lumière en créant de curieux effets continuels.

Die auf den die Theke umlaufenden Rand montierten, aus unzähligen Dias gefertigten Lampen schaffen ununterbrochen seltsame Lichteffekte.

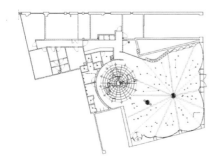

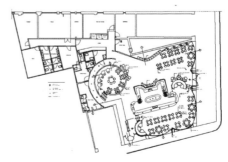

Café Berlín

Sandra Tarruella Esteva, Isabel López Vilalta

Barcelona, España
2000
Photography | Photo | Fotografie: Martí Llorens.

Neither avant-garde design, nor the most furiously up-to-date trends. The proposal of Sandra Tarruella and Isabel López is based on the freshness and ambivalence of its areas. The locale, small and triangular in shape, was reformed to take maximum advantage of the space. The basic elements are a large bar in two sections and a bench with tables for breakfast, lunch or having a drink, positioned in line with the front wall. The abundance of natural light and the predominance of light colors turn it into an open space. The back wall provides the color contrast. Here a striking, mainly red mural leads to a staircase down to the cellar. This second level downstairs is much more intimate. The structural whites are offset by the more intense hues of sofas and easy chairs. Undoubtedly, the warm lights of the numerous candles and lamps intensify the atmosphere of seclusion.

Ni design d'avant-garde, ni tendances rageusement actuelles. La proposition de Sandra Tarruella et Isabel López est basée sur la fraîcheur et l'ambivalence de ses zones. Le local, de surface triangulaire et peu de mètres carrés, a été rénové de façon à pouvoir profiter au maximum de la place. Un grand comptoir en deux parties et un banc avec des tables alignés le long de la façade pour prendre le petit déjeuner, le repas ou un verre, sont les éléments de base. L'entrée, bien éclairée à la lumière naturelle, et les tons clairs prédominants contribuent à ouvrir l'espace. Le contraste chromatique est donné par le mur décoré d'une belle fresque dans les rouges conduisant à l'escalier qui mène au sous-sol. La proposition est, à ce second niveau, plus intime, et les blancs structuraux sont atténués par les tons plus intenses des canapés et des fauteuils. Les lumières chaudes des nombreuses bougies et les lampes intensifient la sensation de recueillement.

Weder avantgardistisches Design, noch brandneue Tendenzen. Das Projekt von Sandra Tarruella und Isabel López zeichnet sich durch die Gewagtheit und Ambivalenz seiner Bereiche aus. Das kleine dreieckige Lokal wurde so umgebaut, daß die zur Verfügung stehende Fläche bestmöglichst ausgenutzt werden konnte. Eine L-förmige Theke und eine an der Fassadenwand stehende Sitzbank mit Tischen, wo man frühstücken, zu Mittag essen oder einen Drink nehmen kann, stellen das Grundmobiliar dar. Da viel Tageslicht vorhanden ist und helle Farbtöne vorherrschen, wirkt das Lokal wie ein offener Raum. Den Farbkontrast bildet die hintere Wand, die in rötlichen Tönen bemalt wurde und den Weg zur Kellertreppe weist. Im unteren Geschoß herrscht eine intimere Stimmung, die in weiß gehaltenen Strukturelemente kontrastieren mit den dunkleren Farben der Sofas und Sessel. Das warme Licht der zahlreichen Kerzen und die Lampen steigern die besinnliche Stimmung.

The linearity of its structural elements means the space available can be fully used.

Les lignes des éléments structuraux permettent de profiter au maximum de l'espace disponible.

Die Linearität der Strukturelemente ermöglicht, daß die zur Verfügung stehende Fläche bestmöglichst ausgenutzt werden kann.

The dominant light tones contrast with the red of the mural painted on the back wall.

Les tons clairs dominants contrastent avec le rouge de la fresque sur le mur du fond.

Die vorherrschenden hellen Farbtönen kontrastieren mit dem Rot der Wandmalerei.

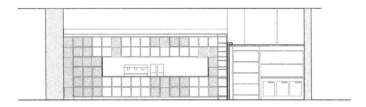

Candles and lamps help create
a much warmer atmosphere
on the lower floor of the locale.

*Bougies et lampes contribuent à créer
une atmosphère plus accueillante au
niveau inférieur du local.*

Kerzen und Lampen schaffen eine viel
wärmere Atmosphäre im unteren
Geschoß des Lokals.

Café Berlín

White is the cellar's dominant color,
though the furniture provides a
perfect color contrast.

*Le blanc prédomine au sous-sol mais
le mobilier offre le contrepoint
chromatique parfait.*

Weiß herrscht im Kellergeschoß vor,
die Möbel bilden einen idealen
Farbkontrast dazu.

Kosushi Bar

Arthur de Mattos Casas Arquitetura Design
São Paulo, Brasil
1999
Photography | Photo | Fotografie: Tuca Reinés.

The Kosushi Bar is an extremely well-known Japanese bar-restaurant in Sao Paulo. Despite this Brazilian city's important Japanese community, Japanese cooking was only introduced to the Western population some twenty years ago. Arthur de Mattos Casas explains the Kosushi Bar as an agreeable and hospitable setting decorated basically with Brazilian furnishing from the 1950s and 1960s. Colonial furniture in Brazilian wood, sofas positioned along the wall and a ceiling that shows the reinforced beams with metal and bamboo finishes are the basic features of its inner landscape. Undisputed star attractions are the affectionate sepia photographs of ordinary faces, that offer the customer a look back at a now distant time. Not in vain, one of the owners and also the sushi man of the Kosushi Bar affirms that these are portraits of his ancestors. Placed both on the walls and on totally independent modular systems, the images create an environment of great plastic force.

Le Kosushi Bar est un bar-restaurant japonais très renommé à Sao Paulo. Cette ville brésilienne, même si elle compte avec une importante communauté japonaise, n'a introduit la cuisine japonaise que depuis vingt ans. Arthur de Mattos Casas décrit le Kosushi Bar comme une ambiance agréable et accueillante, dont le décor est basé sur le mobilier brésilien des années cinquante-soixante. Bois du Brésil pour le mobilier colonial, canapés disposés le long du mur et plafond aux poutres apparentes renforcées par des finitions métalliques et du bambou sont les traits principaux du paysage intérieur. Les photographies sépia de visages touchants et humbles, protagonistes indéniables, offrent au client un regard vers un temps passé et lointain. Ce n'est pas en vain qu'un des propriétaires, sushi man du Kosushi Bar, affirme que ce sont les portraits de ces ancêtres. Placées sur les murs et sur les systèmes modulaires totalement indépendants, ces photos créent un environnement d'une grande force plastique.

Kosushi Bar ist ein renommiertes japanisches Bar-Restaurant in São Paulo. Obwohl in dieser brasilianischen Stadt eine wichtige japanische Kolonie vorhanden ist, machte sich die japanische Küche erst vor zwanzig Jahren bei der westlichen Bevölkerung breit. Arthur de Mattos Casas konzipierte das Kosushi Bar als ein angenehmes und gemütliches, hauptsächlich mit brasilianischen Möbelstücken der fünfziger und sechziger Jahre dekoriertes Ambiente. Im Kolonialstil gehaltenes Mobiliar aus brasilianischem Holz, an der Wand stehende Sofas und eine Decke, deren Balken mit Metallelementen und Bambus verstärkt wurden, sind die Grundmerkmale der Innenausstattung. Im Mittelpunkt stehen zweifellos die verblaßten Fotografien von freundlichen und bescheidenen Gesichtern, welche die Gäste in eine längt vergangene Zeit zurückversetzen. Nicht umsonst behauptet einer der Inhaber und zugleich sushi man des Kosushi Bar, daß es sich dabei um die Porträts seiner Vorfahren handele. Die sowohl an den Wänden als auch an den freistehenden Modulelementen angebrachten Bilder schaffen eine sehr plastische Umgebung.

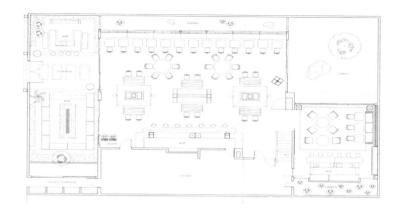

Wood is the main item making the Kosushi Bar a warm and pleasant place. The ceiling is of Brazilian wood and bamboo, strengthened with a metallic frame. The furniture is of natural textile fiber in the colonial style.

Le bois, surtout, transforme le Kosushi Bar en un espace chaud et agréable. Le plafond, revêtu de bois du Brésil et de bambou, est renforcé avec un système métallique, et les meubles sont en fibre textile naturelle de style colonial.

Die Wärme und Gemütlichkeit des Kosushi Bar ist hauptsächlich auf die Verwendung von Holz zurückzuführen. Die Decke wurde mit brasilianischem Holz und Bambus verkleidet und mit Metallelementen verstärkt; die Möbel im Kolonialstil sind aus Naturtextilfaser.

Kosushi Bar

Riva

KLMN Enterprises (Stefan Kulhorn, Nihaus Machicau)
Berlin, Deutschland
1999
Photography | Photo | Fotografie: Pablo Castagnola.

Impact and color. Riva is undoubtedly one of the most fashionable cocktail-bars in Berlin. Located under a viaduct, this bar is a renovated cellar whose warmth of shapes and tones makes every sip of our cocktail a delight. A large oval bar receives us as soon as we cross the door. Around it stand the red leather-topped revolving stools. Arches have been created in the ceilings and walls to make the surrounds of the bar not a conventional rectangle, but a new extremely wide ellipse that serves as a theatre proscenium. The orange and reddish colors used are by Oskar Putz and follow broad edges that turn into more oval lines. To both sides of the bar, groups of tables, chairs and red leather sofas are positioned. At the back, a large curtain of transparent gauze separates the room from the entrance.

Impact et couleur. Riva est, sans doute, un des établissements berlinois à la mode. Situé sous un viaduc, cet établissement est un sous-sol rénové où les formes et les couleurs chaudes invitent à savourer avec plaisir chaque gorgée de boisson. Un grand comptoir ovale nous accueille en entrant. Tout autour s'alignent les tabourets tapissés en rouge. Les plafonds et les murs sont en arc pour, que le périmètre du local ne reste pas un rectangle conventionnel, mais une nouvelle ellipse de grandes dimensions, servant de cadre scénique. Les tons orangés et rougeâtres appliqués sont l'oeuvre de Oskar Putz et décrivent de larges franges qui deviennent d'autres lignes ovales. De chaque côté du comptoir l'ensemble des tables, des chaises et des canapés en cuir rouge sont bien disposés. Au fond un grand rideau en tulle transparent sépare la salle de l'entrée.

Wirkungsvoll und farbenfroh. Riva ist zweifellos eine der Berliner Mode-Cocktail-Bars. Das unter einem Viadukt gelegene Lokal ist ein renovierter Keller, in dem die warmen Formen und Farben den Gast dazu einladen, seinen Drink bis auf den letzten Tropfen zu genießen. Gleich am Eingang befindet sich eine große ovale Theke und darum stehen mit rotem Leder gepolsterte Drehhocker. Um den herkömmlichen rechteckigen Umfang des Lokals in eine große elliptische Szenerie zu verwandeln, wurden Decke und Wände gewölbt. Die in orangenen und rötlichen Farbtönen gehaltenen breiten Streifen, ein Werk von Oskar Putz, betonen die im Lokal vorherrschende ovale Linienführung. Auf beiden Seiten der Theke befinden sich Sitzgruppen, bestehend aus Tischen, Stühlen und roten Ledersofas. Ganz hinten trennt ein großer durchsichtiger Vorhang aus Gaze den Saal vom Eingang.

The edges and rectangles of warm
colors used on the walls and ceiling
are the work of Oskar Putz.

Les franges et les rectangles aux couleurs
chaudes appliquées aux murs et au
plafond sont l'oeuvre de Oskar Putz.

Die in warmen Farben gehaltenen
Streifen und Rechtecke der Wände und
der Decke stammen von Oskar Putz.

Riva

Around the large oval bar stand the rotating stools upholstered in striking red leather.

Autour du grand comptoir ovale s'alignent les tabourets tournants tapissés en cuir rouge vif.

Rings um der großen ovalen Theke stehen mit leuchtend rotem Leder gepolsterte Drehhocker.

Anima Mia

Marcello Panza, Maria Borrelli, Claudio Giunnelli
Napoli, Italia
1999
Photography | Photo | Fotografie: Matteo Piazza.

From the night club to the soft piano bar. Contemporary irony from the '70s. With openly declared feeling, as the bar's name suggests, Anima Mia recovers the breath of a period that was highly creative in both music and design, the 1970s. Right in the old centre, next to the Piazza dei Martiri, heart of Naples' night life, a four-sided space has been upgraded, with the ceilings of chestnut beams left visible and its arches on the outside. The vigor of this structure contrasts with the interior decor full of colors: a theatre stage on which reds, greens and blues alternate. The mirrors wink at that recovered past when the use of plastic sheets, velvets, wood imitations and paper lamp-shades had just begun. The motifs are chosen with the utmost precision so as not to invade the space, leaving it free and diaphanous, space where even the piano takes on a dream-like appearance.

Du nigth club au soft piano bar. Ironie contemporaine des années 70. Comme le nom l'indique, avec un profond sentiment, l'Anima Mia récupère l'âme d'une époque très créative que ce soit quant à la musique que quant au design. Situé en pleine vieille ville, tout près de la Piazza dei Martiri, centre de la vie nocturne de Naples, l'espace tétraédrique a été rénové, en laissant apparaître les poutres en bois de châtaignier du plafond et les arcs de la façade. La vigueur du support contraste avec la décoration intérieure aux multiples couleurs: une scène théâtrale avec alternance des rouges, des verts et des bleus; les miroirs jettent un clin d'oeil à ce passé recréé où on a commencé à utiliser les laminés en plastique, les velours, les imitations du bois et les lampes en papier. Les motifs ont été sélectionnés avec grande précision pour ne pas trop envahir l'espace, préserver la liberté, la clarté où le piano devient protagoniste de rêve.

Von Nightclub hin zur Soft-Piano-Bar. Zeitgenössiche Ironie der 70er Jahre. Wie der Name der Bar schon besagt, wird offenbar in Anima Mia der Geist der 70er Jahre, einer sowohl auf dem Gebiet der Musik wie auch im Design sehr kreativen Epoche, zurück ins Leben gerufen. Das Lokal liegt mitten in der Altstadt, am Piazza dei Martiri, dem Mittelpunkt des neapolitanischen Nachtlebens. Der tetraedrische Raum mit den nun sichtbaren Deckenbalken aus Kastanienholz und den Bögen an der Fassade wurde umgebaut. Die kraftvollen Stützelemente kontrastieren mit der farbenfrohen Innendekoration: eine Szenerie bei der sich rote, grüne und blaue Farbtöne abwechseln; die Spiegel reflektieren die im Lokal evozierte vergangene Zeit, in der man begann, Laminate, Samtstoffe, Holzimitationen und Papierlampen zu verwenden. Die Motive wurden sorgfältig ausgewählt, um den Raum diaphan und übersichtlich erscheinen zu lassen, wo sogar das Klavier die Gäste zum Träumen einlädt.

The homage to 1970s creativity is totally contemporary. For example, areas such as this bar in the corner bring to mind images of night clubs from the past, without converting them into yellowing snap-shots. The toilets with silhouettes of people on the doors recall the plastic graphics of that period.

L'hommage à la créativité des années 70 est totalement contemporain. Ainsi, les zones créées comme ce comptoir dans un coin ravive les images passées de night clubs, sans les convertir en instantanées jaunâtres. Les toilettes avec les silhouettes indicatrices sur les portes rappellent les graphisme plastique de cette époque.

Die Ehrung der Kreativität der 70er Jahre ist ganz aktuell. So rufen die geschaffenen Bereiche, wie die abseits stehende Theke, Bilder von Nachtclubs aus der Vergangenheit wach, ohne daß sie wie vergilbte Fotos wirken. Die Waschräume mit den Silhouetten an den Türen erinnern an die plastische Graphik jener Epoche.

Anima Mia

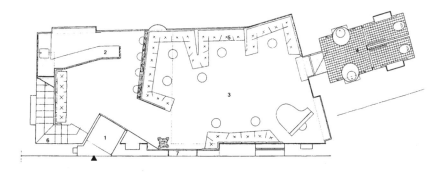

A diaphanous, free space has been achieved. It lets the motifs from the '70s breathe, such as the Falkland lamps, by Bruno Munari, or the plastic by Karim Azzabi that was so popular in its day and is used now in various decor items.

Un espace diaphane a été obtenu, libre qui laisse liberté aux motifs des années 70, comme les lampes Falkland, de Bruno Munari, où le plastique de Karim Azzabi, si populaire à son époque et employé aujourd'hui en différents éléments de décoration.

Es wurde ein diaphaner und übersichtlicher Raum geschaffen, in dem die ausgewählten Motive der 70er Jahre -die von Bruno Munari entworfenen Falkland-Lampen und der damals so beliebte und heute bei verschiedenen Dekorationselementen verwandte Kunststoff von Karim Azzabi - voll zur Geltung kommen.

Bica do Sapato

Margarida Grácio Nunes, Fernando Sanchez Salvador

Lisboa, Portugal
1999
Photography | Photo | Fotografie: Ana Paula Carvalho,
Fernando Sanchez Salvador.

In Pessoa's city, fusion takes the name of Bica do Sapato. Choosing with the most exquisite taste the best French taste, the oriental fashion for sushi and spectacular decor, and mixing it all up with Portuguese sensibility, are the strong points of a spot where the most modern characters of the Lisbon night meet, a highly sophisticated clientèle. Located in the always magical quarter of Alfama, it emerges from a former two-storey warehouse. On the line of trends in other European cities, the proposal is of a restaurant functioning as the ante-chamber of a disco. There are three separate areas. On the ground floor are the cafeteria and restaurant, separated by a small waiting-room, dominated by a futuristic panel wrapped in a huge metal screen that rises to the top floor which contains the sushi-bar. Well worth noting are the extravagant objects brought together here, especially those harking back to the 1950s imagination. A light-filled innovative recipe.

Dans la ville de Pessoa, la fusion prend nom de Bica do Sapato. Choisir avec un très fin sens le meilleur des saveurs françaises, la tendance orientale du sushi et une décoration spectaculaire, le tout avec le romantisme portugais, sont les réussites d'un lieu où se donnent rendez-vous les personnages les plus modernes de la nuit de Lisbonne, clientèle très cosmopolite. Situé dans le quartier de l'Alfama, qui n'a pas perdu de sa magie, émerge de ce qui était autrefois un magasin duplex. En suivant la tendance d'autres villes européennes, la formule du restaurant fonctionnant comme antichambre de la discothèque, a été proposée. L'espace se divise en trois aires. Au rez-de-chaussée, la cafétéria et le restaurant sont séparés par une petite salle d'attente où un panneau futuriste enveloppé dans un grand écran en métal s'élève jusqu'à l'étage supérieur où se trouve le sushi-bar. Il faut remarquer la réunion d'objets extravagants, en particulier ceux qui rachètent de l'imagination les années cinquante. Une recette lumineuse et innovatrice.

In der Stadt Pessoas heißt die Verschmelzung Bica do Sapato. Die sorgfältige Auswahl der besten französische Gerichte, der orientalische Sushi-Trend und eine spektakuläre Dekoration, gemischt mit portugiesischem Feeling, sind der Clou eines Lokals, das von den modernsten Kreisen des Lissaboner Nachtlebens, einem sehr kosmopolitischem Publikum, aufgesucht wird. Bica do Sapato liegt im magischen Lissaboner Alfama-Viertel und ist in einem ehemaligen zweistöckigen Lager untergebracht. Dem Trend anderer europäischen Städte folgend, wurde das Lokal als ein Vor-Disko-Restaurant konzipiert. Der Raum ist in drei Bereiche gegliedert. Im Erdgeschoß befinden sich die Cafeteria und das Restaurant, voneinander getrennt durch einen kleinen Warteraum, wo sich ein auffallendes, von einem Metallvorhang eingehülltes Wandpaneel bis zum zweiten Stockwerk, in dem die Sushi-Bar untergebracht ist, erhebt. Hervorzuheben sind die hier ausgestellten seltsamen Objekte, insbesondere diejenigen, welche den Erfindergeist der 50er Jahre wieder in Erinnerung rufen. Ein leuchtendes und innovatives Rezept.

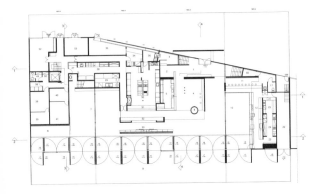

The unmatched views over the River Tagus and its style as a restaurant and bar make Bica do Sapato one of the sophisticated musts of Lisbon. Various suggestive mixtures of retro effects and art pieces mingle under a single roof. The panel on the wall is one of the locale's original successes.

Les vues exclusives sur le fleuve Tage et la proposition comme local restaurant-bar font de Bica do Sapato un des référents cosmopolites de Lisbonne. Différentes propositions sous un unique toit intercalent des effets rétro et des exemples artistiques. Le panneau sur le mur est une des réussites innovatrices.

Der einmalige Ausblick über den Tejo und das vorgeschlagene Konzept als Restaurant und Drinkbar lassen Bica do Sapato zu einem Begriff für die kosmopolitischen Kreise Lissabons werden. Verschiedene Möglichkeiten unter einem Dach, bei denen sich Retro-Effekte und Kunstwerke einander abwechseln. Das Wandpaneel ist eines der innovativen Glanzstücke des Lokals.

Bica do Sapato

Some of its decorations come from exceptional collections. The large panel in the picture, with its strong futuristic symbolism, is one of the plastic art-works to be found in this most up-to-date meeting-place. Luminous balloons and other bizarre kinds of lamps are an apt and witty way of lighting the locale.

Certains des objets décoratifs font partie de collections privilégiées. Le grand panneau montrant l'image, avec un fort symbole futuriste, est une des créations plastiques qui se donnent rendez-vous en ce lieu à la modernité la plus actuelle. Des ballons lumineux et d'autres lampes hétéroclites apportent une solution curieuse à l'éclairage.

Einige der hier ausgestellten Dekorationsgegenstände gehören zu renommierten Sammlungen. Das große Wandpaneel, auf dem futuristische Symbole dargestellt sind, ist eine der plastischen Kreationen, die in diesem Treffpunkt der Modernität zu besichtigen sind. Leuchtkugeln und andere ungewöhnliche Lampen sind einfallsreiche Lösungen zur Beleuchtung des Lokals.

La Verònica

Julia Schulz-Dornburg

Barcelona, España
1996
Enlargement | Agramdissement | Erweiterung: 1999
Photography | Photo | Fotografie: Miquel Bargalló.

The Verònica is divided into two almost symmetrical parts on either side of the central axis that is the kitchen and services area. As such, it looks almost exactly the same at both its entrances: one from the George Orwell square and the other from the Verònica square that gives this bar-restaurant its name. Right in the middle of Barcelona's Gothic quarter, this connection, highlighted inside by a line of lights from one door to the other, is the locale's most original feature. The bare bulbs hanging from the ceiling are countered by a range of warm colors on the walls, with alternating colors inspiring diversity and contributing towards the feeling of depth. The white compound-wood benches are also unifying, their set-in lights stretching out on both sides. They serve a triple function: to muffle surrounding noise, give background light and be a comfortable place to sit.

La Verònica se dédouble en deux parties presque symétriques sur un axe central qui constitue la zone de cuisine et les services. Ainsi, les deux entrées offrent une image identique: l'une est sur la place George Orwell et l'autre sur la Place de la Verònica qui lui donne le nom. En plein quartier gothique barcelonais, ce bar-restaurant est connu par cette particularité soulignée à l'intérieur grâce à une ligne de lumières traversant le local. Le nudité des ampoules suspendues au plafond est en contraste avec une gamme de couleurs chaudes sur les murs, en alternance avec les nuances différentes qui inspirent une diversité et qui contribuent en plus a augmenter la sensation de profondeur. Les bancs en DM blanc contribuent à l'unité avec leurs lumières encastrées qui s'étendent de chaque côté et qui ont une triple fonction: mitiger le bruit ambiant, être une source de lumière générale et en un endroit où s'asseoir confortablement.

La Verònica ist in zwei fast symmetrische Teile gegliedert, wobei der Küchen- und Dienstbereich die Mittelachse darstellt. Dies hat zur Folge, daß das Lokal von den beiden Eingängen her ein fast identisches Bild abgibt. Diese befinden sich jeweils am Plaza George Orwell und am Plaza de la Verònica, nach dem das Lokal benannt wurde. Wichtigstes Merkmal dieses mitten im gotischen Viertel Barcelonas gelegenen Bar-Restaurants ist die durch eine Linie von Glühlampen hervorgehobene Verbindung von einer Eingangstür zur anderen. Die Schlichtheit der an der Decke hängenden Glühbirnen wurde mit den warmen Farben der Wände ausgeglichen. Jede Wand weist eine andere Farbe auf, was Abwechslung in den Raum bringt und ihn gleichzeitig optisch vergrößert. Eine vereinheitlichende Wirkung haben auch die Sitzbänke aus weißem DM mit eingebauten Lichtern, die auf beiden Seiten stehen und eine dreifache Funktion erfüllen: den Lärm im Raum dämpfen, Licht spenden und eine bequeme Sitzgelegenheit bieten.

The whiteness of ceilings,
benches and furniture contrasts with
the range of warm tones
on the walls of the locale.

*La base blanche formée
par les plafonds, les bancs et le mobilier
de base contrastent avec la gamme de
nuances chaudes appliquées sur les
murs du local.*

Das Weiß der Decken, der Sitzbänke
und des Grundmobiliars kontrastiert
mit den warmen Farbtönen der
Wände des Lokals.

La Verònica

Each wall is painted in a different color to give a feeling of diversity as well as achieve a feel of greater depth.

Chaque mur a été peint d'une couleur différente pour renforcer la sensation de diversité et augmenter l'effet de profondeur.

Jede Wand wurde in einer anderen Farbe gestrichen, um Abwechslung in den Raum zu bringen und ihn gleichzeitig optisch zu vergrößern.

Toast

4^{IV}

London, United Kingdom
1999
Photography | Photo | Fotografie: Chas Wilshere.

Toast is a bar-restaurant in Hampstead that turns into a dance hall on Monday nights for those eccentrics who like to put a good face on the start of the damp, cold London week. Restrained good taste creates the effect of a high-class department store. It boasts clean finishes and soft lines that often, however, merge into the very sharpest design trends. The furniture, for example, consists of chairs imported from Milan and tables of varnished walnut. In the VIP area, a curving wall has been padded with caramel-color leather; and, in contrast, the other walls have a rough varnish in cream colors. However, the most interesting part is hidden behind the matt black granite bar, where the black back wall has been covered with smoked glass. The lighting breaks the refined monotone of the decor: it consists of thin tubular lamps and circular ceiling mirrors that trick the eye.

Le Toast est un bar-restaurant de Hampstead qui se transforme en une salle de danse le lundi soir pour les excentriques aimant affronter les humides et froides semaines londoniennes avec bonne humeur. Un prudent savoir-faire le dévoile comme un de ces grands magasins à la finition chic. Il se vante de ses finitions nettes aux lignes douces qui souvent emboîtent le pas aux tendances les plus aiguisées du design. Ce n'est pas en vain que le mobilier comprend des chaises importées de Milan et des tables en bois de noyer verni. Dans la zone vip, un mur courbe a été tapissé de cuir couleur caramel. Pour harmoniser, le restant des murs a reçu un vernis aux nuances beiges inégales. Mais l'autre zone, plus intéressante, se cache derrière le comptoir en granite noir mate, sur le mur arrière noir où on a appliqué des verres fumés. L'éclairage, à partir de minces lampes tubulaires et des miroirs circulaires qui, du plafond, trompent l'oeil du client, rompt la monotonie raffinée de la décoration.

Toast ist ein in Hampstead gelegenes Bar-Restaurant, das sich montags in einen Tanzsaal für Exzentriker, die die feuchte, kalte Londoner Woche lustig beginnen wollen, verwandelt. Wegen seines klassischen Aussehens könnte es mit einem eleganten Kaufhaus verwechselt werden. Die reinen und sanften Linien verfallen jedoch oft in die gewagtesten Designertrends. Nicht umsonst stellen aus Mailand importierte Stühle, sowie lackierte Tische aus Nußbaumholz das Mobiliar dar. Im Vip-Bereich wurde eine nach innen gewölbte Wand mit karamellfarbenem Leder gepolstert. Zur Abstufung wurde an den übrigen Wänden cremefarbener Lack unregelmäßig aufgetragen. Aber das Interessanteste verbirgt sich hinter der Theke aus schwarzem mattem Granitstein, denn die schwarze Wand wurde mit Rauchglas versehen. Die Beleuchtung mit schlanken röhrenförmigen Lampen und an der Decke angebrachten runden Spiegeln, welche den Gast optisch täuschen, steht im Kontrast zur eintönigen, vornehmen Dekoration.

The sober and elegant furniture contrasts
with an excellent set of lights and circular
mirrors which, in an amusing visual trick,
tests out the onlooker's perception.

*Le mobilier au style sobre et élégant contraste
avec un excellent jeu de lumières et de miroirs
circulaires qui, comme un drôle de trompe-oeil,
met à l'épreuve la perception du spectateur.*

Das schlichte und elegante Mobiliar steht im
Kontrast zum außergewöhnlichen Spiel der
Lichter und runden Spiegel, das mit einer lustigen
optischen Täuschung die Wahrnehmungsfähigkeit
der Gäste auf die Probe stellt

Toast

The glass in this bar-restaurant shows a Toast logo reminiscent of the classic Lucky Strike logo.

Les verres de cet établissement révèlent un logo du Toast qui semble réviser la classique iconographie des Lucky Strike.

An den Glasscheiben des Lokals prangt das Logo des Toast, welches an das Markenzeichen von Lucky Strike erinnert.

Sushita

Jorge Varela
Madrid, España
2000.
Photography | Photo | Fotografie: Juan Pérez Iscla.

A sushi-bar located in a building in Madrid's nineteenth-century expansion. The former structure of Sushita, that consisted of small rooms off a corridor, has been converted into a wide space which respects the emblematic sides and recovers the original floors. In addition, a profound refit has sought to recreate the atmosphere of ordinary popular restaurants in Japanese cities. Large strips of paper run along the walls and roof, creating a subtle and ethereal skin that softens the austerity of the surfaces. Back-lit steel disks with saturated color that complement the light from the paper lanterns, and wooden hoardings lined with collages of Japanese newspapers, cage-lanterns and large-format printing illuminations have also been introduced. They highlight the sushi-bar's image of an alleyway lost among chaotic buildings.

Un sushi-bar situé dans un bâtiment du dix-neuvième dans l'ensanche madrilène. La structure ancienne de Sushita, qui était formée de petites pièces articulées autour d'un couloir s'est transformée en un large espace où les paramètres latéraux et emblématiques ont été respectés, et les sols d'origine ont été récupérés. De plus, un profond travail scénique a été réalisé pour recréer l'esthétique des locaux de soupe populaire typiques des quartiers japonais. De grandes bandes de papier longent les murs et le plafond créant une peau subtile et éthérée qui nuance l'austérité des surfaces. Des disques en acier rétro-illuminés avec une couleur saturée complètent la lumière des ballons en papier et, en plus, des panneaux en bois recouverts d'un collage de presse japonaise, des lampes cages et des luminaires typographiques au grand format rehaussent cette image d'impasse perdue parmi de chaotiques édifices.

Eine in einem Madrider Gebäude des 19. Jahrhunderts untergebrachte Sushi-Bar. Die ehemalige Struktur des Sushita, bestehend aus kleinen, von einem Flur ausgehenden Räumen, wurde zu einem großflächigen Raum umgestaltet, bei dem die charakteristischen Seitenwände beibehalten und die ursprünglichen Fußböden wiederhergestellt wurden. Außerdem wurde mit Sorgfalt die Ästhetik der einfachen Gasthäuser der japanischen Arbeiterviertel nachgebildet. Breite Papierstreifen sind an Wand und Decke entlang gespannt und schaffen eine hauchfeine, ätherische Hülle, welche die Kargheit der Oberflächen mildert. An den Wänden hängen von hinten beleuchtete Stahlscheiben, deren sattfarbenes Licht das der Papierkugeln ergänzt. Installiert wurden außerdem mit Collages aus japanischen Zeitungsausschnitten bezogene Holzpaneele, Käfiglampen und große typographische Leuchten, die den Eindruck einer zwischen chaotischen Gebäuden liegende, verlassene Gasse noch verstärkt.

A single twelve meter-long table
stretches throughout the Sushita,
unifying its character of sushi-bar
and spontaneous dining-room.

*Une unique table de douze mètres
de longueur s'étend tout au long du
Sushita, ce qui souligne le caractère
de sushi-bar et de salle-à-manger
spontanée, planifiée dans le local.*

Ein einziger, zwölf Meter langer
Tisch erstreckt sich über das
Lokal und verbindet die beiden
Zweckbestimmungen des Sushita:
Sushi-Bar und Speiseraum.

Long strips of Japanese paper run along
the walls and the ceiling, breaking the
dominant color. Wood hoardings holding
collages from Japanese newspapers have
also been installed.

*Les grandes bandes de papier japonais
parcourent les murs et le plafond
et rompent les couleurs dominantes.
Des panneaux en bois ont été installés,
sur lesquels a été appliqué un collage
de presse japonaise.*

Die breiten Streifen aus japanischem
Papier sind an der Wand und der Decke
gespannt und stehen im Kontrast zur
ansonsten farbenfrohen Dekoration.
Es wurden auch mit Collages aus
japanischen Zeitungsausschnitten
versehene Holzpaneele installiert.

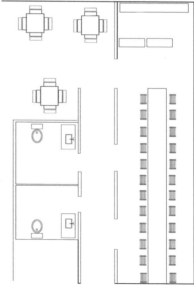

Sushita

Code

Stefano Severi

Carpi, Italia
2000
Photography | Photo | Fotografie: Alberto Ferrero.

In a restored old building, Code combines in masterly fashion traditional elements with avant-garde design. Its wooden ceilings with beams exposed have been recovered, along with other former structures. However, they have been given a new treatment through the introduction of color and new materials. This is the case of the white marble of some walls or of the bronze lighting from the false round windows. In addition, new pieces in strong shapes and colors have been introduced. Examples include the false ceilings with orange backgrounds, the wood furniture varnished white and the stainless-steel chairs with red leather cushions material also used in the upholstery of the benches at the sides. A final touch. Code has a highly impressive source of warm lighting: the neon along the front of the broad bar.

Installé dans un ancien bâtiment rénové, le Code se caractérise par une combinaison magistrale des éléments traditionnels avec le design d'avant-garde. D'une part, ses plafonds en bois avec des poutres apparentes ont été refaits, ainsi que d'autres structures existantes, rénovées par la couleur et les nouveaux matériaux appliqués; par exemple certains murs en marbre blanc ou bien l'éclairage couleur bronze de certaines fausses lucarnes rondes. D'autre part, des pièces nouvellement créées aux formes et aux couleurs très caractéristiques ont été ajoutées. Les faux plafonds aux fonds orangés, le mobilier en bois laqué blanc ou les chaises à la structure en acier inox, les sièges en cuir rouge, matière tapissant également les bancs situés le long du mur, sont quelques exemples. Une dernière touche, l'éclairage du local part d'une source chaude à grand effet: les néons qui délimitent le panneau du vaste comptoir.

Das in einem alten, renovierten Gebäude untergebrachte Code zeichnet sich durch die geniale Kombinierung von traditionellen Elementen mit avantgardistischem Design aus. Auf der einen Seite wurden die Balkendecken, wie auch andere schon vorhandene Strukturen, restauriert, obwohl dies auf innovative Art und Weise unter Verwendung von Farben und neuen Materialien geschah. Es handelt sich dabei um den weißen Marmor mancher Wände und um die bronzefarbene Beleuchtung der runden blinden Fenster. Auf der anderen Seite kamen neue, stark von ihren Formen und Farben geprägte Elemente hinzu. Die abgehängten Decken mit orangenem Hintergrund, das Mobiliar aus weiß lackiertem Holz, sowie die Stühle mit Strukturen aus rostfreiem Stahl und Sitzen aus rotem Leder - ebenso bei den seitlich angeordneten Sitzbänken zu finden- sind einige Beispiele dafür. Abgerundet wird die Dekoration von den die Vorderfront der großen Theke abgrenzenden Neonlichtern, einer auffallenden Lichtquelle, die Wärme ausströmt.

The ceilings with their beams
exposed contrast with avant-
garde design items, such as the
stainless-steel chairs and tables.

*Les plafonds en bois aux poutres
apparentes contrastent avec les
éléments de design d'avant-garde
comme les tables et les chaises à la
structure en acier.*

Die Balkendecken kontrastieren mit
den im avantgardistischen Design
gehaltenen Elementen wie die
Tische und Stühle mit Stahlstruktur.

The orange neon highlights the edge of the false ceilings, just as the red and blue neon strips light up the front of the bar.

Les néons couleur orange suivent le périmètre des faux plafonds comme les tubes lumineux rouges et bleus rehaussent le panneau du comptoir.

Die orangenen Neonlichter zeichnen den Außenrand der abgehängten Decken ab, so wie auch die roten und blauen Leuchtröhren die Vorderfront der Theke hervorheben.

Code

IllyCaffé

Claudio Silvestrin architects

Trieste, Italia
2000
Photography | Photo | Fotografie: Alberto Ferrero.

An oasis of well-being in periods of frantic movement. Recover the "luxury of pausing" appears to be the commission that Claudio Silvestrin's team has carried out in the first Illy Caffé cafeteria, by making natural values run in tune with the chosen materials. A contemporary space, but also an archaic one, through this look into the past that is revealed by the use of the earth/water duality. Earth is present in the paving stone and the bottom of the walls; in the opaque marble at the top of the walls that surround completely the site; and in the wood and rusted brass that reflect the color of coffee. The blue lights and the bowl of water bring in the element of water. A huge arch, protected by a large sheet of beveled glass which is sliced in the middle by a transparent thin opening, emerges: a window for looking both inwards and outwards. Privacy is the area's dominant sensation. Finally the halogen lamps give the soft light that helps you appreciate a good cup of coffee.

Une parenthèse de bien-être dans un temps d'agitation frénétique. Récupérer le "luxe de la pause" semble être la tâche que l'équipe de Claudio Silvestrin a su mettre en évidence dans le premier établissement de Illy Café, en faisant en sorte que la valeur de la nature se développe en syntonie à partir de matériaux sélectionnés. Un espace contemporain tout en restant archaïque en raison du regard vers le passé qui apparaît dans le binôme terre/eau. La première, présente dans la pierre du sol et la base des murs, dans le marbre opaque, sur la partie supérieure des murs qui contournent sans fin les lieux, et dans le bois et le laiton oxydé rappelant la couleur café. Les lumières bleues et le bassin d'eau rapprochent l'élément aqueux. Comme une devanture commune à l'intérieur et à l'extérieur, émerge un grand arc protégé par une grande plaque en verre poli, coupé juste au milieu par un faisceau transparent. L'ambiance est dominée par une sensation d'intimité. Finalement, les lampes halogènes offrent la lumière diffuse qui convient si bien à la dégustation d'un bon café.

Eine Oase in der Hektik des modernen Lebens. Den Genuß des "Luxus einer Pause" wieder möglich zu machen ist anscheinend der Auftrag, den das Team von Claudio Silvestrin in der ersten Cafeteria von IllyCaffé erfolgreich ausgeführt hat, indem die ausgewählten Materialien harmonisch zusammenspielen. Ein zeitgenössisch wirkender, aber wegen des hier verwandten, die Vergangenheit wachrufenden Binoms Erde/Wasser zugleich archaisch anmutender Ort. Der Stein des Fußbodens und der Wandsockel, der undurchsichtige Marmor am oberen Teil der Wände des ganzen Lokals und schließlich das Holz und der oxydierte Messing, welche an den Farbton des Kaffees erinnern, stellen die Erde dar. Die blauen Lichter und das Wasserbecken repräsentieren das flüssige Element. Als Fenster nach außen, wie auch nach innen hin, erhebt sich ein großer Bogen, der mit einer genau in der Mitte von einem durchsichtigen Glasstreifen unterbrochenen durchscheinenden Glasscheibe verschlossen ist. Dadurch herrscht im Lokal eine intime Atmosphäre. Schließlich reicht das diffuse Licht der Halogenlampen zum Genießen eines guten Kaffees völlig aus.

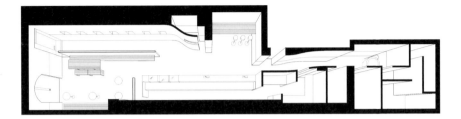

Visible order, the use of natural materials and the delicate lines on the furniture are synonym of a staging that looks for the natural effect. On the continuous wall, parallel to the monolithic bar, cavities with light built in exhibit the collection of Illy cups and other items used to serve coffee. Behind the bar other small holes take the sugar bowls and various bottles.

L'ordre si visible, l'utilisation de matériaux naturels et les lignes délicates du mobilier sont synonyme d'une mise en scène revendiquant l'effet naturel. Sur le mur continu, parallèle au comptoir monolithique, des cavités avec des lumières encastrées accueillent une collection de petites tasses Illy ou d'autres ustensiles du service de café. Derrière le comptoir, d'autres petites cavités accueillent les sucriers et différentes bouteilles.

Die sichtbare Anordnung der Elemente, die Verwendung von aus der Natur stammenden Materialien, sowie die feingezeichneten Linien des Mobiliars weisen darauf hin, daß die Natur bei der Gestaltung des Lokals im Vordergrund stand. Die parallel zur wuchtigen Theke verlaufende Wand hat beleuchtete Nischen, in denen die Illy-Tassensammlung und andere Service-Teile ausgestellt sind. Hinter der Theke berherbergen weitere kleine Nischen die Zuckerdose und verschiedene Flaschen.

IllyCaffé

Hakkasan

Jestico & Whildes, Christian Liagre
London, United Kingdom
2001
Photography | Photo | Fotografie: Chas Wilshere.

Absolutely disconcerting and mysterious. This is Hakkasan, a large bar-restaurant located in Hanway Square, London. The shine of the neon and blue lights illuminating the front of the long bar and the back walls are an outer-space context for this setting half-way between an updated industrial aesthetic and the exotic Oriental touches contributed by certain concrete items. The wood with which the chairs and tables are made, the shutters and light panels separating the dining area from the rest of the premises and some private areas with sofas, poufs and low tables make up the warm half of Hakassan. Then, the omnipresent blue lighting, the use of glass and other cold materials such as steel complete a suggestive but contradictory setting.

Tout à fait déconcertant et mystérieux. Ainsi est Hakkasan, un grand bar-restaurant situé dans la place londonienne Hanway. L'éclat des néons et des lumières bleues sur la partie frontale du long comptoir et les murs du fond constitue le cadre galactique de ce scénario à mi-chemin entre l'esthétique industrielle révisée et mise à jour et les nuances exotiques et orientales de quelques éléments concrets. Le bois des tables et des chaises, les jalousies et les panneaux légers séparant les zones de salle-à-manger du reste du local et la conception de certains privés avec canapés, poufs et tables basses constituent cet hémisphère chaud du local. Par contre, le bleu omniprésent dans l'éclairage, l'utilisation du verre et d'autres matériaux froids comme l'acier conforment le cadre général aussi contradictoire que suggestif.

Echt verwirrend und geheimnisvoll. So ist Hakkasan, ein geräumiges, am Londoner Hanway Square gelegenes Bar-Restaurant. Der Schein der Neonlampen und blauen Lichter an der Vorderfront der langen Theke und an den hinteren Wänden schafft dieser Szenerie, die sowohl von der aktualisierten Industrie-Ästhetik als auch vom exotischen und orientalischen Hauch einiger Elemente geprägt wird, eine galaktische Atmosphäre. Das Holz der Tische und Stühle und der Gitter und leichten Paneele, die den Speisesaal vom übrigen Teil des Lokals trennen, sowie die Ausstattung mancher Séparées mit Sofas, Puffs und niedrigen Tischen stellen die warme Hemisphäre des Lokals dar. Das allgegenwärtige Blau der Beleuchtung, sowie die Verwendung von Glas und anderen kalten Materialien wie Stahl schafft dagegen einen gegensätzlichen und suggestiven Schauplatz.

The entire dining area is separated off by shutters and panels that could well have been inspired by Oriental decor.

Toute la zone de la salle-à-manger est séparée du reste du local par des jalousies et des panneaux qui semblent avoir été inspirés des décorations orientales.

Der gesamte Bereich des Speiseraums wird durch orientalisch aussehende Gitter und Paneele vom übrigen Teil des Lokals getrennt.

Hakkasan

The basic lighting comes
from the blue panels on the back walls
and the front of the long bar.

*L'éclairage général du local provient
de panneaux aux nuances bleues placés
sur les murs du fond et sur la partie frontale
du long comptoir.*

Die blauen Leuchtfelder der hinteren Wände
und der Vorderfront der Theke stellen die
Hauptbeleuchtung des Lokals dar.

Piccolo Bar

Andrea Meirana

Savona, Italia
1998
Photography | Photo | Fotografie: Alberto Ferrero.

The Piccolo Bar, in a XIX th-century building in a central street of Savona, was originally a closed space with limited views. For this reason, it was decided to decompose the visual lines in order to create an effect of expanded space. Following a line around the idea of reduction, as a purifying element of space, each detail in the decor was reduced to its natural essence. The result is forms and materials that evoke spaces and atmospheres that belong to our collective imaginations. Aesthetically, the solution is a Piccolo Bar dominated by straight lines, rigorous shapes, minimalism, borrowing a repertoire from theatre architecture. In this context, the bar is the stage for the work of the barman, the new actor in a magical space.

Le Piccolo Bar, situé dans un édifice du XIXe siècle d'une rue du centre de Savona, était à l'origine un espace fermé aux perspectives limitées. C'est pourquoi on décida de décomposer les plans visuels pour créer un effet de dilatation de l'espace. En suivant une ligne de recherche autour du concept de réduction, comme facteur purificateur de l'espace, chacun des éléments de la décoration a été reprise dans son essence naturelle. Le résultat est un produit de formes et de matériaux évoquant des espaces et des atmosphères appartenant à l'imaginaire collectif. Esthétiquement, la solution dernière nous présente un Piccolo Bar où prédominent les lignes droites, les volumes minimalistes, par l'emprunt au répertoire de l'architecture théâtrale. Dans ce contexte, l'établissement est la scène de travail du barman, maintenant converti en auteur dans un espace de magie.

Die in einem in der Innenstadt Savonas gelegenen Gebäude des 19. Jahrhunderts untergebrachte Piccolo Bar war ursprünglich ein enger, unübersichtlicher Raum. Aus diesem Grunde wurden zur optischen Vergrößerung des Raumes die visuellen Felder zerlegt. Auf der Suche des Reduktionkonzeptes als Reinigungselement des Raumes wurde jedes einzelne Detail der Dekoration nach seiner natürlichen Bestimmung eingesetzt. Das Ergebnis sind Formen und Materialien, die zum allgemeinen Gedächtnis gehörende Räume und Atmosphären evozieren. Rein ästhetisch gesehen ist das Endergebnis eine Piccolo Bar, in der gerade Linien, ganz klar abgezeichnete Formen und minimalistische Räume vorherrschen, wobei typische Merkmale der Theaterarchitektur übernommen wurden. In diesem Kontext wird das Lokal zum Schauplatz der Arbeit des Barmans, welcher hier die köstlichsten Drinks zaubert.

Whether from inside the bar or
from the street, breaking down the
lines of vision creates a Piccolo Bar
perceived as a wider space.

*Sia dall'interno del locale che dalla
strada, la scomposizione dei piani visivi
produce l'effetto di far apparire il
Piccolo Bar come uno spazio
percettivo dilatato.*

Sowohl vom Inneren des Lokals aus
als auch von der Straße her gesehen
schafft die Zerlegung der visuellen
Felder eine optische Vergrößerung
der Piccolo Bar.

The Piccolo Bar searches for
a line of essentials and purity
in all its elements. The result
is a venue of straight lines,
rigorous shapes, and minimalism.

*Il Piccolo Bar punta su una linea
di ricerca a favore dell'essenzialità
e della depurazione di tutti gli
elementi. Il risultato è una proposta
basata sulle linee rette, le forme
severe ed i volumi minimalisti.*

In der Piccolo Bar setzt man
auf die Suche nach dem
Wesentlichen und auf die
Beseitigung aller überflüssigen
Elemente. Das Ergebnis sind
gerade Linien, klar abgezeichnete
Formen und minimalistische
Räume.

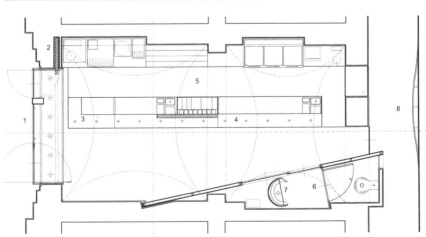

Piccolo Bar

Isola a

Andrew Martins
London, United Kingdom
2001
Photography | Photo | Fotografie: Chas Wilshere.

Perfect for solitary souls, Isola is a refuge for lovers of fast food and so of velocity itself. It is no coincidence that this is the only locale in Europe whose upholstery is made by the Ferrari car company. The famous red of the Italian escutcheon and brand-name is also the guiding principle of Isola's decor. Present in the PVC covering the restored poufs, chairs, stools and sofas, its extremely vivid color contrasts with the white of the basic structures, the metal of the circular columns and some finishes, and of the panels lining the floor, the bar front and the back wall. These lighter tones are reinforced by the abundant natural light that penetrates through the wide windows, where red is also featured in the locale's logo.

Idéal pour les âmes solitaires, l'Isola est le refuge des amateurs de fast-food et par conséquent, de la vitesse. Ce n'est pas pour rien que c'est le seul lieu d'Europe dont les tapisseries ont été confectionnées par la maison automobile Ferrari. Le rouge de l'emblème de la marque italienne est aussi le fil conducteur de la décoration de l'établissement. Présent dans le skay tapissant poufs, tabourets, et sofas récupérés, son extrême vivacité contraste avec le blanc des structures de base, par exemple le métal des colonnes cylindriques et de certains détails de finition; le rouge est également présent dans les panneaux recouvrant le sol, le devant du comptoir et le mur du fond. Ces éléments aux nuances plus claires sont renforcées par l'abondante lumière naturelle qui passe par les grandes baies vitrées où le rouge se retrouve sur le logo du local.

Für einsame Seelen ideal. Isola ist ein Zufluchtsort für Fans des Fast-Foods und folglich der Geschwindigkeit. Nicht umsonst handelt es sich dabei um das einzige Lokal Europas dessen Sitzbezüge vom Equipe und Automobilhersteller Ferrari stammen. Das typische Rot der italienischen Marke ist außerdem das Leitmotiv der Dekoration des Lokals. Der äußerst intensive rote Farbton des Kunststoffleders der Puffs, Stühle, Hocker und restaurierte Sofas steht im Kontrast zum Weiß der Grundstrukturen, zum Metall der runden Säulen und anderen Elementen, sowie zu den Holzpaneelen des Fußbodens, der Vorderfront der Theke und der hinteren Wand. Diese in helleren Farbtönen gehaltene Elemente werden durch das Licht, das durch die großen, mit dem roten Logo des Lokals versehenen Fenster hereinströmt, noch mehr hervorgehoben.

The red PVC of Ferrari can be seen in the chairs, stools, poufs and sofas throughout the locale as a unifying element.

Le skay rouge apporté par la maison Ferrari est présent sur les chaises, tabourets, poufs et canapés comme élément unifiant l'ambiance du local.

Das von Ferrari stammende rote Kunstleder ist an Stühlen, Hockern, Puffs und Sofas zu finden und macht das Lokal zu einem einheitlichen Ganzen.

Isola_

The basic white structures and the
metallic columns offset the dominant
red of the furniture perfectly.

*Les structures de base blanches et les
colonnes métalliques sont en contraste
parfait avec les nuances rouges
dominantes sur le mobilier.*

Die weißen Grundstrukturen und die
metallischen Säulen schaffen einen
scharfen Kontrast zu dem
vorherrschenden Rot des Mobiliars.

The enormous bar is
designed to facilitate the
speed of Isola's food.

*Le comptoir aux grandes
dimensions est placé de
façon que la dégustation
rapide de l'offre
gastronomique de l'Isola
soit facilitée.*

Die große Theke des Isola
wurde so gestaltet, daß ein
schnelles Servieren der
Speisen möglich ist.

Each room is conceived to give each animation or exhibition breathing-space. To guess the new identity of Renault, the option is given to look at their cars elsewhere than on the tarmac. If the spectator sits on pieces that can be de- and re-assembled like sofas or chaise-longues, looking becomes a visionary and daring spectacle.

Chacune des salles est conçue pour que chaque animation ou exposition soit dégagée. Pour pouvoir deviner la nouvelle identité de Renault, l'option est d'admirer les voitures sur un autre que l'asphalte. Si le spectateur s'installe dans les modules comme les canapés ou les chaises longues, la contemplation devient un spectacle visionnaire et audacieux.

Jedem Saal wurde ein Event bzw. eine Ausstellung zugeordnet. Zum Erkennen der neuen Identität von Renault können die Autos hier auf einer anderen Ebene als auf der Fahrbahn einer Straße betrachtet werden. Setzt sich der Zuschauer auf auseinandernehmbare Elemente, wie Sofas und Chaise-longues, bietet sich ihm ein visionäres und gewagtes Schauspiel dar.

ACKNOWLEDGEMENTS

Bar Decors is a book collecting the best proposals in design, interior decor and architecture in places with atmosphere, whether cafeterias, bars or discothèques. It could not have been put together without the invaluable contributions of all those professionals, leisure-loving amateurs and tireless explorers whose great ideas have suggested places, addresses and professional contacts.

Thanks to Sara for her disinterested contribution to documenting the French part of the project, and to Ariadna for her input on architecture.

Thanks to the team of leisure-loving researchers: Maite, in London; Núria, in Barcelona; and Paola, in Milan. Luckily there are no limits to the Italian creative imagination!
To Oscar for drawing our attention to lesser known bars; without him, they might well not be published here.
A special mention for the Lounge group who helped a mere project become hard reality with such enthusiasm.
Lastly, to the College of Interior Decorators of Catalonia, the Barcelona Design Centre, the Official College of Architects of Catalonia, the office of the FAD prizes in Architecture and Interior Design, and particularly to Paula from the Portuguese Design Centre.

REMERCIEMENTS

Bar Decors est un livre accueillant les meilleures propositions de design, de décor d'intérieurs et d'architecture tournant autour des établissements tels que cafétérias, bars ou discothèques. Son élaboration n'aurait pas été possible sans l'aide inestimable de tous les professionnels, les amateurs de loisirs et les explorateurs infatigables aux idées géniales, qui nous ont suggéré des endroits, des adresses et des contacts.

À Sara pour sa contribution désintéressée dans la documentation française du projet et à Ariadna pour ses apports au sujet d'architecture. À l'équipe de recherche des oisifs : Maite, à Londres; Nuria, à Barcelone; Paola, à Milan. Heureusement, la créativité italienne n'a pas de limites!
À Oscar, qui nous a déniché des projets inconnus, toujours recommandables; sans lui, ils n'auraient peut être pas présentés ici.
Un souvenir spécial pour le groupe Lounge, qui a rendu possible que ce projet devienne une enthousiasmante réalité.
Finalement, au Col.legi de Decoradors de Catalunya, au Barcelona Centre de Disseny, au Col.legi Oficial d'Arquitectes de Catalunya, au bureau Prix FAD d'Architecture et décor d'intérieurs et très spécialement à Paula du Centre Portugais de Design.

NACHWORT

Im Buch Bar Decors werden die besten Designer-, Innendekorations- und Architekturvorschläge für Cafeterias, Bars und Diskotheken präsentiert. Ohne die wertvolle Unterstützung aller Fachleute, Nachtschwärmer und unermüdlichen Entdeckungsreisenden, die Lokale, Adressen und Kontaktpersonen vorgeschlagen haben, wäre dieses Werk nicht möglich gewesen.

Wir möchten uns bedanken:
Bei Sara, für ihre großzügige Hilfe bei der französischen Dokumentation des Projekts; bei Ariadna, für ihren architektonischen Beitrag.
Bei dem Freizeitdetektiven-Team: Maite in London; Núria in Barcelona; und Paola in Mailand. Zum Glück ist die italienische Kreativität unerschöpflich!
Bei Oscar, weil er uns interessante, unbekannte Projekte näherbrachte, ohne ihn wären sie vielleicht in diesem Buch nicht erschienen.
Wir möchten uns bei der Lounge-Gruppe besonders bedanken, denn das Projekt wäre ohne ihre Begeisterung nicht zustande gekommen.
Und schließlich, beim Col·legi de Decoradors de Catalunya, beim Barcelona Centre de Disseny, beim Col·legi Oficial d'Arquitectes de Catalunya, beim Veranstalter der FAD-Preise für Architektur und Innendekoration und ganz besonders bei Paula vom Centro Portugués de Design.

PHOTOGRAPHIC CREDITS | *CRÉDITS PHOTOGRAPHIQUES* | FOTONACHWEIS

© **Ron Arad Associates:** Adidas.

© **Miquel Bargalló:** La Verònica.

© **Nuno Borges de Araujo:** No Rio Douro.

© **Oscar Brito, Lara Rettondini:** Bbar.

© **Ana Paula Carvalho, Fernando Sanchez Salvador:** Lux, Bica do Sapato.

Pablo Castagnola: Caroshi, Lore, Kurvenstar, Jubinal, Schwarzenraben, Riva.

© **Peter Cook (VIEW):** Tavern on the Green.

Paola D'Amico: Makia, Julien Launge Bar, Light, Barbugatti, Clip's, Ragoo, Cuore, Il Volo, That's amore, Le Biciclette.

© **Uxio da Vila:** Café Larios, Cool.

Pep Escoda: Santé Café, Rita Blue, Medusa, so_da, The Pop Bar, Salero, Milk.

© **Alberto Ferrero:** Atlantique, Mohmah, Lodi, Lot 61, Mamamia, Zapping, Code, IllyCaffè, Piccolo Bar, Spielbank Saarbrücken, Pharmacy.

© **Chris Gascoigne (VIEW):** Vertigo. Tower 42.

© **Fabrice Guyot:** Le Trabendo.

© **António Homem Cardoso, Fernando Sanchez Salvador, IPPAR (Instituto Portugués do Patrimonio Arquitectónico):** Palácio Nacional da Pena.

Martí Llorens: Fonfone, Café Zurich, Café Royale, El Café que pone Muebles Navarro, Sidecar, Café Schilling, Manaus, Dot, Café Berlín.

© **Ari Magg:** Astro.

David Manchón: Fuse, Living, Club 22, Café Salambó, Seltz.

© **Olivier Martin Gambier (ARCHIPRESS):** Atelier Renault.

© **Mihail Moldoveanu:** Musée de la Publicité, Pershing Hall, Long Bar, Renoma Cafe Gallery.

Luis Olivas: Suite Café-Club.

© **Juan Pérez Iscla:** Sushita.

© **Matteo Piazza:** Magritte, Anima Mia.

© **Tuca Reinés:** Kosushi Bar.

© **Philippe Ruault:** Palais de la Bière.

© **César San Millán:** Kaiku, Plaza.

© **Claudio Silvestrin:** Kornhaus Cafè.

© **Hervé Ternisien:** Café Gavoille.

Chas Wilshere: Light Bar, Wapping Project, The Social, Alphabet, Cinnamon, West Street, Lab, Gold Bar Café, Purple Bar, Detroit, Toast, Hakkasan, Isola, Grand Central.

© **James Winspear (VIEW):** Norman Bar.